On a Voiceless Shore

STEPHEN MINTA

On a Voiceless Shore

Byron in Greece

~

A MARIAN WOOD BOOK

HENRY HOLT AND COMPANY   NEW YORK

Henry Holt and Company, Inc.
Publishers since 1866
115 West 18th Street
New York, New York 10011

Henry Holt® is a registered
trademark of Henry Holt and Company, Inc.

Library of Congress Cataloging-in-Publication Data
Minta, Stephen.
On a voiceless shore: Byron in Greece / Stephen Minta.—1st ed.
p.   cm.
"A Marian Wood book"
Includes bibliographical references and index.
ISBN 0-8050-3778-0 (alk. paper)
1. Byron, George Gordon Byron, Baron, 1788–1824—Journeys—Greece.
2. British—Travel—Greece—History—19th century. 3. Poets, English—19th
century—Biography. 4. Greece—Description and travel. I. Title.
PR4384.M56   1998
821'.7—dc21   97-11474
[B]   CIP

Henry Holt books are available for special promotions
and premiums. For details contact: Director, Special Markets.

First Edition 1998

Designed by Michelle McMillian
Map designed by Jackie Aher

Printed in the United States of America
All first editions are printed on acid-free paper. ∞

1   3   5   7   9   10   8   6   4   2

Acknowledgments

Travel and writing are lonely pastimes. So it is a relief to remember how many people helped along the way. From among those, I should like to thank in particular: Jack Donovan, Maria Prosperi, Paolo Baranti, Donatella Raspaolo, Romano and Silena Baino, Thoma and Lindita Simaku, and Panagiota Batsaki. My thanks also to the staff of the British School at Athens, for their legendary hospitality; to the staff of the National Library of Greece and to those in charge of the General State Archives (Athens); and to the British Academy, for financial assistance.

My thanks as always to my agent, Anthony Goff. Above all, with gratitude and affection, to my editor Marian Wood.

and where art thou,
My country? On thy voiceless shore
The heroic lay is tuneless now—
The heroic bosom beats no more!
And must thy lyre, so long divine,
Degenerate into hands like mine?

—*Don Juan*, Canto III

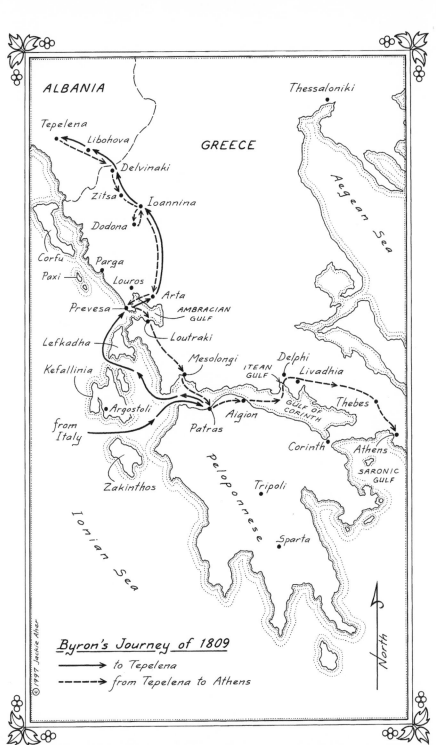

ALBANIA

Thessaloniki

Tepelena • Libohova
Delvinaki   GREECE
Zitsa
Dodona   Ioannina

Aegean Sea

Corfu   Parga
Paxi   Louros
Prevesa   Arta
              AMBRACIAN
              GULF
Lefkadha   Loutraki

Kefallinia   Mesolongi   ITEAN   Delphi
                                 GULF   Livadhia
Argostoli   GULF OF   Thebes
                        Patras   Aigion CORINTH
from   Athens
Italy   Corinth   SARONIC
                                                  GULF
Zakinthos   Peloponnese
                                    Tripoli

Ionian Sea
                                        Sparta

© 1997 Jackie Aher

North

Byron's Journey of 1809
⟶ to Tepelena
⤑ from Tepelena to Athens

On a Voiceless Shore

One

Be young as long as you can. . . .

—Byron to Hobhouse, 12 December 1818

There is no better time of day, no softer season, no finer approach. Yet it was only by chance that Lord Byron's first view of Greece came on a morning in late September, as he sailed in from the west across the Ionian Sea.

He had by then spent three months on a Grand Tour of Europe, though it had so far been something less than grand. It was 1809, and the Napoleonic Wars had closed most of the best sights to British travelers. Portugal, Gibraltar, Malta, Sardinia: these were not the obvious places for a first-time sightseer, but in the western Mediterranean there was nowhere else to go.

Byron had touched at each of these places on his way out to Greece. Touched them lightly, seeing and judging with virgin eyes and all the unreflective vividness of being twenty-one years old. He had set out in July, "sadly flea-bitten," from the Cornish port of Falmouth, where, he wrote, "I never saw so many handsome youths of both sexes in my life." He had been fascinated to see a woman there whipped over a cart for "evil speaking." "She was much whipped," he remembered, "but exceeding impenitent."

From Cornwall, he had sailed to Portugal. He had swum across the River Tagus at Lisbon, a feat much admired by his friend and traveling companion, John Cam Hobhouse. Then they had gone on horseback into Spain, across a peninsula at war. He had admired from afar Spain's "dark-glancing daughters." Turning down an invitation to bed with his hostess at Seville, he had departed with a lock of her hair three feet long.

Cádiz, he thought, was the "prettiest town in Europe," Gibraltar "the dirtiest most detestable spot in existence." Desire mingling with nationalistic pride, he concluded: "I must confess the women of Cadiz are as far superior to the English women in beauty as the Spaniards are inferior to the English in every quality that dignifies the name of man."

From Spain they had taken a ship for Sardinia, where, on a short ride into the interior, they had seen three human heads nailed to a gallows. Then on again by sea to Malta, and for Byron the gorgeous inevitability of his first foreign romance. Her name was Constance Spencer Smith. She had a past more exotic than any twenty-one-year-old had a right to expect, and Byron would remember her, from time to time, as he traveled in Greece.

In Malta, they had paused while Byron fell in love; then they wondered where to go next. The East was what they had left England to see. They thought of Turkey, which lay at the very edge of contemporary tourism. Then the governor of Malta eased their way onto a ship bound for Greece, and on 19 September they set sail.

They awoke on that Saturday morning, 23 September 1809, as the ship passed up the channel between two islands in the Ionian Sea. Kefallinia was to the north, Zakinthos to the south, and they had three leisurely sailing days still to run before they made their first landing on Greek soil at the port of Patras. It was one of the last of those magical days, sandwiched between the tearing heat of a Greek summer and the gentle warmth of autumn.

We know what Hobhouse felt at the moment of awakening, for he made the following entry in his diary: "First saw ancient

Greece." This curious way of putting it was much in the fashion of the time. Ancient Greece, especially the Athens of the fifth century B.C., was what most travelers then came to find. Which explains why so many of them left Greece disappointed, baffled at the changes of the intervening two and a half thousand years. Hobhouse, bookish, a little dogged, had arrived in search of a beloved past framed by the landscape of the present. He wanted a Greece of inscriptions and monuments, backed by the mountains and plains that ancient writers had once made famous. In general, he took a measured view of what he saw. "Agreeable" for him was a term of high praise; if he found something "peculiarly agreeable," it was beyond compare.

Byron was an altogether different character. They made for a time a complementary duo of travelers, but they were far apart on many of the things that mattered. What Byron thought as they looked out toward the western coast we do not know. But when he came to write *Childe Harold's Pilgrimage* a few months later, he too created a landscape to match his expectations. Byron had little interest in monuments. For him a classical Greek column would be something to carve his name on, or to sleep under. Byron, in the most old-fashioned of ways, had come to the East in search of adventure.

More exotic, more sexually provocative, than the idea of Greece was the fantasy of Albania. It was then, as it is now, the least-visited country in Europe. The historian Gibbon had once commented on the paradox of a country "within sight of Italy" that was yet "less known than the interior of America." The frontier between Greece and Albania was conveniently fluid in Byron's time; and so it was the approach to the Albanian coast that he chose to remember in *Childe Harold*:

> *Land of Albania! let me bend mine eyes*
> *On thee, thou rugged nurse of savage men!*

Already, Byron appears as the creator of a myth that years later would draw him back again to the East. His Greece was a wild land; a place of strong men and passionate action, a place to come of age. It was here that he would return to pay homage to his youth, to recover his battered fortunes, and to die in 1824.

Unpredictably, the Greece of Hobhouse and the Greece of Byron would meet in the end. When the War of Independence broke out in the 1820s, Hobhouse poured his boundless political energy into organizing support for the Greek cause. He helped to found the London Greek Committee; and he played a major part in a process that was to lead his old traveling companion back to Greece and to death by the marshes of Mesolongi.

It was thirty years since I had been to the west coast of Greece, and often, in that time, I had renewed a mental note not to go back. From the sea, as you approach, the land is softened by an eternal haze. You see only gray shapes, sometimes long and low, disappearing into the horizon; sometimes rising high into the air, with all the mystery of those wild mountains behind. Everything is distanced, out of focus. From a boat, the country looks untouched, ripe for discovery, the alluring end of so much blue water and sky.

Once you go ashore, however, it's a long series of disappointments. From the modern Albanian frontier, south to the entrance of the Gulf of Corinth, there are few settlements, all of them drab. Most of the time the road is squeezed to the edge of the sea by the mountains, which draw back only around the port of Igoumenitsa and from the plain to the north of Prevesa. The mountains, bare and bleached and deserted, show scattered patches of white that, from a distance, look like houses, but are only rock reflecting the sun. These mountains, too, lose their promise as you come closer, revealing themselves to be merely monotonous.

It wasn't casually, then, or by chance that I went back. Nor was it planned. Although now, in retrospect, it seems inevitable that it was Byron I was looking for, I didn't register that at the time. It was only later, when I'd followed him into towns and villages, across mountains and through the remnants of the Greek forests, that, finally, I became interested in the stories that had brought him there, too, 180 years before.

In truth, I've never wanted to follow in anyone's footsteps. Even when I'd been nowhere outside the tiny island where I grew up, I already knew that footsteps have a short life span. At an age when everywhere in books is exciting, when there is as yet no difference between Cairo and Calcutta, I read all the travel books I could find. I went off happily with their authors on the heels of the long dead, in search of Alexander the Great and Genghis Khan. But I was never a true believer. Alexander and Genghis remained out of reach, no matter how many deserts we crossed, how many mountains we climbed. And the past refused to be measured in miles, or in difficulties overcome.

There was something else, too, that I discovered then and that I have never been able to shake off. Something that went deeper than a simple adolescent suspicion of the improbable. It came to me gradually, during those crisp, throaty days in December, when we used to gather to sing carols in a chapel by the sea. For as we sang, I began to realize that, whatever happened to me in life, I did not want to be that page boy who followed Wenceslas.

It was on a wild and snowy night that Wenceslas looked out. On the Feast of Stephen. He saw a poor man gathering firewood in the dark and was moved to pity. He summoned his page and together they went off, "through the rude wind's wild lament," on a famous errand of mercy.

But out there, in the bitter weather, the page lost his nerve, daunted by the possibilities of the night. He survived, eyes on the ground, only as a slave to the master before him:

> *In his master's steps he trod,*
> *Where the snow lay dinted. . . .*

They gave the poor man his Christmas dinner; then, I suppose, returned home, the king to be a saint and the page to carry on being a page.

A memorable journey. Even so, it was hard to believe, at the age of twelve, that life held nothing better than the promise of a great man's coattails.

Now, increasingly, I begin to see things differently, and I can understand the marvelous security of following on behind. On those dull days of travel, caught between buses in a small town where you have nothing to do, it's easy to envy that page boy. His horizon was limited, but his job, after all, was clear, and he had, I suppose, no second thoughts about where he was going. . . .

Still, these reflections belong to the end of a journey, not the beginning. The journey out is always simpler. On a day in late September I returned to the west coast of Greece. This book, with all the distortions of memory and the years, is the result.

As they passed by the island of Kefallinia, Hobhouse registered the great emptiness of the Greek countryside, its unforgettable desiccation. The island, he wrote in his book *Travels in Albania*, "appeared a chain of high rocks to the north with a few villages scattered at their feet, and presented a prospect of universal barrenness." Ahead of them were the mountains of the Greek mainland. Just to the north lay Ithaca, the island of Odysseus.

They reached Patras on 26 September 1809 and, at 10:30 A.M., landed for the first time in Greece. The country was then under Turkish occupation, as it had been for almost four hundred years. The sight of Turks at the landing place, with pistols and daggers in their belts, was something different from anything they had come across before in Europe. This, at last, was real traveling. Hobhouse rose to the sight of the minarets of the mosques catching the early rays of the sun, the groves of orange and lemon trees, and the mountains behind. This was joy after the "white waste of Malta" and the barren rocks of the Greek coast.

They had just an hour before the ship turned around and made for Prevesa. They wandered into a currant field and practiced pistol shooting. This was a time, Byron later recalled, when he could split a walking stick at twelve paces with a single bullet. It was an art that added greatly to his prestige in Greece, both then and later, and especially in the frontier atmosphere of Mesolongi in 1824.

On their way to Prevesa they passed Mesolongi. Neither then nor later did either of them have much to say about the place, though Byron's death there would make it one of Europe's most famous unvisited towns. Even in the revised edition of Hobhouse's book, published in 1858, he refers simply to "a distant view of a town called Mesolonghi." It is set on the shore of a great lagoon, protected on the eastern side by a long, narrow strip of land that curves around in a horseshoe. Behind the town rise inevitable mountains.

They turned north, with Ithaca to their left, and, as it grew dark, the island was lit up by the fires of shepherds in the mountains. They rounded Cape Dukato at the southern end of the island of Lefkadha. Here, according to an unreliable tradition, the poet Sappho threw herself over a cliff into the sea to escape the ravages of unrequited love. " 'Twas on a Grecian autumn's gentle eve," Byron recalled in *Childe Harold*, that they saw

> Leucadia's far-projecting rock of woe,
> And hail'd the last resort of fruitless love. . . .

It was a place that fascinated him by its association. Sappho, like him, a poet, like him, bisexual, apparently fated. He would remember "burning Sappho" in the most famous lines he ever wrote about Greece.

In the evening of 28 September, they reached Prevesa, at the entrance to the Ambracian Gulf. A Greek who was one of the acting British vice-consuls for the town came onboard and studied their letters of introduction, which he could not read. Then they went ashore.

Prevesa. Now the name is remembered only in the travel brochures. It has an airport that takes in tourists heading for the

limited delights of western Greece, sending sun followers up the
coast to the resort of Parga, or south to the island of Lefkadha.
But this is a place that was once famous in history, for an empire
was lost in the narrow strait that separates the airport from the
town. Here, in 31 B.C., the Battle of Actium was fought, which
marked the end of Antony and Cleopatra and the line of the
Macedonian rulers of Egypt.

In Byron's day, too, Prevesa had a fame of sorts. It went back
to events ten years before he and Hobhouse arrived. When
Napoleon's extraordinary European expansion took his armies
into Italy in 1797, one of the minor consequences was that the
French seized a number of towns and islands in western Greece,
Prevesa among them. A year later, the Albanian chieftain Ali
Pasha, anxious about what a strong French presence in the area
might do to threaten his own ambitions, attacked Prevesa and its
occupying French forces.

Prevesa was almost completely destroyed. There was butchery
of a kind that shocked outsiders who were used to more disci-
plined ways of killing. The Albanians made a grand pyramid
from the heads of the French soldiers who had died in the fighting. Accounts of the battle grew ever wilder in the telling. "Like
the Angel of Death," wrote an early-nineteenth-century author,
Ali Pasha "hovered over the smoking ruins of Preveza."

One hundred and sixty Greeks who had fought on the French
side were executed and, according to the same author, the task
was so terrible that "the arm of the executioner . . . became nerve-
less, his knees shook . . . and he fell upon the bodies of his still
reeking victims, and expired." One hundred and fifty French soldiers who survived the fighting were marched across northern
Greece to Constantinople, through one of the worst winters ever
remembered.

This was the beginning of the legend of Ali Pasha, who was to
play an important role in Byron's Greece. Prevesa made Ali
famous; and Lord Nelson, passing through the Aegean Sea, sent
an officer to congratulate him on his success. The town, though,

remained desolate. It had been a decent center of commerce, but its population halved between 1798 and 1809. All the best houses were in ruins; the rest were simple huts made of branches and plastered with mud. Forty years on, when Edward Lear was in Greece, he noted that "the whole place has an air of melancholy desolation" and that "even now, after the lapse of so many years, a foreigner perceives that the awful name of Ali Pasha is hardly pronounced without a feeling akin to terror."

It is not surprising that Hobhouse was gloomy. They landed in a shower of rain. "Few places," he wrote, "will bear being visited in a rainy day, least of all a Turkish town, and such a town as Prevesa." He gathered some stories about the local Turks from the master of an English ship in harbor; saw the unpaved streets, deep in mud, and the wooden huts. The Turks, who had appeared delightfully exotic at Patras, now looked merely savage, with their pistols and long knives sticking from their belts— symbolic of their power over the unarmed Greeks. This was the downside of travel. As Hobhouse wrote, he and Byron were "just fresh from Christendom." They had imagined better of Greece, after so long an anticipation.

And I, too, landed at Prevesa in the rain. I had watched the storm coming from over the water, the west wind driving the waves white, and the rain following. It bent the trees along the shoreline, draining away the sea's warmth, the last memory of the summer months of fire.

Whenever I come to a place for the first time, I still have old dreams of seeing it with uncluttered eyes. But as the boat or train or bus gets closer, small irrational fears begin to eclipse the excitement of discovery. Where to stay? Where to eat? What to do, alone, in the evenings to come? Long before I landed at Prevesa, I had already given in to the easy tyranny of false knowledge, and opened my guidebooks. They didn't agree, of course. "Unprepossessing," said one. "Not without its charm," said the other. In time, though, they could be reconciled.

It was the worst moment of the day to enter a southern town. Midafternoon, and the rough straggle of concrete, so typical of places like this, was almost empty of life. I sat in a café and drank black coffee and watched the ferries crossing the gray water to the promontory of Aktion with its Venetian fort. A couple went by on a motorbike; then a priest: black gown, black beard, black hat, black umbrella, a small girl holding on to the flow of his dress. Then two women in straw hats with white shorts. Lost holiday-makers, confused by the early rain, they now looked as incongruous by the waters of the Ambracian Gulf as they would have been by the Thames in autumn.

By late afternoon the wind had shifted and the rain moved away. A young girl riding a bicycle far too small for her ran into me; she fell to the ground and laughed. From then on Prevesa was not without its charms and I began to imagine the place in the sun, with people and noise. The sun shining on the calm waters of the gulf and, farther out, the white water of the real sea.

Already, in Malta, Byron and Hobhouse had decided that when they got to Greece they would go and see Ali Pasha. His reputation as a wild and wily Albanian chieftain had a natural appeal for two young Englishmen just down from Cambridge. No one ever quite knew where Ali was: that was part of the romance. But his name was always tied to the northern Greek city of Ioannina. He had seized control of the city in 1788 and it was there that he held court on the most lavish scale. So it was to Ioannina that they now prepared to travel.

First, though, they would go and visit a memorial to the past. This area of Greece is poor in monuments and sites. It is the dismay of the travel agencies, who struggle each summer to attract their clients to the few undistinguished piles of ancient stones. Just to the north of Prevesa, however, are the ruins of the city of Nikopolis. Its name means Victory City in Greek and it was founded by Octavian to celebrate his defeat of Antony and Cleopatra at Actium.

There seems something awesome and a little ridiculous about Octavian's gesture. "Here I fought, here I pitched my tent, here I will build a great city." It was a miserable site. Low-lying, unhealthy, swept by the winter rains from off the sea. It was far from centers of population and so the city was filled by the forced evacuation of other places. It had, however, strategic and mercantile importance and it flourished, for a time. Relative to its importance, it has been called the most neglected archaeological site in Greece.

"More extensive than magnificent," was Hobhouse's comment on the ruins. The site is sprawling and hard to read; and today the main road north from Prevesa passes straight through it. The great Roman city was plundered by Vandals and Ostrogoths. Restored, it flourished again in the sixth century, before going eventually, like almost everything else in Greece, into long, unrecorded decline.

Hobhouse, with his desire for a wholly classical Greece, a place of slender columns and stately control of space, could only be disappointed by his first Greek monument. Yet the brick walls of Nikopolis have, in the afternoon sun, a dilapidated grandeur. Goats browse high among them. Down below is a tangle of undergrowth, where, from time to time, you fall over the debris of five hundred years of pagan and Christian culture.

Above the crumbling theater of Nikopolis is the Monument of Augustus, Octavian's own memorial to himself. It's a set of massive stone blocks, now surrounded by a barbed-wire fence. Here Octavian stood watching the battle. The view is vast and open. I sat until evening, until the goats began to pass on their way home to the village nearby. Farmers greeted each other, shouted across the gathering half-light. One of them spoke to me. It was a long time since I had spoken Greek and I felt again the pleasure that comes when half-remembered words bring a smile of recognition to the eyes of a stranger.

Emperors and generals, vandals and destroyers, Romans, Arabs and Slavs, Crusaders, Venetians, Turks: it's a miracle the

Greek language ever survived all the physical assaults on Greece. A language protected from oblivion only by its immense age, its prestige as the medium of Homer and then, later, of God.

Greece retains its remarkable capacity to absorb. This is a country that has known no settled history, only a succession of intrusions. A place where changes of fortune have often meant no more than changes of foreign ownership. It's been truly ravaged by time. Yet, by that strange paradox that strikes all travelers sooner or later, Greece has remained in possession of itself. How often still, even in the face of the final levelings of late-twentieth-century tourism, you find yourself saying, for better and for worse, this could only be Greece.

In Byron's time there were two obvious ways from Prevesa to Ioannina. There was a direct route leading north beyond the ruins of Nikopolis. It turned east toward the village of Louros, then north again through the mountains. Hobhouse noted that the countryside around Louros "was at that time not quite safe"; and so they chose the longer route, via the city of Arta.

They began by taking a boat across the Ambracian Gulf. They had with them a man they called George, an all-purpose and not entirely satisfactory guide to Greece whom they had hired in Patras. They also had a single English servant, Byron's valet, William Fletcher.

Fletcher had already been in Byron's service for two or three years and he was to remain with him through every twist and turn of the next fifteen. He would be there, faithful to the last, at his bedside in Mesolongi. It's clear that Byron trusted Fletcher implicitly. We never hear much about him in the course of Byron's travels, but he is always there, doing the multiplicity of things servants are supposed to do. Occasionally, he is given a voice, which is invariably one of complaint. For Fletcher seems, not unreasonably, to have spent much of his time on the road with Byron wishing he were somewhere else.

There is no doubt that Fletcher was miserably homesick.

"English servants are detestable travellers," Byron wrote to his mother in March 1810. And in another letter to his mother, in January 1811, he talked of Fletcher's "perpetual lamentations after beef & beer, the stupid bigoted contempt for every thing foreign, and insurmountable incapacity of acquiring even a few words of any language," all of which "rendered him like all other English servants, an incumbrance." Hobhouse felt the same: "English servants are rather an encumbrance than otherwise in the Levant," he wrote. "Their inaptitude at acquiring any foreign language is, besides, invincible."

On 1 October, the four of them set off across the gulf, bound for Salaora, the port of Arta. They took seven trunks of luggage, three beds, with bedding, and two light wooden bedsteads. Byron never traveled either lightly or quietly. "I am on the rack of setting off for Argos," he wrote in August 1810, "amidst the usual creaking swearing loading and neighing of sixteen horses and as many men." In 1821, when he moved from Ravenna to Pisa, he asked Shelley for eight horse-drawn wagons to carry away his belongings.

In those days, there was nothing strange about traveling in style. Yet Hobhouse sounds almost apologetic. "Our baggage was weighty," he wrote, "but, I believe, we could not have done well with less." Bedsteads, he noted sensibly, were useful for overnight stays in private houses, since they protected the traveler from the damp of mud floors and the explorations of vermin. Then, too, he said, if you travel fast and can't have your clothes cleaned, "a large quantity of linen is necessary."

That last detail is appealing. Hobhouse, along with so many English of the time, had a passion for clean clothes and an aversion to washing. No one ever seems to wash in Hobhouse's world, however long and dusty the journey. Byron was the exception: he loved the physical pleasures of bathing and mocked his friend's "noble contempt for that 'oriental scrupulosity.' " For both of them, however, a large quantity of clean linen was the mark of a well-born traveler.

The trip across the bay of Salaora is about ten miles. To the north are the characteristic bare mountains of Greece, which, at Louros, reach down almost to the sea. Gray rock, with low trees here and there, and patches of red earth. In early October, rain clouds are already forming over the mountains, while the sea is summer-blue and the sun still warm.

The Ambracian Gulf reminded Hobhouse of Loch Lomond in Scotland. It is so landlocked that indeed it seems more a lake than a part of the sea. It should be a romantic place, but today it is beautiful only at a distance. Few villages lie by its shores and the water is, for most of the year, entirely without movement. In the heat of summer, people search out places to swim among tin cans and wrapping papers and plastic bottles. Small resorts like Menidhi, on the eastern edge of the gulf, dissolve under weekend invaders, and wherever you stop to look out over the beauty of the sea, there are piles of rubbish lying there indolent, shameless.

In a poem of November 1809, Byron celebrated the romance of the gulf by night:

> *Through cloudless skies, in silvery sheen,*
> *Full beams the moon on Actium's coast. . . .*

It might still be romantic, if you drove on a moonlit night along the eastern shore. You could go north from the town of Amfilokhia, which lies, like a cork driven into the neck of a bottle, at the very head of the gulf. The gulf soon opens out, as if toward open water, and, on a summer's night, the smell of baked earth and fish frying in small tavernas, the sound of crickets, and the unmoving sea might restore the balance of the day.

Byron and Hobhouse arrived in Salaora to find it was no more than a single house and a two-room army post. They spent the night with ten Albanian soldiers: "It was impossible for any men to have a more unsavoury appearance," wrote Hobhouse. But appearances were deceptive, since, he added, "we found them exceedingly mild and good-humoured." On their second day at

Salaora it rained hard and on the morning of the next they set off with ten lean horses for Arta.

The bus was half empty, half full of Greeks out for the day in Arta. I thought I was the only foreigner among them and I sat at the back and listened to the rise and fall of conversation, as the bus swept on through the rain. Then suddenly, a few seats away, two bodies came to life in the gathering light of early morning. They stretched, disengaged, spoke.

English words on foreign lips. The woman was Greek, with youthful, ravaged skin and brittle hair. Her lover was a large, sleek northerner, German or Dutch perhaps. English was the only language they had in common. He spoke it mechanically and without pride, as the ultimate language of convenience. She hardly knew it at all, but understood, or pretended to.

There's a world of romance in foreign languages, but not where they're foreign to both parties in a relationship. If he had spoken Greek or she had learned his mother tongue ... But English was all they had, remnant of the sweated classroom, emptied of intimacy.

They had reached the moment of crisis in their holiday affair when there is only the choice between pushing on or saying good-bye forever. He wanted to take her back home, to live with him in the north, and her face was already marked by the struggle, liberation and loss, temptation and regret.

He would begin his sentences with the words "In my country," inviting her to a faraway place that was always what Greece is not. "In my country," he said gloomily, "it is cleaner than here." There was a long silence. We passed through a village, by mounds of rubbish, unkempt streets, and, for a moment, I saw it through his eyes. A fatal solidarity, since if you are to survive for long in Greece, you must learn to live with its vast debris, the wreckage of the present no less than the past.

"In my country," he began again, "you have more choice than here. If you want to buy something in the supermarket, you have each time four or five different, but here you have different only two or three."

She thought this over for a long time. For hundreds of years Greeks have left their country in search of the better life abroad, and now here it was, opening all before her. In her silence she measured the claims of Düsseldorf or Rotterdam. Then the bus stopped, more people got on, and I couldn't see her face anymore. A few times after that I heard the man's voice, tireless, monotonous; and once hers, as she dredged her memories and wondered: "Why?"

If Byron and Hobhouse had taken the land road along the northern edge of the gulf, they would have passed within a few miles of the famous Monastery of Zalongo; and if they had visited Zalongo, Byron would have seen one of the holy places of modern Greece. He would also have learned something about the Suliotes, a tribe that fascinated him but whose story he never really understood. He mythologized the Suliotes in *Childe Harold* and celebrated their bravery in some famous lines:

> *Oh! who is more brave than a dark Suliote,*
> *In his snowy camese and his shaggy capote?*

When Byron returned to Greece in 1823, he brought the fascination back with him and it cost him dearly in the last months of his life.

The Suliotes were remnants of a group of Greek/Albanian Christians. Centuries before, falling back in the face of an advancing Islam, they had taken refuge on a high plateau above the Black River, the ancient River of the Dead, to the north of Prevesa. Though they are always called Suliotes, as if they were a single tribe, they were in fact a collection of small groups with little mutual sense of purpose. They came together only in time of war. They lived the harsh life of the Greek mountains, as shepherds and bandits, and all through the eighteenth century the Pashas of

Ioannina tried to bring them to order. Ali Pasha led three thousand men against them in 1790; ten thousand in 1792; and as many again in the very early years of the nineteenth century.

Always the Suliotes held out. Until, in December 1803, victims of blockade, hunger, and the treachery of some of their leaders, they agreed to surrender. They were given a guarantee of safe conduct out of the mountains to wherever they chose. After so many years of struggle, however, Ali Pasha was not a man to let them escape. Two thousand of the Suliotes fought their way to Parga, from where they were able to cross to the Ionian Islands. Another thousand made for Zalongo, where they were almost immediately besieged by Ali's troops.

From Prevesa, the road to Zalongo lies across a wide plain. Then there is a sudden climb into the mountains. When you turn off the main road, you see, far away and above you, the line of a high cliff. On the very edge of the cliff, a few matchsticks that, at a distance, look like fir trees bent in the wind. By the time you reach the village of Kamarina, just below Zalongo, the fir trees turn out to be a monument in stone, an abstract group of figures, descending in size from right to left.

As you climb still higher, with a view over the coast and the bay of Nikopolis, you see the ruins of the ancient city of Kassope to the left. To the right is the Monastery of Zalongo and, above it, a well-manured path rises quickly through the tree line. If you take this path and climb until the ruins of Kassope below are only an indistinguishable clump of stones, you reach the monument that was raised in honor of the women of Suli. It records an event that took place on 18 December 1803 and it is famous as a place of pilgrimage.

Besieged in Zalongo, and with no hope of escape, sixty Suliote women gathered here, a sheer precipice before them and mountains all around. It was said that those with children kissed them good-bye before throwing them down onto the rocks below. Then the women joined hands in a round dance, slipping one by one over the cliff to rejoin their children in death.

Edward Lear came to the village of Kamarina in the rain in May 1849. It was then, he wrote, "a straggling hamlet of white-washed houses and reed-built cabins." He was prevented by the weather from seeing Kassope or the rock of Zalongo, but he met women in Kamarina who remembered the "terrors of those evil days," and he understood that what had happened here was the beginning of genocide. By his day, the Suliotes had become a people without a country or a name.

Some of the Suliotes were to return to the mainland of Greece in the 1820s, after years of exile. Some fought heroically in the Greek War of Independence. But already by the time of Byron's first visit to Greece, the "dark Suliote, / In his snowy camese" was a romantic anachronism, for which in the end he would pay the price.

Hobhouse and Byron crossed on the stone causeway that still links Salaora to the mainland. In the marshes, which border much of the northern shore of the Ambracian Gulf, they saw flocks of wild swans. The rain was violent and unceasing, until they came within sight of the city of Arta. Then the clouds rolled back and the sun shone. The approach today has probably changed little. Orchards of orange and lemon trees, olive groves, pomegranate and fig trees line a road that runs absolutely straight for ten miles across flat land. When Byron came this way, the ground was swampy and the baggage animals frequently fell under their load of trunks and bedsteads.

They liked Arta. Everyone who passed through it in those days did and most people still do. It's famous for its packhorse bridge, which dates from the seventeenth century. According to a tradition that was once widespread over Greece and Albania, the master builder of the bridge walled up his wife in one of the piers, in order to strengthen the foundations. She, in death, cursed her fate, saying, in the words of the Greek folk song: "May this bridge shake like the gillyflower, and may those passing over it fall like leaves from a tree." Whatever the truth of the story, it's a fine-looking bridge.

Arta has a dimly understood classical past, symbolized by a massive chunk of wall that sits incongruously in a busy street, just off the Athens road. It has a medieval castle that had gone to decay in Byron's time. Its marvelous circuit of defensive walls goes back to the days in the twelfth and thirteenth centuries when Arta was an important trading center. It was again prosperous in the early years of the nineteenth century, and had become, after the destruction of Prevesa, the second commercial town in western Greece.

If the length and wealth of its past must contribute something to the atmosphere of modern Arta, it is the setting, in a wide loop of the Arakhthos River, that makes it such a fine place to stay. Greece is a country poor in rivers, and few towns or cities have any memorable connection with them. Arta is different. Nowhere, wrote Edward Lear, could be "more superbly situated than this."

The city has, and had, other, more mundane virtues, too. It was, said Hobhouse, in his dogged way, "tolerably clean . . . and free from unpleasant smells"; and they had somewhere decent to stay, after the horrors of Prevesa. It's only when you've seen many Greek towns, the unplanned sprawl and the anonymity that comes from lack of civic pride, that you recognize how special Arta is. It's clean and neat, quietly rich. The right size for a city. You can hear birdsong in the central square and, well into October, the sound of crickets at night.

The most interesting sight in Arta is what Lear called "a very curious old Greek church." It had fallen into ruin when Hobhouse and Byron were here. In any case, neither of them were much interested in Greek churches or religion. "A more abandoned race of miscreants cannot exist than the lower orders of the Greek clergy," was Byron's commonplace view.

The church is of the Virgin Paregoretissa and dates from the last years of the thirteenth century. From the outside, it looks more like a palace than a place of worship. A huge, blocklike structure, rising three stories high and topped by five domes. Inside, two things strike you at once. First, that the whole place looks as if it's about to fall on your head, for the central dome apparently rests on an impossible system of crumbling columns and stone outcrops. The *Blue Guide*, authoritative, reassuring as ever, says it "cannot be as unsound as it appears."

Second, there is a marvelous mosaic of Christ in Majesty, surrounded by cherubim and seraphim, high above in the dome. He has that wonderful quality of peace that the Byzantine artists gave to Christ. He has long, thin fingers, and, gazing down, refuses to meet your eye, looking away into his sublime majesty. It is all so different from those products of medieval Christendom, all those tortured Christs who showed western Europe the way to a terrifying, fatal realism.

I spent a happy week in Arta, though it rained a good deal. No other part of Greece has as much rain as this and nowhere else in Greece do the rains begin so early in autumn. In Byron's time, the month of October was the season of fever, a season that traditionally opened with the first rains and closed with the first gales of November.

Most travelers then thought Greece an unhealthy place. Malaria, plague, and dysentery were endemic. Partly this was due to the general backwardness of the country. Partly to the fact that, until the twentieth century, when a program of marsh drainage was completed, Greece was a land of swamps. Most of the north coast of the Peloponnese was marshland; so was the plain between Prevesa, Louros, Salaora, and Arta.

Now Greece is one of the healthiest countries you can visit. Life expectancy, for men at least, is higher than in Great Britain. It's also a very safe country, and, looking back on that first week in Arta, the feeling of safety is what I remember more than any other. Greece remains one of those places where the night holds no fears. Coming back into the city in the early evening, you pass young girls walking alone along deserted roads, old men driving flocks of goats. In the city itself, people walk along dimly lit streets, dragging huge shadows behind them, confident, easy.

From my room I looked down every evening on the relaxed street theater of Mediterranean life. This was a vital part of Byron's Greece and added to his distaste for the more rigid cultures of the north, not least of his native land. On my first night I watched a middle-aged man carrying a suitcase up a steep flight of steps. An Englishman doing the same thing conceals the effort, grits his teeth, for there is always in the action a possibility of ridicule. But a Greek carrying a heavy suitcase advertises the hard work. He mutters, mops his brow, waves a free hand, and talks happily to no one in particular, a privilege that in England is reserved only for the insane.

I watched a man talking to a friend on a motorbike, his arm loosely around another man in casual embrace. Physical presence here is always social. An Englishman might ride a hundred miles sitting next to you in a railway carriage and never speak, never catch your eye, hardly even seem to breathe; and he could do it with a naturalness that doesn't offend. But a Greek mistrusts the idea of private space, looks always for a point of contact.

The first really heavy rains came early one evening. In a few minutes the gutters were full of water and the debris of months of summer drought. The wind blew hard, bringing down a flutter of leaves, and people said to each other as they passed by in the street: "It's autumn."

The mayor of Arta was making a speech in the open air. He was a small man, almost invisible behind his microphone, with a banner-draped podium before him and a large yellow awning above, to shield him from the weather. It was election time and he had much to say, and he did not, I'm sure, abbreviate one word of his prepared speech in deference to the rain. Aristotle, in a famous phrase, said that man was by nature a political animal. He was *politikos*, born to be gregarious. The passion is still unshakable in modern Greek life.

Greek politics is many things and it would be foolish to be sentimental. Much of the passion is old-fashioned, pork-barrel business after all. It's about jobs and favors, about what outsiders call corruption. But it's more than that, too. A wave of political graffiti follows you everywhere in Greece. Nowhere, not in the most miserable ruined hut in the mountains, can you escape it; and if it's true that people cover walls with their most intimate urges, then an outsider could only conclude that Greeks are more concerned with politics than with sex.

The mayor of Arta had set out on one of those tours of history and culture that are popular with Greek politicians. Given the immensity of the Greek past and his determination to do it justice, this was a speech that could only go on forever. I thought of speeches I'd heard in Central America. Hours spent in hot dusty squares, listening to Castro or Ortega in full voice. There was the same easy commerce with the past, the same confidence in a political culture still uneroded by the sound bite. Here was an audience that wouldn't stand up and walk away.

I listened for a time and then went to find something to eat. There was nothing but lukewarm *patsas*, a pigs' feet and tripe soup that is a delicacy in the Balkans, and which often tastes even worse than it sounds. During this time, the mayor must have threaded his path through the period of Roman domination and the Middle Ages, for on my way back across the square he was deep in the Independence struggle of the nineteenth century. I waited, until, sure as autumn, the name of Lord Byron sounded out over the square. Then I went for coffee.

Passing by one last time, on my way to bed, I found we had reached the twentieth century. The mayor's voice rose with enthusiasm and emotion. The lightning flashed, the thunder rolled around him. Still people listened, grouped in doorways, under overhanging eaves. Or they carried on eating or having their hair cut or buying a new pair of shoes; but every so often they would whistle or clap their hands, to show they were still there, the mayor was not alone.

An old friend of my family was famous among us for having gone to fight in the Spanish Civil War in the 1930s. He was one of the survivors of the Battle of the Jarama River and, if you asked him often enough, he would sing the civil war ballad that began: "There's a valley in Spain called Jarama." Two-thirds of the international volunteers who fought at Jarama lost their lives, along with nearly all their officers. The stories we heard, over and over again, fixed forever in my mind certain images of war: the incompetence of generals, the heroism of fighting men, the sad duplicity of lost causes.

Just outside Arta, on the eastern side, is the village of Peta. What Jarama was to Spain, Peta was to Greece. The Battle of Peta, in July 1822, was an equal tale of muddled leadership, heroism, and disintegrating idealism. Two-thirds of the foreign volunteers in the Philhellene Battalion and all their higher-ranking officers were slaughtered here, trying to defend a small hill against an overwhelming Turkish attack. Ten months later, in May 1823, Byron met a German survivor of Peta in Genoa. It was his first chance to discover what a return to Greece would be like.

William St. Clair gives the best modern account of the Battle of Peta, in his thoroughly disenchanted study of the Greek War of Independence, *That Greece Might Still Be Free*. The European volunteers who fought there were under the command of General Normann, a veteran of Napoleon's march on Moscow. His name survives in Norman Street in the modern village of Peta. He was chief of staff to Alexandros Mavrokordatos, the Greek political leader who would be at Mesolongi waiting to welcome Byron in January 1824. Normann led the Philhellene Battalion on a long march up from Corinth and, against his better judgment, was drawn into battle. His men were outnumbered, weak from fever, fatigue, and poor food. Defeat was inevitable and with it came the defeat of an international idealism. The image of Peta might well have remained the defining image of the Greek war had it not been for Byron's so much more famous intervention in the following year.

Peta today is a quiet place. Nothing is left of the old village, which was burned to the ground after the battle. It's a hard climb up from the Athens road and the modern settlement lies across the steepest of slopes. There's a children's playground, with rusting swings and a slide, and a Monastery of St. George. Arta is clearly spread out below, its walls superb through binoculars. To the right are small hills rising to a high peak, with another high mountain closer at hand, utterly barren. To the left are low wooded slopes.

I stood there in the windless heat of early October and looked down at the smoke rising from a dozen small fires in the plain below. Here died Germans, Italians, Poles, French, Swiss, a Dutchman, and a Hungarian: the international roll call of the Battle of Peta, which conceals the commitment and the futility, the hopes and disappointments of the men who preceded Byron in the pursuit of Greek freedom.

Thirteen years before the Battle of Peta, when Byron was first in Greece, the very idea of Greek freedom seemed far away. In *Childe Harold*, the important question could still be raised in a way that was abstract, rhetorical, and romantic:

> *Fair Greece! sad relic of departed worth!*
> . . . .
> *Who now shall lead thy scatter'd children forth,*
> *And long accustom'd bondage uncreate?*

There was a pragmatic strain in Byron's character that saved him from ever truly believing he could play Moses to the oppressed Greeks. Even so, the gap between the romance of *Childe Harold* and the miserable realities of the Greek War was one he struggled to bridge until the end of his life.

Not far from Arta, a little to the east of where the Arakhthos River reaches the Ambracian Gulf, is a place called Aliki. It appears on some maps, a brief dot on the edge of the blue expanse. It's not even a village. When I went there one summer I saw just three buildings: a ruined house, roofless and cracked; a smart new house alongside; and a café with a red-tiled roof and bright blue and yellow chairs outside. A pole that had once carried the name "Aliki" lay overturned, the metal rusting in the dust.

One house in ruins, one newly built. Aliki is an image of the strange world of Greek tourism. Your first thought on coming here is that it would be one of the last places on earth to spend a summer vacation. The land is marshy, it swarms with mosquitoes, and the sea is the color of bathwater in which half the world has already bathed. This little strip of land, tucked into the northeast corner of the gulf, is airless, without charm and without promise.

Yet now in October the place was alive with the optimism of development. There was hammering, sawing, and cursing, all the sounds of every building site in the world. Women passed back and forth with trays of food, shouting at unseen husbands or lovers over the noise of a radio that howled by the roadside. Here was a confidence that crowds would soon be arriving in Aliki, to eat, drink, and swim, pass a honeymoon or an idle weekend.

The confidence seems absurd, but, on reflection, it is natural in the history of Greek tourism. When waves of visitors began to arrive in Greece about two hundred years ago, they came mostly to gaze on the remains of antiquity. They traveled as comfortably as circumstances allowed, following each other around a circuit that quickly became traditional and that still draws millions to this day.

In the early 1960s, however, a different kind of traveler appeared. These were the mainly young and they came in search of the places where no one went. They fanned out across the islands of the Aegean and found bare rocks on which to spend the summer. These rocks were often inhabited by only a handful of old men and women, those who had clung on when everyone else had fled the boredom and poverty of island life. There were no monuments, little to eat, and nothing to do. But the new wanderers lay happily in the sun, spent whatever money they had, and rescued a dying world.

Nowhere was too remote or too uncomfortable in those days. Anywhere with a glimpse of the sea was potential paradise and travelers waited for days on end in the port of Athens, hoping for the boat that never came, the one that would drop you off on that ultimate outcrop of rock that no one else had ever seen.

The Greeks, incredulous at first, got used to these odd cravings, saw opportunities; and so now, last of the line, wretched Aliki awaits its saviors.

Hobhouse slept badly at Arta. He was troubled, he wrote, by a party of Greeks "fiddling and dancing in the room next to us." The complaint is familiar enough. The music, though, would be different today. Now you would have to search a long time to hear the eastern sounds of traditional Greece, the music that one nineteenth-century traveler compared ungenerously to "the howling of dogs in the night."

They left Arta for Ioannina on 5 October. It was an easy road to travel, "thro out tolerable for horses," as Hobhouse noted. Such roads were one of the most visible signs of Ali Pasha's authority. Recognizing that wealth depended on the free flow of goods through a safe country, Ali had worked to make life comfortable for those who moved about.

There were also plenty of places to stay on the road north. These places were called by the Turkish word *han*, meaning an inn. To Europeans these *han*s were usually worse than nothing, being dark, dirty, and overconvivial. But their existence in large numbers was always a sign of the commercial importance of an area.

There were, for example, almost no *han*s in the vicinity of Athens, a backwater in the days before Independence. Byron once struggled through the rain on a journey from the Peloponnese to Athens and then complained bitterly to the chief of the British Embassy in Constantinople because he could find nowhere to rest his head.

Byron and Hobhouse took two soldiers with them for protection. On their way out of Arta they met long lines of horses loaded with goatskins. For this is the time of the grape harvest. On the road beyond, they met only two parties of armed Albanians. It was no season to be moving through the mountains. "We had begun our . . . tour a month too soon," wrote Hobhouse, once the misery of traveling in the rainy season had become clear to them.

In the dark and rain they reached the *han* of Ayios Dimitrios, about thirty-five miles north of Arta. Those who had arrived earlier were already camped out in the stable. Byron and his party were forced to share a room with four Albanians and a priest. Almost everyone slept with their hand on their pistol, "not so much out of caution as custom," said Hobhouse, since apparently no one was in the slightest danger. "The fashion was new," he added, "and somewhat disagreeable to us."

Today the main road from Arta to Ioannina follows the Louros River for much of the time. It carries a great deal of traffic and crosses a pass at over two thousand feet. There is another way, to the east of this main road, which avoids some of the hardest climbing; and a third route to the west, much more difficult, and dominated by Mount Tomaros at six thousand feet.

Byron and Hobhouse took the more easterly road and they traveled without incident. For once, as they came in sight of Ioannina, the sun shone on them, and they were able to gaze down in peace on the domes and minarets of what was then the finest, most cultured city in Greece.

Approaching from the south, as they did, one notices that the geography of the Ioannina area stands out clearly. The city lies at about fifteen hundred feet, in a narrow plain beside a lake. Mitsikeli, the classic bare mountain, rises on the other side of the lake, overlooking a small island where Ali Pasha was assassinated in January 1822. Ioannina has a difficult climate. Far from the sea, it is fearsome in the heat of summer, while the winters are long and bitter. Edward Lear came here in the middle of May 1849. It rained and he was so cold at night that he could hardly sleep.

Ioannina excited everyone in those days. It was, said one

traveler, "the Athens of modern Greece." Lear, as an artist, loved both the natural and the human landscape. In the mountains, plain, lake, and buildings, he found an "inexhaustible store of really beautiful forms." The city, he wrote, "will always hold its place in memory as one of the first in interest of the many scenes I have known in many lands."

Lear's enthusiasm almost conceals the fact that he was looking at Ioannina in decline and his reference to "its present and utterly melancholy condition" comes as a surprise, after so much praise. But it was indeed a different and fallen city in his time. Byron and Hobhouse had the luck to see it in its absolute prime.

Most European travelers in the nineteenth century were massively disappointed with Greek towns and villages; still today, there are few that you remember for their style or their buildings. The almost universal view in pre-Independence days was that Greece was cursed with the backwardness it deserved, though none went further than the Englishman Finch, who declared that "many of the Greeks resemble monkeys and baboons." Travelers came to dread the approach of night and the need to find shelter. The Greeks lived in hovels of sun-dried bricks, with no comforts or decoration. The narrow streets were often full of mud, often mere gutters or ditches. Worst of all were the small villages and the dirt and disease of their mud huts.

Against this general background, Ioannina was a revelation. It was the most prosperous and populous city for miles around, a trading center on the route that linked the Ionian island of Corfu with the eastern Greek city of Thessaloniki across the Pindus Mountains. Its small traders exported hides to Italy, imported manufactured goods from Trieste and rice from Egypt. It had a population of about thirty-five thousand, more than three times the number who lived in Athens.

Ali Pasha's rise to power had coincided with the destabilizing events of the Napoleonic Wars; and, since no one knew what might emerge from the complexities of Balkan politics, his capital had become the object of intense diplomatic activity. Russia,

Turkey, France, and England all sought, at different times, to intervene, and Ali found himself flattered by the attentions of those who were far more powerful than he.

His city was cosmopolitan and full of life. There was a great covered market, like the famous one in Constantinople, a hospital, and a college where Latin and French were taught. Since the city had fallen to Ali, many of the settled Turkish and Greek families had left, preferring the security of other places to the spotlight of Ali's massive ambitions. So Ioannina thronged with temporary visitors: merchants from the Levant; Turkish, Albanian, and Moorish soldiers; gypsies. There, too, were hostages, held by Ali as surety for the actions of people in other parts of his domain; black slaves for the seraglio; and a wild collection of renegades and foreigners on the run.

As Byron and Hobhouse came down into the outskirts of the city, they passed a butcher's shop and saw something hanging from the branch of a large tree. They took it to be a piece of meat. As Hobhouse went closer, he discovered it was the arm of a man "with part of the side torn from the body, and hanging by a bit of string tied round one of the fingers." It was, he learned later, part of the body of a priest who had been executed five days before as the leader of a band of robbers. The rest of his body was scattered on exhibition around the city.

It was a shocking entrance, but Hobhouse shrewdly refused to draw the obvious stereotype. Before we think of the Turks as savage and brutal, he wrote, let us remember that a stranger coming into London fifty years ago might well have thought the same about the English. Even the French consul general in Ioannina, who had every reason to loathe Ali Pasha, recognized that Ali's brutal methods had cleared a large area of Greece and Albania of bandits. As Hobhouse noted, Ali had burned them, hanged them, beheaded them, and impaled them. His growing empire had been made safe for commerce.

The price, of course, had been high. Pouqueville, the French consul general, tells how he once went to call on Ali at night and how, on his way home across a dimly lit courtyard in Ali's castle, he fell over a pile of newly severed human heads. In some ways, violence and insecurity had simply been transferred: ceasing to be part of the anarchy of a bandit-infested countryside, they had become one of the dominant features of Ali's Albanian state.

Byron and Hobhouse carried a letter of introduction from the governor of Malta to the English resident in Ioannina, William Martin Leake. Leake had arranged a house for them on what is now, inevitably, Lord Byron Street. A later visitor, the Reverend Thomas Smart Hughes, has left a detailed description of the place, which also gives some idea of the way of life among middle-class Greeks at the time. The house, Hughes wrote,

> affords perhaps as good a specimen as can be met with of a modern Greek mansion. From the street we enter by a pair of folding doors, into a large stone portico or piazza, enclosing three sides of an area or court fronted by a garden ... very near the folding doors a flight of stone steps leads up to a fine picturesque gallery or corridor supported on the stone arches of the portico and shaded by the long shelving roof of the house; this is a place of exercise for the inmates in bad weather, and of indolent repose during the violence of the heat: at one end is seen a species of summer-house fitted up with seats and cushions, called the kiosk, where the family sit to enjoy the refreshing breeze, and the master frequently receives his visitors; at the other end is a bath. From this gallery we enter at once into the dwelling rooms, the principal of which are the apartments of the men fitted up with a divan, or low sofa, raised about a foot from the floor, and furnished with cushions, which serve the purpose both of chairs and beds, for in the same room wherein the Greek sits, and eats, and drinks, and smokes all day, he sleeps also by night, divesting himself only of a small part of his clothes, and covering himself with a species of thick

quilt. . . . At a different part of the gallery a passage leads into the gynaeconitis or gynaeceum, the apartments of the women. . . .

Leake knew more about Greece than anyone at the time. Of him it could almost literally be said that, during his vast excursions, he had left no stone unturned. He was a true professional. The four volumes of his *Travels in Northern Greece* remain one of the classic works of Greek topography. He found the two young English visitors who had been thrust upon him irritating amateurs, which was perhaps not unfair. There was, after all, something of the poseur in both Byron and Hobhouse. They strutted about the city in regimental uniforms and seemed to believe they were creating a great impression.

Pouqueville, too, despised the new intruders. He wrote of "ces mirliflores" (these dandies), of these "two self-styled noblemen," though Hobhouse says that Pouqueville held himself aloof during their visit, because England and France were then in a state of war, and that they did not meet him in Ioannina.

On the day after their arrival, Leake called on them. He was ill with a cold, "which disease seemed to be communicated to his manner," Hobhouse noted in his diary. Byron met Leake again two years later in England and found him then much improved. "I had a visit lately from Major . . . Leake," he wrote in September 1811. "He is grown less taciturn, better dressed, & more like an (English) man of this world than he was at Yanina."

On Hobhouse, however, Leake took his revenge. For when Byron's companion published his *Travels in Albania* in 1813, Leake set out to undermine its credibility; in his own *Researches in Greece*, published the following year, he devoted forty pages to listing the errors, large, small, and imaginary, into which Hobhouse had fallen.

Byron and Hobhouse were to spend six days in Ioannina. Ali Pasha's secretary called on them and took care to flatter them immensely. He spoke to them in French, told them that Ali had gone north into Albania to finish off a small war ("une petite guerre"); that he had left instructions for them to follow on, accompanied by an armed escort. It was to be all expenses paid, as Byron naively enthused in a letter to his mother. So, with the prospect of the most interesting city in Greece before them, they settled down to enjoy themselves.

$\mathcal{T}wo$

*I see not much difference between ourselves & the Turks, save that
we have foreskins and they none, that they have long dresses and
we short, and that we talk much and they little....*

—Byron to Henry Drury, 3 May 1810

The city, of course, is much changed. But there are still few
places in Greece finer than Ioannina on a fine October
morning. The old quarter lies down by the lake and the entrance
to it is still through high fortification walls. Once inside you find
yourself in a pattern of narrow lanes, between houses with overhanging balconies. This, the most intimate part of Ioannina, was
once defended by a moat and drawbridge. It is unbearable in
summer, as the heat bounces from wall to wall with no escape.
Here it is easy to imagine the world of intrigue, of unseen events,
that characterized the capital of Ali Pasha's empire.

On the south side of this fortified sanctum is an inner citadel,
walled within walls. There is a mosque here with its minaret
and, perhaps, Ali Pasha's tomb—though, if so, it must contain his
body only, since his head finished on a platter in Constantinople.
This is where Ali brought his Suliote captives, to be flayed alive
or roasted on spits. Nearby, there were once four palaces: the old
palace of the Pasha, with its harem; then, a little to the south,
Ali's newer palace of Litharitza, a place Leake called "the finest

artificial feature in the beautiful scenery of Ioannina." Then a palace each for Ali's two sons, Moukhtar and Veli.

Byron and Hobhouse did the tour of the palaces: "splendid, but too much ornamented with silk & gold," Byron wrote to his mother. Above the entrance to Moukhtar's palace was a mural that showed him in the act of torturing a prisoner; Veli's palace had a painting depicting piles of severed heads. Byron best remembered calling on Mahmoud, son of Moukhtar, who was holding court in the absence of his father. He was ten years old, Byron wrote, "with large black eyes which our ladies [in England] would purchase at any price."

Mahmoud admired Byron's sword and asked him how he came to be traveling so young with no one to take care of him. Precociously, he asked the two Englishmen whether they were members of the House of Commons or the House of Lords. One of the luckier members of Ali's family, Mahmoud would survive the death of his grandfather. He lived on, in the rags of a dervish, until 1863, in Constantinople. His father and his uncle would both die violent deaths, their heads, like that of Ali, ending up as exhibits in the Turkish capital.

Overlooking the lake and the walls of the fortress is the Aslan Mosque. Built in 1618, it is now the Municipal Museum. Its very existence is a symbol of cultural discord, for on this site was once the Greek Orthodox Church of St. John the Baptist. It was destroyed in reprisal for a Greek uprising against the Turks in 1611, and the mosque built in its place, as an act of revenge.

Four communities, frequently antagonistic toward each other, have made Ioannina what it is. Three of them—Turkish, Greek, and Jewish—are represented in the museum. No attempt has been made here to impose false harmony on the past. Each of the three cultures is simply given a room of its own, in memory of the fact that, for five hundred years, they shared the same narrow space within the fortress walls.

Ioannina remained in Turkish hands long after the Greek War

of Independence. It became Greek only in 1913. Many Turks stayed on after that, in the city that had been their home for generations. Then in 1922, after a catastrophic war between Greece and Turkey, all were returned to Asia Minor, in the final admission that Greeks and Turks could not live together. The Jewish community, too, once flourished here and a synagogue still functions inside the walls. But, of the 5,000 Jews who lived in Ioannina before the Second World War, only 150 remain.

Of the fourth community that played a part in the making of Ioannina, the museum says little. Ali Pasha and his dreams of a greater Albania are still too close. Most of the Albanian Muslims in this part of Greece were massacred by Greek nationalist troops after the Second World War in a process of ethnic cleansing. Today, Albanian refugees, in flight from the poverty of their native land, are universally despised in Greece.

From the bus station in Ioannina there is a regular service to the Albanian frontier at Kakavia. I watched two young men boarding the evening bus. They had a collection of cheap plastic lampshades tied to their backs and they struggled up the steps, tugging on a dozen thin plastic bags. One of the bags broke open, spilling out bottles of baby shampoo, tins of tomatoes, floor cleaner, and condensed milk. All they could carry from the supermarkets in Ioannina. By chance, I saw them again a few days later, restocking bare shelves in a warehouse in southern Albania.

With the darkness of evening it got cold. I walked along the red mud of Lord Byron Street where, earlier in the day, a bulldozer had been re-laying the tarmac. In a shop doorway, red with the blood of slaughtered meat, there was a sign advertising a public meeting on the causes and prevention of cholera. There was an epidemic, it seemed, in Albania.

How much Greece has changed. When I first came here in the 1960s, things moved so slowly, as if the whole country had still not recovered from the misery of an unlucky past: war, occupation, then civil war and famine. It was like watching an old man who, having suffered for years from some incurable illness, was yet miraculously alive, haunted by everything that had gone before. Children looked hungry then and animals starved.

Even so, the harsh old world of Greek rural life looked a paradise to the outsider. The eternal round of habits, the darkness and peace of the country at night, fields full of asphodels in spring, the stillness of midafternoon in the summer heat. It was a place where people knew the economy of storytelling; for nothing was too small to lead to a story, and, like the clothes people wore or the farm implements they owned, every story could be reused over and over. It was an easy paradise, troubled only by the awareness that many who lived there would have chosen, if they could, to be somewhere else.

Sometimes, in the last few days, I had come across the debris of this almost forgotten world. Outside Arta, I saw an old woman in black walking her sheep against the traffic on a busy highway, her head held high, her face an anachronism, lined and vacant. On the way to Ioannina, there was an old man by the side of the road, pulling on the carcass of a dead goat, while two skeletal cows chewed among the stones behind him. A rural world of dying continuities that I would find again, time-trapped, in Albania.

Ioannina is Greek, but its streets are international. It is a bright, transparent, altogether modern city. I joined the crowds for the evening *volta*. This is one of the glories of southern life and redeems a time of day that in northern Europe is the very death. Suddenly, after dark, the streets fill with people of all ages. Young children in the arms of sisters or mothers; students carrying notebooks and packets of colored pens; later, businessmen with their briefcases; grandfathers, great-aunts, the boys next door. *Pame volta,* people say: "Let's go for a walk." And they do. Up and down the same few streets. It's hard to believe there's anyone left indoors. The shops are open and you can do all the things that in English towns you can do only on weekends or in an hour stolen from the day.

In places like this, people say to each other a dozen times as they pass: "Where are you going?" As if there were a thousand possibilities. The formalities observed. Handshakes, smiles, the raising of the hat, the farewell of the hand, endlessly repeated, evening after evening. It's a marvelous pageant, though nothing in Greece, perhaps, can make the outsider feel so oppressively alone.

The next morning, I checked out of my hotel. In a voice of ancient gravel, the one-eyed owner wished me a safe journey. *Kalo taxidhi, Mr. Bristol,* he said. . . . In Greece I have often been Mr. Bristol. Many Greeks speak English, but not all of them read it well; so, since my passport faithfully registers the place of my birth, the confusion is understandable. It has happened so many times that, even when I'm a long way from Greece, the name of Bristol brings back the soft, oily smell of Greek plumbing and the unsparing white walls of cheap hotels.

In the cool early morning I was hungry. Ahead was a long walk to the Monastery of Zitsa, which had been Byron's first stop beyond Ioannina, on the way to find Ali Pasha. I had never been to Zitsa before. Byron had said that it lay among some of the finest scenery in Greece. A gloriously benign phrase that suggested the walk could only be uphill.

Breakfast is a difficult time in Greece, a time of stale bread and broken biscuits, since most Greeks manage on coffee until lunchtime. Still, it is, no doubt, better than the sadness of the great English breakfast where, amidst kippers and sausages, toast and marmalade, you have to accept that the best meal of the day is over before you're even properly awake. I chewed on a remnant of days past and walked out in the sunshine.

Byron and Hobhouse had a good time in Ioannina. They didn't sleep well, it is true. It was the feast of Ramadan and they were disturbed by the heavy drum, which called the faithful to prayer at midnight, and by the hours of carousing that followed the end of prayers at one o'clock. Hobhouse had some complaints, as he always did. There was no one in the city who could mend an umbrella and only one poor Italian who could mend a bedstead. These, though, were minor problems. They had dabbled unself-consciously in the politics of Ioannina, playing the Englishman abroad to little princes in palaces. They had been entertained and flattered by Ali's family. Moreover, as far as Byron was concerned, Ioannina had begun to reveal the sexual possibilities of contemporary Greek life.

In the city, Hobhouse observed, you never saw unmarried women. They were held in seclusion, as was the way throughout the Turkish Empire. Consequently, there was room for sexual pleasure only with married women or with men. So, as Hobhouse saw things, there was "some excuse for pederasty—which is practised underhand by the Greeks, but openly carried on by the Turks."

This last observation he concealed in his diary. He would never have repeated it in print. In the England of his time, homosexuality was "an unnatural crime," "an abominable offence," in the contemporary language of the newspapers. It was a hanging matter; or, if not that, something that could easily lead to humiliation and violent abuse, through exposure in the pillory. If a writer wished to speak of homosexuality, the rule was either to condemn it or to deny its very existence.

Among a thousand examples, here is Leake, in the course of his *Researches in Greece*. He is talking of a subject about which few people in England knew anything at all: Greek folk poetry. He explains that the Greeks have two kinds of song: the warlike or heroic, on the one hand; the erotic, on the other. The erotic songs, he says, are known by the general name *poustika*, "a word highly characteristic of the manners of those who have adopted it, and derived from a Turkish word [*pust*, meaning a sodomite], for which we have happily no corresponding term in the English language."

Hobhouse had some toleration for homosexuality. In December 1819, when he was detained in Newgate Prison for writing a radical pamphlet, he heard a man being executed for sodomy.

"Tis dreadful hanging a man for this practice," he recorded in his diary. Yet he knew full well the limits of his society and he looked on with increasing concern the development of his friend's own intimate Greece.

Late one evening, during their stay in Ioannina, Byron and Hobhouse went to the public baths. This detail, too, finds no place in Hobhouse's book, only in his diary, and the reasons again are obvious. They did not, he says, venture as far as the "inner room," frightened away by the presence of an old man. But in that inner room, they were told, the washing took place, performed by *bei giovani* (beautiful young men). Even in his diary, Hobhouse is discreet, leaving everything to the imagination. Byron, in a letter to his publisher in 1819, put it more directly: "a Turkish bath," he wrote, "that marble paradise of sherbet and sodomy."

On their way back through Ioannina, at the end of October, they were to make a different sort of excursion, this time to an apparently innocuous Turkish puppet show. The event throws further light on Hobhouse's capacity for discretion, reveals how already he was performing a mission he would pursue until the end of his long life: that of protector of Byron's reputation.

The Turkish *karagöz* (the name means a person with dark eyes) is the Punch figure of a shadow-puppet tradition that was once popular all over Greece. A single shadow theater still survives, or did until recently, by the harbor in Prevesa.

The show in Ioannina was performed in a dirty coffeehouse. It was "in the corner of the room," Hobhouse wrote in his diary, "the figures being shown on a piece of greas'd paper a yard or so in length & breadth. The hero of the representation was a personage with an immense head & body [and, it is clear from Hobhouse's book, an immense penis] . . . towards the conclusion a certain divertissement was introduced between this man & a lady—which was highly to the taste of the audience, which consisted mostly of young boys—nothing could be more beastly—but Ld B. tells me that he has seen puppet-shows in

England as bad, and that the morrice-dancers in Nottinghamshire are worse."

Whatever unorthodox sexual practice Hobhouse saw is scarcely relevant. What is interesting is the way he treats the incident in his book. There he repeats the view he had expressed in his diary, that the show "was too horribly gross to be described"; but he concludes by saying simply: "Those who have seen the morrice-dancing in some counties of England may have a faint idea of it." No mention of Byron. Even the reference to Byron's home county of Nottinghamshire is carefully removed.

Byron and Hobhouse left Ioannina for Zitsa on 11 October. They had with them Ali Pasha's secretary, the Greek Spiridion Colovo. He was an important man and during Ali's last days he would be tortured to death by the Turks to make him reveal his master's secrets. They also took an Albanian soldier named Vasili. He was in Leake's service at the time and was recommended by him "for his Albanian virtues of activity and fidelity," though not, Leake added, for his intelligence.

The way to Zitsa first passes over level ground to the west, then becomes a steep climb as you turn north. They saw the tents of grape harvesters, crossed a large tract of marshy land, and then began the climb into the stony hills. As evening came on, Hobhouse reached Zitsa and the rain began to fall in torrents. At this time of year, when late holiday-makers are still burning by the sea, it is already autumn in the mountains.

Byron had lagged behind with the luggage and servants, and Hobhouse soon realized that his friend was lost out in the storm. A storm, Hobhouse says, that he never in his life saw equaled. He lay down in his greatcoat on the mud floor of the cottage in which they had arranged to stay the night. In the intervals of peace, between the howling of the wind and the roaring of thunder, he listened to dogs barking and shepherds calling to each other in the surrounding hills. Then, a little after midnight, "a man, panting and pale, and drenched with rain, rushed into the room."

The man reported that the baggage horses had fallen and everyone had lost their way. Not until 3:00 A.M. did Byron and the servants arrive to tell the tale of the storm. How they had wandered, lost in the driving rain, finally stopping by a waterfall, near some Turkish tombstones; and how their guides had run away in fear. Hobhouse was dismayed at the fickleness of the natives and drew a lesson for the future: "In this country," he wrote, "it is absolutely necessary to be always accompanied by a soldier, to enforce obedience."

Byron was less concerned with the insubordination of his guides, more charmed by the romance of the storm. He later published a poem that, he claimed, he had composed during his hours out in the wind and rain on that night of 11 October 1809. It's hard to believe this literally, for the poem is over seventy lines in length, which is a very long poem even for a great storm. But the story is romantic enough and has long formed part of Byron's biography. In the midst of it all, he said, he thought back to the married woman he had left behind in Malta:

> Clouds burst, skies flash, oh, dreadful hour!
>   More fiercely pours the storm!
> Yet here one thought has still the power
>   To keep my bosom warm.

It was a long time, Hobhouse remembered, "before we ceased to talk of the thunder-storm in the plain of Zitza."

They stayed at Zitza the whole of the next day and night to dry out; and, in the afternoon, they climbed up out of the village to the monastery that Byron would make forever famous in *Childe Harold*. The monastery is empty now, but still secure behind its high walls, the doors and windows barred. The grounds are a little overgrown and birds screech from the silent bell tower. There's a plaque on the wall that gives some mistaken dates for Byron's visit and then, in English, the opening lines from stanza 48, book 2, of *Childe Harold*, which record just how much he loved the place:

Monastic Zitza! from thy shady brow,
Thou small, but favour'd spot of holy ground!
Where'er we gaze, around, above, below,
What rainbow tints, what magic charms are found!
Rock, river, forest, mountain, all abound,
And bluest skies that harmonize the whole. . . .

Just beyond the monastery, there's a large open space, shaded by tall fir trees. In autumn the shade is cool, but in the sun the light still reminds you, like a distant relation, of the season that has passed. Here, on summer evenings, villagers come to sit and talk and escape the heat. Looking south, you can see the way Byron must have come and the forest of oak trees where the guides lost their bearings. The mountains, as always just ahead or behind, here in a horseshoe before you.

It is a beautiful site, but Byron would see wilder, more breath-taking views as he went up into Albania. Edward Lear came south this way, full of the splendor of the mountains farther north, and he was inevitably disappointed. Zitsa, he wrote, was "a place I had looked forward to visiting as much as to any." But, he concluded, "all my enthusiasm regarding 'Monastic Zitza' . . . vanished as the rain came down . . . and the wind blew so hard as to make sitting on horseback difficult."

There were only three or four priests living here in Lear's time. One of them remembered clearly Byron's visit thirty-nine years before. They talked, but Lear admired Byron and gives only the merest hint of what was said. "I shall not add," he writes, "to the list of crude absurdities too often tacked to the memories of remarkable men." He left, "in (be it confessed) no satisfied humour."

Both Hobhouse and Byron, though, had the same enthusiasm for Zitsa. With the air of men who had traveled everywhere and seen it all, they both reached the same judgment. "Perhaps there is not in the world a more romantic prospect than that which is viewed from the summit of the hill," wrote Hobhouse. And Byron to his mother: the monastery was "in the most beautiful Situation (always excepting Cintra in Portugal) I ever beheld."

Zitsa was a poor village in Byron's time. A place of about 150 houses, inhabited almost entirely by Greeks. The best land belonged to the monastery, which paid no taxes. The full weight of Ali Pasha's greed fell on villages just like this, and Hobhouse saw clearly that the people were starving in the midst of plenty. Their flocks, wine, corn, and meat were produced only for sale, so that they could pay the impositions of Ali's empire. Hobhouse spoke to a priest, dirty and miserably dressed. "I never saw a Welsh curate," he noted in his diary, "but cannot suppose any one so poor as this man."

Today the roads that lead northwest from Zitsa toward the Albanian frontier are still rough and untraveled, for Zitsa is a terminus, not a route to somewhere else. As Leake noted dryly, Byron and Hobhouse were only taken that way because Zitsa had more comfortable accommodation than any of the surrounding villages.

They were, as they almost always were, unlucky with the weather and traveled only four hours or so beyond Zitsa before the rain forced them to halt. They stayed at the house of a poor priest, "who . . . seemed to have as much reason to be miserable," Hobhouse wrote, "as the people whom we had just left."

I followed them out of Zitsa on a dirt road that would have dissolved into mud with a day's heavy rain. I passed through small villages, places far too small for the names they carried: Vassilopoulo, Ieromnimi, Parakalamos. For miles you see and hear no one. Wooded slopes and deep ravines, with only the sound of birds. A few red-tiled roofs from time to time. Outside Vassilopoulo, an open-air basketball court, the gift of a nostalgic Vassilopoulan who, thousands of miles away, had looked back gratefully on an idyllic childhood beside this dirt track. An odd memorial to youth, in a village now given over only to the very old.

Sometimes these nostalgic émigrés return, from Australia or the United States. Someone who's spent thirty, forty years in Melbourne or Chicago takes the great decision and comes back here, to build one of the pretty houses with the red-tiled roofs, completing the fantasy that's kept them going during all those years in the wilderness. Then they sit on their veranda and look over the deserted mountains with, sometimes, in the distance, the smoke of a fire, proof that someone else is still alive in this silent countryside. They watch the fields of ripening corn, the oak trees that give such wonderful shelter in summertime, and they think . . . Well, I'm not sure what they think. For I've long been fascinated by these returnees, who are so much a part of modern Greek life, and have often spoken with them, but I've never understood how they feel about coming home.

The conversation goes:

"Do you miss America/Australia/wherever?" A wide wave of the hand, up toward the ear then down again. Absurd notion.

"So you like it here?"

"It's quiet"; or "We have fresh air." Or something else so unchallengeably true that it always seems a warning against further questions.

There's good walking country north of Zitsa. Easy and unspectacular. In the autumn sun it's as beautiful as the best summer's day in England. But if you have rain it's miserable among these half-abandoned villages. Eventually, you reach the main road that runs west from the town of Kalpaki to the Albanian frontier. I passed a small lake, blue with white waves, like the sea; perhaps the same lake Byron and Hobhouse saw as they came this way, beginning their ascent to their favorite mountain village, Delvinaki.

The frontier between Greece and Albania in their day was ill defined politically. Greece and Albania were, after all, merely provinces within the Turkish Empire. But Delvinaki, "dear Delvinachi," as Byron called it, was traditionally recognized as the last Greek village before Albania. To the north, travelers noticed the signs of change, the presence of a different culture, and one which, to Byron and Hobhouse, was still more exotic than the Greek.

While he was traveling through Germany in May 1816, after the collapse of his marriage, Byron wrote to Hobhouse to say how much the countryside there reminded him "of the old scenes" in Greece and especially of the valley that leads out of Delvinaki. The resemblance, he wrote, with a facetious thought for his ever faithful servant, was one that "struck even the learned Fletcher."

Today Delvinaki lies about ten miles from the frontier and just a few miles north of the main road into Albania. It's a remarkably pretty village, at the bottom of a deep chasm. The approach is through wooded gorges, with mountains closing you in on all sides. In the sun it looks a neat and self-contained sort of place, like a prosperous spa town.

Byron and Hobhouse found that Ali Pasha had passed through Delvinaki eight days before and was probably, by now, in Libohova in Albania. Hobhouse was happy to rest for a while. He took a walk behind the village to watch Delvinaki at sunset. He spent a rare few minutes at peace, quietly pastoralizing over a scene that has changed little since that time. Animals browsing, the ever present goat, the tinkling of bells.

They left the following morning, traveling northwest through what is still densely wooded country. Three hours after leaving Delvinaki, they entered the valley of the Drinos River. In the hills on the western side of the valley they could see a succession of towns and villages, "which appeared," said Hobhouse, "like the goats of Virgil, to hang upon the rocks."

The area was heavily populated then, unlike today. They met parties of other travelers, on horseback or on foot. When they exchanged greetings, the language they heard was no longer

Greek. The dress of the peasantry, too, had changed, from the loose woolen trousers of Greece to the cotton tunic of Albania. "The wild Albanian kirtled to his knee," as Byron remembered in *Childe Harold*. There were, of course, no tame Albanians in his mythology.

Today, it is impossible to follow their path exactly, for the only crossing into Albania is by a road a little farther to the south. That road is almost deserted. You pass one or two jeeps or an abandoned car rusting in the sun. The fields, too, are empty. The border is troubled and small groups of Greek soldiers patrol the back roads, looking for the refugees I would later see coming down toward the frontier from the other side.

The modern road climbs through the woods and then, at a sudden turn, you look down a long way to the Drinos Valley and the border crossing. As I came closer, I walked for several miles beside a long line of gasoline tankers. They wait here, at the edge of nowhere, to clear Greek passport control, then trundle slowly forward, the lifeline servicing Albania's recent passion for the motorcar.

Once you walk into Albania, the change is as sudden as all the clichés in all the books would have you believe. This is the place where time stands still, the museum of the living past. After a while, such metaphors are inadequate, but they serve for a day or two and help the traveler survive the first bouts of incomprehension. Suddenly nothing is familiar from the modern world, but everything reminds you of things you once read, in history and travel books of generations ago.

Until the late 1980s, Albania was almost completely sealed off from the rest of the world by a socialist government of outrageous tenacity. It is, by a long way, the poorest country in Europe. You see the poverty hanging over everything from the moment you arrive. Over the dust in the customs office, over the bare walls, the cracked tables and chairs, the dirty sofa. Behind are the steel gates that guard the way into Greece; ahead a quiet crowd of hopeful émigrés, waiting and watching on a patch of waste ground, as a few people pass over from one world to another.

When Byron and Hobhouse crossed the frontier, they skirted the hills on the eastern side of the Drinos Valley, making for the town of Libohova. Today, the main road follows the west bank of the Drinos, heading north toward the city of Gjirokastra, with the turning toward Libohova about a dozen miles down the way.

Libohova was the home of Ali Pasha's sister, Chehnissa. As passionate, and as passionately cruel, as her brother, she had been devastated by the early death of her eldest son and had withdrawn from the world into her palace. It was almost certainly to see her that Ali had come to Libohova, a few days ahead of his young English admirers.

Byron and Hobhouse met Chehnissa's youngest son, Adam Bey, somewhere on their way through Albania. He, too, was to die prematurely. After this second blow, Chehnissa destroyed all the mirrors and ornaments in her palace and had all the windows painted black in mourning. She was, in every respect, the ogress out of a fairy tale. A woman who is never mentioned without a shiver of fear.

Chehnissa and Ali were responsible for one of the most memorable massacres in a period of Albanian history when such things were commonplace. The details of what happened say much about the characters of the two and the kind of feuding culture to which they belonged, and Byron's response to the news of the massacre says something interesting about him and his attitude to what he had seen in Albania.

A long time before, perhaps as far back as 1762, Ali Pasha's mother had been taken prisoner in the village of Gardiki. This is the modern Kardhiq, which lies not far from Ali's Albanian stronghold of Tepelena. It was a minor incident in a long history of intercommunal feuding. Some accounts say that Ali's mother was captured along with her daughter Chehnissa, others that she was taken alone. Stories of gang rape circulated in the aftermath of the event, though there is little evidence to support them and they were almost certainly untrue.

In feuding cultures, the sharpness of memory is not blurred by the passage of time. The writer James Pettifer recalls a modern instance in 1992, in Tirana, Albania's capital. A man was beheaded there with an ax in the lobby of a hotel, in revenge for a crime committed by his father more than forty years before. Whatever happened to their mother in prison, Ali and his sister retained a lifelong hatred of the inhabitants of Gardiki; and, when Ali seized control of the village in 1812, the insults of half a century before were as vivid in his mind as they had ever been.

He had almost the entire male population of the village shot by the banks of the Drinos as he looked on. The women, about a thousand in all, were then raped by Ali's soldiers and brought to hang their heads in shame before the terrible Chehnissa. Vengeance finally achieved.

Byron learned of the massacre at Gardiki from Henry Holland, a traveler who had been in Albania and who, coincidentally, brought back, in 1813, a letter written in Latin from Ali Pasha to Byron. In this letter, Ali addressed Byron as his "most excellent & dearest friend" and asked him for an English gun.

Byron wrote to at least two correspondents, passing on the details of the story that Holland had told him about Gardiki. Here is the version he gave to Lady Melbourne on 7 September 1813:

> What do you think was "dearest friend's" last exploit?— Forty two years ago the inhabitants of a hostile city seized his mother & 2 sisters & treated them as Miss Cunegonde was used by the Bulgarian cavalry. Well—this year he at last becomes master of the aforesaid city—selects all the persons living in the remotest degree akin to this outrage (in *Turkey* these are affronts) their children grand children— cousins &c. to the amount of 600—& has them put to death

in his presence.—I don't wonder at it—but the interval of 42 years is rather singular. . . .

The story, as Byron has it, is only slightly garbled. He accepts the account of gang rape, through his allusion to the fate of Cunégonde in Voltaire's *Candide*; and there are now two sisters, where there can only have been one at most and, very possibly, none at all. But if the details are more or less right, it is the tone that strikes us now as strange: Ali's delight in blood domesticated for the gossiping circles of Regency London.

Byron, as we shall see, was never fooled by Ali. He knew something of the score of cruelty and treachery that lay behind the man's fame. Still, Ali was a kind of hero for the young Byron. He was ruthless, daring, utterly committed to his own independence. He was also sexually addicted, with a harem not even Byron in his Italian days would be able to rival. Byron was exhilarated by Ali's power; while Ali, with his insouciance, could have been—if he hadn't been so old and so commendably exotic—almost one of the boys.

But there was also a lesson here, in his fascination with Ali, one that is important to the whole of Byron's development. To experience what Byron once called "the poetry of life" is, after all, to deny the world a share of its essential ordinariness. The imagined Greece of Byron's youth was almost all extraordinary, a wild place, always on the edge: Ali Pasha, the Suliotes, the land of Greece itself. Later he came to see the limitations, needed to engage with a real world unredeemed by the imagination. Life as fact or as fantasy: the return to Greece in 1823 would be a last attempt to confront an old dilemma.

Hobhouse was exasperated that no one in Libohova appeared to know whether Ali Pasha was there or not. He put it all down to the fact that Libohova was a Turkish village and that the Turks were "the most lazy and incurious race of beings on earth." His hostility toward the culture did not, however, prevent him from enjoying the food. Many dishes, he wrote, "are very palatable to an English taste, much more so, indeed, than those to be met with in Portuguese and Spanish cookery."

They discovered eventually that Ali had moved on again and was now in his hometown of Tepelena, thirty miles to the north. Held up, as ever, by torrential rains, they finally left Libohova on 17 October for what was to be the final destination of their outward journey.

At this time of year, however fine the weather, you always travel with an eye on the clouds. As I crossed into Albania they were piled up on the horizon, white as summer, with the promise of easy days to come.

In the customs office I met two old friends, both much changed, both victims of the new Albania. One used to be a poet, the other a folk dancer. Their former lives have become a symbol of the bad old days, when the state controlled the arts, as it controlled everything else. So they, along with poetry and folk dancing, have fallen on hard times. They work six or seven days a week, twelve hours a day, and struggle to avoid nostalgia.

There's always a sadness, as well as an excitement, in moments of transition. The excitement in Albania today is about the possibility of a future outsiders already know, so it is the sadness that remains most striking, the loss of old ways, the fear of what lies ahead.

There were almost no cars here until three years ago. Now the public transport system is breaking down and the car has become the symbol of freedom, as elsewhere in the world. People attend to their machines with the love they might give to children, a love that reflects all the pleasure of a once unthinkable release. About 70 percent of Albania is mountainous. In the old days, to go "over the mountains" was a major business; now, it's an affair for any weekend, if you can afford the gasoline. To see and be seen; to meet old friends, recover lost relatives.

It's a freedom that colonizes the spaces of the past. On the road north from the border, donkeys, cows, pigs, and sheep are still more numerous than cars, but the cars dominate effortlessly. Old men and women have suddenly become the flotsam of this new world. Abused, they take refuge with their animals in the ditch. The car rushes by, magically reducing the size of a country that is only slightly larger than the state of Maryland, but which, for a thousand years, has seemed enormous by its geography and its seclusion.

The excitement, the sudden dream of riches, are both real enough. Everyone here is trying to make money. I had only been in Albania for an hour when someone gave me a cigarette, and asked me to go into business with them.

"What business?"

"American cigarettes."

"But I don't smoke."

It's no good saying you know nothing, because that is the position most people start from.

"But we could do it, you and I." The man pleads, smiles, encouraging; talks on and on in unidiomatic Greek.

My two Albanian friends were exhausted. So, for a while, they dozed on the broken sofa, while I sat stamping passports for them. Once in a while an expensive car would come through. Then someone from a back office, with an animal instinct for the intruder, would shake himself out of sleep and begin the long process of taking the car to pieces. Partly, out of a remnant of bureaucratic pride; partly, out of the desire for revenge on a changed world.

When the long shift was over, we drove toward Libohova in the dark. We stopped at a restaurant by the side of the main road. Inside it was dimly lit, full of smoke, and there were no women to be seen. My friends ordered *kokoretsi*, which the dictionary defines as grilled sheep's entrails, a proposition reality all too quickly confirms. We talked with everyone in the crowded room. I was lost in the flow of language, from Greek to Albanian and back again. At the end, the waiter collected the leftover cold entrails and we took them with us in a paper bag.

On our way, we picked up a Serb who lived in northern Albania. He was trying to get home with his Greek girlfriend for a family reunion. She was so obviously his girlfriend, but he always called her his wife. He never seemed to notice how much this amused everyone else, as they drove back to a troubled domesticity of real wives and children, to apartments without heating and with running water for only a couple of hours a day.

The most impressive city in the south of Albania is Gjirokastra, which is about nine miles to the northwest of Libohova. Now a UNESCO World Heritage City, it has a famous ruined castle. The castle is vast and romantic and lies high above the city. The wind howls through the low trees that grow over the ruins, and shepherds graze their flocks on the rough grass. The city is rugged, austere, overlooked by bare mountains the color of cement. For generations Gjirokastra was important because of its control of the Drinos Valley. Every conquering army bound for Greece came this way, most recently the motorized divisions of the Italian and German armies in World War II.

Edward Lear noted that from afar the houses of Gjirokastra appeared "as one great pyramid of dwellings against the mountainside." Hobhouse, too, was impressed by the sight of the city, but he never saw it close at hand. Until 1812 it lay outside Ali Pasha's control. As Ali's guests in hostile territory, they thought it safer to keep their distance.

Many people still speak Greek in this area, as they have for millennia, but Hobhouse noted at once that the Albanian Greeks of his time were different from the Greeks across the border to the south. Above all, they were more prosperous and more confident. Stopping, by chance, for the night in a small village not far from Libohova, Hobhouse was surprised to find comfortable lodgings in a neat whitewashed cottage. Their host was kind and welcoming and in his face, Hobhouse wrote, there was nothing "of the cringing, downcast, timid look of the Greek peasant." In Albania the idea of Greek freedom was less absurd than it seemed in Greece.

Leaving Gjirokastra to the west, Byron and Hobhouse went north. They noticed, with surprise, a gang of women working with pickaxes and spades and they passed a large fountain "where there were many women washing with sticks and stones, in the Scotch fashion, and drawing water." Neither sight would be strange in today's Albania. The rhythms are still those of the old countryside. As you travel, you have the illusion that nothing moves but you. A boy, squatting by the roadside, is still there an hour later when you return, his sheep almost motionless in dry pasture. An old woman works a furrow with a wooden pick, ancient and alone in a vast field of brown grass and stones.

All this land in Ali Pasha's time was full of life. As Byron and Hobhouse finally drew near the town of Tepelena, Ali's Albanian capital, it was clear from the activity all around them that there would be much to see here and remember. Byron recorded the descent into Tepelena in *Childe Harold*:

> *The shades of wonted night were gathering yet,*
> *When, down the steep banks winding warily,*
> *Childe Harold saw, like meteors in the sky,*
> *The glittering minarets of Tepalen,*
> *Whose walls o'erlook the stream; and drawing nigh,*
> *He heard the busy hum of warrior-men*
> *Swelling the breeze that sigh'd along the lengthening glen.*

He was excited by the extravagance of Tepelena. It was a world that was at once both cosmopolitan and remote, a world of feudal splendor in which anything might be possible. The vision, once caught, held him forever and played its part in that dangerous surrender that would one day draw him back again to the East.

In Tepelena, Byron found contrasts of great power. In a letter home, he recalled the magnificence of Albanian dress. Cloaks trimmed with gold, velvet gold-laced jackets, silver-mounted pistols and daggers. He remembered the sight of Turks in their turbans, Tartars in their high caps, castrated black slaves. Two hundred horses ready to move out at a moment's notice. The beating of kettledrums.

Hobhouse, in his usual way, was less dramatic. But he, too, recognized that they had entered a world that had long disappeared in England. The sight on first going into Ali's palace, he wrote, was "something like what we might have, perhaps, beheld some hundred years ago in the castle-yard of a great feudal lord." The streets of Tepelena were "dirty and ill-built," but this was the most fascinating, extraordinary place he had ever seen.

Tepelena was a symbol of old forms of absolute power, a culture untroubled by the European Enlightenment; and for Byron, in particular, the most intriguing aspect of this old world was its display of sexual power. Already, as they approached Tepelena, they had seen a large party of soldiers escorting a sedan chair in which one of the women from Ali's harem was being carried shoulder-high the last few miles into town. Here was a place of complete sexual control:

> *Here woman's voice is never heard: apart,*
> *And scarce permitted, guarded, veil'd, to move,*
> *She yields to one her person and her heart,*
> *Tam'd to her cage, nor feels a wish to rove. . . .*

But Ali's power did not simply go beyond the limits of ordinary sexuality. What Byron saw in Tepelena was a society in which there seemed to be no sexual limits at all.

His interest in this is almost entirely concealed, appearing only in some canceled lines from *Childe Harold*:

> *For boyish minions of unhallowed love*
> *The shameless torch of wild desire is lit,*
> *Caressed, preferred even to woman's self above. . . .*

These few lines, however, are vastly eloquent about Byron's own sexual feelings. The sight of young boys freely available was a revelation. It is clear that Byron was aroused by what he saw, and that he reflected on it long afterward.

In an entry in his journal for 13 December 1813, Byron wrote: "It seems strange; a true voluptuary will never abandon his mind to the grossness of reality. It is by exalting the earthly, the material . . . by forgetting them altogether, or, at least, never naming them hardly to one's self, that we alone can prevent them from disgusting."

In Ali's court, this transformation of reality was easily made. At home, the sexual love of boys was an almost unspeakable transgression; here, in remote Tepelena, the grossness of sexual appetite could be exalted through another time and space. At home, there was only the harsh word "sodomy" and the fear of social ostracism. Here, the rules were different; it was a place of dimly lit courtyards, secret rooms, silken sofas, sherbets, and sweetmeats, where desire could be infinitely prolonged, made infinitely poetical.

It was the revelation of a freedom that would mark Byron's view of the East until the end of his life. It prepared the way for the vast excesses of his time in Athens, in 1810–11. It also affected the way Byron felt about other forms of freedom and so helped shape the course of a life. For, as he wrote in *Don Juan*, "I was born for opposition."

After the long search and the allure of Ali Pasha's great reputation, the eventual meeting between Ali and the two Englishmen was an anticlimax. At least, neither Byron nor Hobhouse left any memorable account of what passed between them.

They were both still young enough to believe that their social status and their Englishness gave them the balance of power over a minor oriental despot. Ali, on the other hand, had long been used to Europeans. He regularly had foreign newspapers translated for him and he took every opportunity to question travelers passing through his empire.

For Ali, Byron and Hobhouse were minor pieces to fit into the enormous jigsaw of contemporary politics. It could do no harm to flatter them. It might, in the current competition between England and France, be of some limited use. While, for their part, they could only imagine they were bringing Ali something precious and rare.

They met Ali four times during their stay in Tepelena. Hobhouse describes him as having quick, blue eyes and a long white beard. By European standards, he was very short. Most obviously, he was very fat. It is a shame they never had the chance to dine with Ali—he excused himself on the grounds of Ramadan—for Pouqueville, the French consul general, gives an account of lunchtime at the palace in Ioannina that suggests such occasions were extraordinary.

Pouqueville describes how Ali was served a whole lamb weighing twelve pounds. He ate over half, along with some heads of garlic, hard-boiled eggs, and an eel. Numerous other dishes arrived from time to time, served by a brilliant retinue of page boys. Ali would touch the food with a finger, to indicate approval, and the dish would vanish. If he found something not to his liking, he would go into a rage, threaten to hang the cooks, force them to eat their rice boiled in washing-up water. The whole scene was framed by gypsy singing and the dancing of court prostitutes.

Ali was charming toward his English visitors. He was always charming toward his guests and, indeed, toward his enemies, too. Often his last words to a man he had condemned to death were the very essence of affability. A complex man, too much so for the abilities of the young Hobhouse. He can find nothing more stimulating to say than that Ali was "mightily civil," that he yielded "very favourable impressions of his natural capacity."

Byron, as might be expected, saw more deeply. Or, rather, saw how opaque was the surface that Ali benignly offered to them. In *Childe Harold*, he remembered Ali reclining by a fountain in a marble-paved pavilion, surrounded by "soft voluptuous couches." It was the very stereotype of Eastern luxury and repose. But Byron registered that he had not for a moment been taken in by "that aged venerable face." Ali was "a man of war and woes," and "in his lineaments," he wrote, "ye cannot trace, / . . . the deeds that lurk beneath, and stain him with disgrace."

Ali flirted with Byron. Asked him what reason he had for having left his native land so young. "The Turks have no idea of travelling for amusement," Byron wrote to his mother. Even more flirtatiously, Ali admired Byron's small ears, curly hair, and "little white hands." The hands, he said, were proof of high birth, a remark that instantly found one of Byron's sensitive areas.

Clearly, there was a sexual interest at play throughout Byron's stay in Tepelena. Ali sent him "almonds & sugared sherbet, fruit & sweetmeats 20 times a day," begging him to visit him "often, and at night when he was more at leisure." Some writers believe Byron reciprocated the interest, even acted upon it, but, given his exclusive passion for youth, this sounds unlikely.

Byron and Hobhouse were lucky to see Tepelena when they did. They came too early to see the magnificent palace that was built to crown Ali's achievements and which was destroyed by fire in 1818. But, otherwise, they were there for the absolute zenith of Ali's power. Tepelena would be nothing after Ali had gone and Edward Lear, once again, was there to record the desolation of a ruined city. In the autumn of 1848, he wrote of the "deadly cold loneliness" of Tepelena. "The whole of this part of Albania," he noted, "is . . . most desolate and its inhabitants broken and dejected . . . and the once proud territory of Ali Pasha is now ground down into a melancholy insignificance."

It has never recovered. When Lear says that there can be nowhere more sad and gloomy than here, he speaks as much for now as for then. The modern town dates from 1920, when the previous wreck of a settlement was destroyed in an earthquake. It is a miserably poor place, without character, and subject to every kind of social problem.

Today, Ali's citadel is, at one end, a dumping ground for the town's refuse. The view from the other side, however, is no doubt as fine as it ever was, with the water far below and mountains rising in front. Just to the south of Tepelena, the Drinos and Vjoses Rivers meet, and the previously narrow valley opens out, wide and spacious. Looking back, into the funnel that guards the approach to Greece, one can easily understand why Tepelena was once important.

The united river that flows beneath the citadel is crossed by a picturesque bridge of rope and wood. One of its supporting stone towers has crumbled. The bridge was built upon sand and in Ali's time it was regularly swept away by the autumn rains. Ali once sent all the way to Constantinople for advice. An English expert called Baily came and told him the position of the bridge was hopeless. After which, it is said, Baily mysteriously died from the rigors of his journey.

It was mid-October when I reached Tepelena. Little rain had fallen and to the south I watched goats picking their way over the dry bed of the Drinos. When Byron arrived on 19 October 1809, the river at Tepelena was as broad as the Thames at Westminster. When I saw it, it was hardly moving. But the water was beautifully green, lined by a huge expanse of white stones.

A family group sat on the ground a few feet away from me, looking at the head of a slaughtered goat. A cow grazed nearby in the sun and a young boy with large brown eyes came to ask me who I was and why I had come. He spoke to me in English, the old-fashioned English of someone who has never traveled and has learned it all from books and the radio. "I think Byron and Ali were both great men," he told me. "They had great spirit and they loved Albania." Then, uncertainly, after a time, he held out his hand and smiled. "It is a great pleasure for me to have met you."

The name of Byron survives across modern Albania. Once, in a small restaurant near the town of Permeti, a waiter showed me his oil-stained copy of *Childe Harold* in Albanian. And once, when

I was leaving the country through the port of Saranda, an official said to me, in that same immaculate English you only ever hear abroad: "You are from the land of Byron. I read him more now than I did. There is something comforting about him in these difficult times."

As an afterthought, he asked me: "Are you taking anything out of Albania?" Never have I been in a country where there is so little to buy. I shook my head. "Just what you can carry in your head, I suppose," he said. He returned my passport. Then, digging deep, he quoted some lines from *Childe Harold*:

> *Fierce are Albania's children, yet they lack*
> *Not virtues, were those virtues more mature.*

"What do you think your Byron would make of us now?" he asked; but the question was only rhetorical and he waved me onto the boat.

Thoma, one of my friends from the customs office, had taken the day off to bring me in his car to Tepelena. He had done this much against his will, because of the reputation of the inhabitants. He refused to follow me the few yards to the walls of the citadel, sat gloomily in the Ali Pasha café, expecting the worst. "They're all thieves," he said. "And worse than thieves." Some time before, two foreigners who had come to look at Tepelena had been abducted and were lucky to escape death. But that wasn't what he meant. "They're all mad in Tepelena," he said; and the reason, when I doubted him, was simple.

"Ali Pasha was mad. He had a thousand women in his harem. Imagine that. And he had to sleep with all of them, or else they made trouble. So everyone in Tepelena is descended from Ali Pasha. And Ali Pasha was mad. Finish."

We drove slowly out of Tepelena along streets full of rubble. Unemployed men looked on as we passed, hands in their pockets, their faces leached by poverty. As we got onto the road south for Gjirokastra, Thoma began to talk about the past; his past, the past of Albania; to talk in that strange, obsessive way that needs no response, since there is, in the end, nothing for the outsider to say.

After 1944, when Albania was liberated from the Nazis, people lived under one of the most repressive regimes in the world. Thousands died under torture or by deprivation in prison. Anyone in those days could suddenly find they had become a Fascist collaborator, traitor to the state, or enemy of the people. At the labor camp of Burreli, northeast of the capital, Tirana, there was a sign over the entrance that read: "This is Burreli where people enter but never leave."

It was hard then for foreigners to travel in Albania and impossible to travel freely. As the dictator Enver Hoxha put it with characteristic flamboyance: "Why should we turn our country into an inn with doors flung open to pigs and sows, . . . to . . . long-haired hippies, to supplant, with their wild orgies, the graceful dances of our people?"

Both Ali Pasha and Hoxha ruled by a mixture of terror and the intelligent manipulation of the forces around them. There was certainly madness in them both. In 1812, Ali bought a complete alchemical laboratory from Venice, in the hope of finding a cure for mortality. When his scientists failed, after five years' searching, he had them hanged.

Both Ali and Hoxha were the objects of ritual veneration. A Greek from Arta once lay down in a bumpy road to smooth the passage of Ali's carriage. His sacrifice was rewarded with a pension of two and a half pounds of bread each day for the rest of his life.

Gjirokastra was Hoxha's city. Thoma said that, when he heard of his death in 1985, he had gone out onto the streets; people had cried like children for the loss of a father. Then, in August 1991, he had been out on the streets again, when rioting crowds tore down Hoxha's monumental statue.

The apparent contradiction is not so strange. Albania has been invaded, carved up, and humiliated throughout its history. A few rulers, over the years, resisted and earned the respect of their people. Ali Pasha took on the might of the Turkish Empire, kept alive the idea that there was an alternative to being ruled by others. Hoxha, at various times, stood out against the Soviet Union, the United States of America, and China, no mean ambition for a country the size of Albania.

When Hobhouse thought about the advantages and disadvantages of Ali's rule, he concluded: "Albania will be for ever the better for his administration; & should the children of the present slaves become free, they will remember his name with gratitude and forget the injuries of their fathers." Not many today would say the same of Hoxha. Albania, he used to proclaim, can go it alone. The price of this madness is everywhere visible and, once you talk to Albanians, you find it everywhere within.

We returned to Gjirokastra after dark. On our way we passed through a village that reminded me of villages in the mountains of Peru. There were pigs wandering up and down the main street and women sitting on the ground, with things for sale on a cloth in front of them.

By the entrance to Thoma's apartment, in the center of Gjirokastra, there were goats and sheep and a single cow browsing among the loose stones. Hardly a streetlight to be seen. In the dark, you come across people suddenly by the light of their cigarettes. At night there are only men and gypsy women out of doors.

Inside, the bare furnishings of several lifetimes. Three generations of the same family live in the apartment. The floor is stone and, even in October, cold to the touch. The only decoration is a pink rabbit and some plastic flowers. The lighting, harsh and white, makes the women look even more tired than perhaps they are. There's an aged picture of the Virgin Mary, rescued from somewhere. A miraculous survival in a country that Hoxha once proclaimed the first atheist state in the world. In one corner, there are two ancient washing machines, but most of the day there is no water.

Before I left, I walked across the city and climbed up to the castle. It was like being back in Greece thirty years ago. Chickens were pecking along the cobbled streets and there was the same smell of tobacco and dark coffee from crowded cafés. In the old quarter, men in small shops worked at sewing machines. Greek Orthodox priests talked in front of the main hotel. There were gypsy women, in red and yellow dresses and long head scarves. Barefoot, carrying small children, they were the only bright colors against the prevailing shades of brown.

It's a hard, dry, unregenerate city. It has some marvelous fortified houses, dating from the eighteenth and nineteenth centuries, when Gjirokastra was rich. More than anywhere, you can feel here the atmosphere of the late Ottoman Empire that Byron knew, its lawlessness, feuding, and insecurity.

As I drove back south toward Greece, I thought how quickly the eye accepts the normality of what it sees. The decay that is all around so easily comes to look natural. Fields uncultivated, factories that seem untouched since the nineteenth century. The mountain roads are lined by stone walls. Once carefully tended, they have crumbled in many places, leaving a descent wide open into the gorges below. I passed a woman standing all alone, spinning. Then suddenly came upon the lines of refugees.

They were moving slowly down the valley toward the frontier. Men on crutches, old women in black, young mothers with children on their backs, the images of every troubled country in the world. They sit and wait by the border fence, with the promise of Greece just two steel gates away. This is freedom, certainly, and a great improvement on the old days, when simply to talk of leaving might cost a quarter of a century in a labor camp. But it's a freedom that troubles at some primitive level. The sight of people fleeing what is theirs, home, friends, a familiar landscape. The nod of the head every morning toward the known, confirming the known.

*T*hree

I grew up on a farm, surrounded by the rusting carcasses of old cars, the smell of mimosa, and the noise of the sea. We lived near a famous archaeological site; so, if anyone had bothered, we could have traced our origins back a quarter of a million years, to when our ancestors drove mammoth and woolly rhino over the cliffs to their deaths. In that sense, I suppose, it was a settled community. Our house was called the Old House, and we were endlessly sure of our superiority over newer arrivals, who lived above us, in Garden Court, Sunset Lodge, and Villa Gardena.

No one was poor, but land was scarce and, from time to time, people left for places unimaginably far away. So far away that they almost never came back. We learned early on that leaving is always an abandonment before it is anything else.

Around us, though, lived people who were different. People who traveled. We never met them, but we knew that, from time to time, they, too, went away. Only they chose their moments and they came home again when they were tired of it all. At Christmas, for weddings, and for deaths.

As I left Albania, I thought again about the irreconcilable nature of these two kinds of movement, which have in common only that both are a form of surrender. The lucky surrender out of choice, out of the sheer love of the game, the rest from necessity. The two worlds are, indeed, far apart. Byron, however, touches them both; for he was, in his short life, first traveler, then refugee.

Walking at night, past the lighted windows of houses, in a place you've known all your life, it's easy to imagine you understand exactly what people are doing or saying. They may be mere shadows on the wall in the firelight, but you can believe you've shared the meals they're eating, the conversations they're having, their silences in the face of unmanageable events. Those lighted windows reflect the whole paradox of belonging, its warm pleasures, its suffocating attentiveness.

For much of his life, Byron struggled to find a way through the paradox. In his journal, there is a casual, but revealing, entry. He recalls an evening at the Opera House, Covent Garden. Looking around the audience, noticing how people of "quality" rub shoulders with courtesans, he is amused by the hypocrisy of English society. "What an assemblage to *me*," he writes, "who know all their histories."

To know all the histories is, of course, a double-edged privilege. It is power, the mark of being fully at home. But the warm glow of belonging can easily cool. To know the stories so completely is to risk being consumed by them, to inhabit a cloying world where they alone seem to matter. Besides, the capacity of knowing proves that one can, in turn, be known, and *that*, if one has as much to hide as Byron did, is a fearful prospect.

In such circumstances, the desire to leave can become irresistible. To find a place where faces, gestures, and signs are opaque, where not to know is a form of release and a means of protection. Byron's Greece was, for a few months in his youth, a true escape, and the homosexual promiscuity he pursued there as good a symbol as any of his liberation from the knowingness of home.

But the Greece of his youth was a celebration that had to end. England drew him back, idolized him, then cast him out. In the few years after his return to England, Byron exhausted all the conventional possibilities of belonging: family, marriage, country, and reputation. This time, there was no release, and the rest of his life was a drifting search for a home elsewhere, first through love, then, finally, through political action.

When I first came to Greece, I quickly discovered some of the paradoxes of escape. Having left a comfortable world that I believed, naively, I understood too well, I set about trying to make sense of the new world in which I found myself. I settled down in a small house, bought myself a grammar book, and began to learn Greek.

The intrepid travelers of my generation saw Greece only as a kind of refueling stop on the way to the East. They passed through in a few days, carrying beads and prayer mats and lists of places in Kathmandu where you could eat for fifty cents. I followed them in my mind, sometimes envied them. But at an age when you fall easily and painfully in love, I fell in love with Greece and stayed on. Stayed on until the waves of real Eastern travelers began to flow back.

Some of them were exotically ill, their ribs showing through dirty T-shirts. Some we'd seen on the way out had gone native and were never seen again. We used to remember them on cold winter nights, when the tavernas shut their doors against the wind from off the sea. We drank ouzo and felt snug and secure, since, though we'd gone to the edge, we hadn't abandoned home, this was still Europe.

I am, I finally realize, a cautious traveler. If the quality I most admire is adaptability, the quality that most fascinates me is something like its opposite: the stubborn peasant attachment to place, the refusal to be impressed by the wider world. As I look back toward childhood, this attachment seems more and more a kind of sanity, though I think I have spent half a lifetime trying to escape it.

Others had adventures on their travels. They slept in brothels by mistake. They were prey to every danger and discomfort, from bandits to bedbugs. But these things never happened to me. To confuse a brothel with a hotel seemed merely bad judgment; and though I once shared my lunch with a bandit in the mountains of Peru, and though I've seen a myriad of bedbugs, I confess my sleep has never been troubled by either. This native caution is hard to acknowledge, yet over the years, and without my realizing it, it brought me ever closer to Byron.

It has long been fashionable to pour scorn on Byron's youthful travels. To say he came to Greece for all the most predictable reasons. Greece was cheap, the sun shone, sex was easy, and you could swim in the sea in December. This wasn't traveling, this was simply tourism.

There is, behind all such judgments, an implied hierarchy. It runs upward from the despised tourist, through the utterly respectable traveler, to the godlike figure of the explorer at the very summit. Byron's age was the very essence of heroic exploration and, in that light, his journey to Greece was of no significance at all.

In a letter of November 1819, he mentions three giants of his time, whose deeds still rank among the most extraordinary. William Browne, the British explorer murdered by bandits on the road to Tehran; Mungo Park, the explorer of the Niger, who drowned in rapids southeast of Timbuktu; Johann Burckhardt, the Swiss orientalist, who passed himself off as a doctor of Koranic law in the forbidden city of Mecca and who explored so long and so hard that he died of dysentery and exhaustion in Cairo.

These were examples of what could be done by the truly intrepid. Nothing suggests that Byron was ever interested in traveling on that scale. In his letters, it is true, he made the most of what was special about his own journey. "Albania," he wrote to a former tutor, "I have seen more of than any Englishman (but a Mr

Leake) for it is a country rarely visited from the savage character of the natives"; or, to a friend, "We have . . . been very high up into Albania, the wildest province in Europe, where very few Englishmen have ever been." In fact, he went barely fifty miles into Albania and spent only ten days there in all.

But Byron's Greece was not a place for discoveries in the external world. He had come there far too late for that. Generations of travelers had preceded him in the area and now only the details remained to be settled. He knew Hobhouse was wasting his time setting their travels down in a book. Leake had already covered the ground, interminably, and with far greater expertise.

In this sense, Byron wasn't a traveler at all and hardly claimed to be. The only real travelers, the French poet Baudelaire would write, are those who leave for the sake of leaving:

> *Mais les vrais voyageurs sont ceux-là seuls qui partent*
> *Pour partir. . . .*

These lines have fixed forever a romantic ideal of motiveless motion. By that definition, Byron certainly wasn't one of the elect. He found it hard to leave places. Partly, from a natural attachment to people he met; partly, as he says in a letter to Lady Melbourne, from laziness: "I am totally & unutterably possessed by the ineffable power of Indolence."

He could be airily dismissive of Europe: "Europe is grown decrepit—besides it is all the same thing over again," he wrote in August 1819. He talked at various times of going to Persia, South America, South Africa, or Australia. In the end, however, he never left Europe, except for a brief tour of the west coast of Turkey.

Very quickly, Byron became aware that traveling for its own sake was no solution to anything. The prizes of travel were all internal; whatever discoveries were to be made lay within, not around the next corner. In a letter to his mother from Patras, in July 1810, he already suggests that he has seen enough. I could easily go to Egypt or to Asia, he writes, but what would be the point? "I shall only go over my old ground, and look upon my old seas and mountains, the only acquaintances I ever found improve upon me." This is an image of belonging. He had settled down in Greece. He was happy to be away from the cold wet climate of England and he saw no good reason to move.

"If I am a poet," Byron said, "the air of Greece made me one." What was most original about Byron is that he found in Greece not a paradise of monuments, as so many did, but a land of sensation, of sun, sea, and sky; a place of mountains, a rough physicality of sunburn and dust. In a letter written in 1815, he quotes some recently published lines by Wordsworth. These lines show the kind of Greece that was fashionable at the time among those who looked through purely literary eyes. Wordsworth's Greece is a country of:

> rivers—fertile *plains*—*&* sounding *shores*
> *Under a cope of* variegated *sky*. . . .

The lines are not Wordsworth's finest and Byron, who loathed the poets he called "those poor idiots of the Lakes," had no trouble dissecting them. He had been to Greece, he knew what the country was like. In Greece, as he said, "the rivers are dry half the year—the plains are barren—and the shores *still* & *tideless* as the Mediterranean can make them—the Sky is anything but variegated—being for months & months—but 'darkly—deeply—beautifully blue.' "

Byron's Greece was neither the museum of the antiquarian nor the portrait of a pastoral imagination. When the Greek War of Independence began, many outsiders, as well as many Greeks of the Diaspora, cherished the possibility of reviving an idealized Greece of the past. Byron was different. When he came back in 1823, it was to support a country that he knew and where he had once been at home. He brought with him fewer illusions than most.

· · ·

Byron was twenty-one when he first came to Greece; thirty-five, when he returned for the second and final time. On that final visit in 1823–24, he carried an enormous baggage of memories, of failure and guilt, and sheer fatigue. By then he had long been the scandalous outcast of his native land. The baggage in 1809 was lighter, of course, and he came as a private man, where later he would return as one of the most public figures in Europe. The Byron of Albania is still an unformed personality, harder to interpret than the Byron of Mesolongi, and much colored by inevitable retrospection.

Byron was born in London on 22 January 1788, his mother's first and last child. From birth he was the victim of a malformed foot that made his life a misery and has fascinated his biographers ever since. The inability to run at cricket or to take to the floor in dancing was a serious handicap in youth, while the fear of rejection and humiliation was lifelong. This fear may be at the root of his famous capacity for seduction, as it also lies, no doubt, behind his often frustrated desire to do something significant with his life. On a less exalted level, his physical problem explains the passion for swimming and pistol shooting, two sports at which he could excel without the need for conventional mobility.

He was born neither rich nor poor, the son of a spendthrift father and a harassed mother. On both sides of his family there was a long line of unorthodox antecedents. His mother was descended from the Gordons who held the estate of Gight in northern Scotland in the late Middle Ages. They were bandits and murderers until well into the seventeenth century. Their family motto: "Je ne change qu'en mourant" (I change only in death).

On his father's side, the Byrons looked back to the days of Henry VIII, from whom they bought their country house in Nottinghamshire. There was drama in this line, too. Byron's grandfather was shipwrecked on the coast of Patagonia in 1741.

He recorded seeing giants eight feet high and, when threatened by starvation, was forced to eat his favorite dog. He subsequently traveled around the world and was known as "Foulweather Jack."

Byron's great-uncle murdered his cousin during a night of drinking at the Star and Garter tavern in London. Byron remembered that he "always kept the sword which he used upon that occasion in his bed-chamber, where it still was *when he died*." You can see it now, in a glass case, in the Byrons' old home at Newstead Abbey.

It was the maternal grandfather, however, whom the poet believed he most nearly resembled in temperament. Looking back, in September 1821, for the origins of the legendary Byronic melancholia, he told his publisher that his grandfather's death had probably been suicide. He was found drowned in the River Avon at Bath. Rich, respected, "& of considerable intellectual resources," he was scarcely forty years of age. It was a tragedy that had seemed entirely without motivation.

If, on his mother's side, there was evidence of depressive illness, on both there was the reality of early death. This convinced Byron, not entirely against his will, that his death, too, would be premature, as so it proved. His father, "Mad Jack," having squandered away the Gight estate, died in 1791 of overliving, or consumption, or despair. He was thirty-five. His mother died in August 1811, a few days after Byron's return from Greece. She was forty-six. Years later, Byron noted with some satisfaction that "nobody lives long, without having *one parent*, at least, an old stager."

He was little more than two and a half years old when his father left home, to seek refuge in France and to die, a year later, in destitution. Byron claimed to remember him perfectly and to have retained, from the memory of early domestic squabbles, "a horror of matrimony." To the end of his life, he idealized his father, either because he could not accept the truth about him or because some part of that truth came to him through his mother, whose side he could never take.

Byron spent his early years in the northern Scottish city of Aberdeen, where he belonged, through education and social contacts, to the Scottish middle class. It was only by one of those rare coincidences that are almost the rule in the history of great landed families that George Gordon of Scotland became Lord Byron.

From an early age, he knew that the title would one day be his. For on the death of an obscure relative, killed at the siege of Calvi in Corsica when Byron was six and a half years old, he had become heir presumptive to the Byron estates. He had reached the age of ten when, on the death of the fifth lord, his wicked great-uncle, he very seriously assumed his new identity as the sixth Baron Byron of Rochdale.

Rochdale was a Lancashire property that came with the inheritance. Throughout Byron's life, it was merely a legal tangle of quarries and coal mines, one that threatened to keep him poor when it might have made him rich. The Byron country estate of Newstead was far from there, in the county of Nottinghamshire. Newstead Abbey, formerly an Augustinian priory, had fallen into the Byron hands in 1539, after the dissolution of the monasteries. It lies on the edge of what remains of the great forest of Sherwood. Of the old priory church, only the west end survives; and the house, as it looks today, is mainly the result of alterations made after it had passed out of the Byron family.

It is still easy to imagine, however, the joy and awe of a ten-year-old boy seeing Newstead for the first time. Knowing that the house and its gardens, along with thirty-two hundred acres of parkland, farmland, forest, and quarries were suddenly his. His wicked great-uncle had ruined the estate and encumbered it with debt, but that only made it more romantic. In a very early poem, probably written in November 1803, Byron tried to express all his love for this gorgeous disaster of an inheritance:

> *Thro' thy battlements, Newstead, the hollow winds whistle;*
> *Thou, the hall of my fathers, art gone to decay;*

In thy once smiling garden, the hemlock and thistle
Have choak'd up the rose, which late bloom'd in the way.

Today, what Byron once called "the melancholy mansion of my
fathers" is still supremely beautiful. A visitor in search of the poet
might, even so, regret the present order into which it has fallen.
Now the roses are no longer choked up and every path is
decently cleared, with that quiet discipline the English so effortlessly impose on the natural world. Today all is in a state of
motionless preservation. From the fine-clipped grass, and the
loveliest of cricket fields, to the ruin of the priory itself—splendid,
but lacking a little by its confident refusal to crumble. When I last
visited there was a special Byron weekend in progress. On Friday
it was "Byron in Venice"; on Saturday, "Byron in Hell."

The young boy had become Lord Byron. In Greece, it is as if he
could never have been anything else. Always Lord Byron, never
Byron alone. On street signs, on the glass cases of museums, on
people's lips.

After he moved south from Scotland to Nottinghamshire, his
way of life gradually took on the forms that belonged to a young
English lord. Not that he and his mother were much the richer for
the move. While they each lived, money was to be one of their
most constant concerns. Yet somehow, through the economies of
his mother, which he found humiliating, and later, through his
own careless surrender to debt, Byron increasingly lived the life
his title presupposed.

When he was just past thirteen, he was sent to Harrow School,
one of the breeding grounds of English leaders; and from there, at
seventeen, to Cambridge University, one of England's pair of fin-
ishing schools. He loved Harrow, after a time, loved its close,
familial atmosphere, the intrigues and the thrill of high-walled
boyish emotions.

Cambridge, however, was a great disappointment. It marked
the end of the intimacies of Harrow, since nearly every one of his
contemporaries went on to Oxford. It was also the end of boy-

hood. "It was one of the deadliest and heaviest feelings of my life to feel that I was no longer a boy," Byron wrote later, in 1821. "From that moment I began to grow old in my own esteem—and in my esteem age is not estimable." Already, at the age of twenty, he had written:

> *And when we bid adieu to youth,*
> > *Slaves to the specious world's controul,*
> *We sigh a long farewell to truth;*
> > *That world corrupts the noblest soul.*

Growing up, for Byron, was a passage into shadow. To become a man was to learn how to mistrust the world, to know the necessity of being always on guard against a sea of potential enemies. It was a tragic process by which a boy lost what was most attractive in his nature. Clarity retreats and the passionate openness of school days vanishes into the calculation of adulthood.

In a letter of December 1811, he wrote: "In the World every one is to steer for himself, it is useless, perhaps selfish to expect any thing from his neighbour; but I do not think we are born of this disposition, for you find friendship as a schoolboy, & Love enough before twenty." In Athens he was to find again the charm and easy silliness of a boyish world and his stay there was to be one of the happiest periods of his adult life.

Cambridge, in Byron's time, was an intellectual backwater. Aristocratic students did nothing much in the way of study. "This place is wretched enough," he wrote in October 1807, "a villainous Chaos of Dice and Drunkenness." In a poem of the previous year, he had mocked Cambridge's "sons of science":

> *Dull as the pictures, which adorn their halls,*
> *They think all learning fix'd within their walls. . . .*

This slumbering retreat from the world could have no appeal for a boy who had already made the decision to do something momentous. He had written to his mother, from Harrow, in 1804:

"However the way to *riches* to *Greatness* lies before me, I can, I will cut myself a path through the world or perish in the attempt." This boyish either/or would, ironically, fail to do him justice, for, of course, within the next twenty years, he was to do both of these things.

Byron's desire to travel emerges in a letter of May 1807: "I shall travel not over France & Italy the common *Turnpike* of coxcombs & *virtuosos*, but into Greece & Turkey." In November 1808, he talks again of travel, but the tone is still unremarkable: "If I do not travel now, I never shall," he writes, "and all men should, one day or other." He adds: "If we see no nation but our own, we do not give mankind a fair chance, it is from *experience* not *Books*, we ought to judge of mankind.—There is nothing like inspection, and trusting to our own senses."

But then, suddenly, by April 1809, everything has changed. In a letter that month to his lawyer, John Hanson, an altogether different tone takes over, urgent and troubled. Hanson was advising Byron against going abroad, because of the perpetually disastrous state of his finances, to which Byron replied: "If the consequences of my leaving England, were ten times as ruinous as you describe, I have no alternative, there are circumstances which render it absolutely indispensable, and quit the country I must immediately."

Such a change, from the bland, genial vision of travel as a thing everyone should sample, to the imperious view of travel as necessary escape, is something that has never been explained. That it wasn't simply caprice, a passing adolescent self-dramatization, is suggested by a number of later letters. Most famously, a letter to Hanson from Prevesa in November 1809: "I never will revisit England if I can avoid it . . . for it is no country for me.—Why I say this is best known to myself." And then, repeated: "I never will live in England if I can avoid it, *why* remains a secret."

At the age of twenty-one, then, Byron was in Greece and he carried a burden of some kind; on the surface, at least, a guilty one. It certainly can't have been about money. Though Byron was troubled by finances for much of his life, there was nothing coy in his attitudes there. Inevitably, then, biographers turn to his sexuality as the likely explanation for the explosive desire to leave England.

Byron and sex. His heterosexuality, homosexuality, bisexuality, his passion for adolescent boys: much has been written, but in the end the biographer still faces the void between what is said or implied and what is done.

For many writers, there is a neatness to be drawn out of Byron's biography. This would make home, the England Byron came to detest, the site of a guilty homosexual awakening; while Greece, the land he loved, would be the paradise of homosexual consummation. This neat separation would provide the missing motivation for the voyage out; and it allows for the resolution of Byron's fantasies against the most appropriate scenery in the world. For the barren landscape of Greece, the mountains and dust, blue sea and sky, had once been home to the most confidently homoerotic culture Europe has ever seen.

The neatness is attractive, but in the end looks unsustainable. Byron's sexuality was, by his own account, awakened very early. It was stimulated, in ways that will never be clear, by the sexual abuse he suffered, when very young, at the hands of a family maid. It was certainly encouraged by the homoerotic atmosphere of a segregated public school.

That Byron was romantically involved with boys from a young age is beyond doubt. The most important of these relationships was with John Edleston, a choirboy two years his junior at Cambridge. When he heard of Edleston's death in 1811, he wrote of him as "one whom I loved more than I ever loved a living thing, and one who, I believe, loved me to the last." Byron, as this shows, was deeply involved with Edleston and it is clear from later correspondence that his love was not free from guilt.

Nevertheless, none of this proves that Byron had been sexually active with boys. It is hard now to decode the emotions of an age when deep love between friends was still possible without consciousness of sex. Less hard to imagine are the social pressures bearing down on otherwise consenting teenagers. Either way, whatever the degree of sexual consciousness at the time, there seems no reason to doubt Byron's honesty many years later, when, in his journal, he wrote of his love for Edleston as "violent, though *pure*."

Nor does Byron's bravado, his facetiousness when alluding to homosexual practice, necessarily prove anything one way or another. In a letter he wrote from Falmouth in Cornwall, just before leaving for Greece, he noted that Hobhouse was making great preparations for his travel book, stocking up on gallons of ink, dozens of pens, reams of paper; whereas he himself was going to write nothing on the trip, he said, except for a treatise on morals to be entitled "Sodomy simplified or Paederasty proved to be praiseworthy from ancient authors and modern practice."

It is still possible here to argue that the eroticism is all in the bravado and not in the act. That the physical side of his passion for boys was still all in prospect. Two very different details, however, suggest otherwise.

The first relates to an incident in late 1803 or early 1804. Byron and his mother, short of money, as ever, had leased out Newstead Abbey to Lord Grey de Ruthyn, a young man in his early twenties. Byron continued to spend much time at Newstead and got on well with Grey until, at some point, Grey did something Byron found unforgivable. This can only have been a sexual advance of some kind. It is otherwise difficult to account for such remarks as the following, in a letter from Byron to his half-sister, Augusta: "He was once my *Greatest Friend*, my reasons for ceasing that Friendship are such as I cannot explain, not even to you, my Dear Sister . . . but they will ever remain hidden in my own breast."

If there was a sexual advance and Byron rejected it, that would simply be a minor event in his biography. But a long time later,

Hobhouse noted that it was during the months of his friendship with Lord Grey that "a circumstance occurred . . . which certainly had much effect on his future morals." Since Hobhouse knew more about Byron's life in Greece and his future morals than anyone, this statement is hard to interpret, except as an invitation to view Lord Grey as a sexual initiator, one who opened the way toward what was to happen later in Athens.

There is a second piece of evidence, which also suggests that Byron was more than just passionately inexperienced with boys before he went to Greece. In another letter, written from Falmouth in Cornwall, we find the following passage, which is clearly coded: "We are surrounded by Hyacinths: & other flowers of the most fragrant [na]ture, & I have some intention of culling a handsome Bouquet to compare with the exotics we expect to meet in Asia.—One specimen I shall certainly carry off, but of this hereafter." Perhaps this, too, is simple homosexual bravado, but, at a distance, it certainly doesn't seem so.

Looking at the general history of Byron's love affairs, both homosexual and heterosexual, there is a strange irony. As Doris Langley Moore noted, in her book *Lord Byron: Accounts Rendered*, the multiple experiences of this most sought-after lover are framed, at each end of his life, by failure. At fifteen, he fell in love with a distant cousin, Mary Chaworth. At thirty-five, with a fifteen-year-old Greek boy, Loukas Chalandritsanos, who inspired the last three poems he ever wrote.

Both relationships are models of pain, so much more enduring than the experience of success. In 1821, he was still writing in his notebook about Mary Chaworth, as if her rejection of him had happened just a few weeks before. This was the man who, it had long been a cliché to say, had all of Europe at his feet. A man for whom conquest was so facile that, when Lord Ravensworth's wife glimpsed him on the roof of St. Peter's in Rome, she ordered her eldest daughter to avert her gaze, saying: "Don't look at him, he is dangerous to look at."

At the other end of life, too, there is failure. In his final poems to Loukas, he touches a genuine hopelessness, in the face of the impossibility of love between an aging man and a young boy:

> *Thus much and more—and yet thou lov'st me not,*
> *And never wilt—Love dwells not in our will—*
> *Nor can I blame thee—though it be my lot*
> *To strongly—wrongly—vainly—love thee still.—*

Byron's old demons are still with him: passion as destiny, the need for love, the power of guilt. At war with these, the desire to redeem it all through action. The conflict continues to the very end, in the heart of Mesolongi.

The Byron who comes to Greece in 1809 is already, and obviously, too complex a figure for easy summary. Backed by an immense family history, a daunting succession of lives lived in the chaos of adventure, violence, or despair, he began in the solidity of the middle class. By luck, he acceded to the world of the English nobility, which opened the way for him to rejoin the chaos of his ancestors; created space for eccentricity, vast financial indebtedness, sexual license, the casualness of power.

He became a poet when still very young—by 1800, at the age of twelve, on his own testimony. He read enormously, in Latin and Greek, French, Italian, and Spanish, bearing all his learning as lightly as a nobleman and good drinking companion should. By the time he left for Greece, he had experience of love, both for women and for boys, and he carried a secret that, he says, drove him away from his native land. In *Childe Harold*, he pictures himself as the riotous youth, carnal, promiscuous, and proud; concealing his dark secret from the world, and profoundly unloved, he looks back at the vanishing coast of England:

> *"Adieu, adieu! my native shore*
> *Fades o'er the waters blue;*

> The Night-winds sigh, the breakers roar,
>   And shrieks the wild seamew.
> Yon Sun that sets upon the sea
>   We follow in his flight;
> Farewell awhile to him and thee,
>   My native Land—Good Night."

Byron and Hobhouse left Ali Pasha's town of Tepelena on 23 October 1809. The way back to Ioannina was much quicker than the way out. They enjoyed magnificent weather, warm as an English midsummer. They arrived back in Ioannina on 26 October and stayed on until 3 November. It was during this time of rest that Byron began *Childe Harold*, the poem about his travels that would bring him instant fame on its publication in 1812.

The two travelers had a good time in Ioannina, as they had earlier in the month, and there was space now in their plans for a classical site. On Saturday, 29 October, they visited a ruin about fifteen miles to the south of the city and saw what Hobhouse, a little defensively, called the "very fine remains of what Capt. Leake says is the largest amphitheater in Greece."

In his diary, Hobhouse left a blank after the phrase: "The name of this place is . . ." In fact, it was not until 1876 that excavations revealed the significance of the site and gave it back its name. It turned out to be what Hesiod, the shepherd-poet of ancient Greece, calls "far-off, wintry-bleak Dodona," the site of the most ancient oracle in Greece.

There was much speculation in Byron's time about the whereabouts of Dodona. It was a romantic name, touched by a vastly old literary tradition. It was to Dodona that Odysseus came, in order to ask the oracle how best to get home to Ithaca. The god Zeus revealed his will through the rustling leaves of a sacred oak tree and he was honored by priests who remained close to the earth, never washing their feet and sleeping on the ground. For over a thousand years of the Christian era, no one knew what had happened to Dodona. In *Childe Harold*, unaware that he had walked among its ancient stones, Byron wrote:

> *Oh! where, Dodona! is thine aged grove,*
> *Prophetic fount, and oracle divine?*
> *What valley echo'd the response of Jove?*
> *What trace remaineth of the thunderer's shrine?*
> *All, all forgotten . . .*

The road from Ioannina to Dodona rises in long loops out of the Ioannina plain; eventually, it descends into an enclosed valley, at the foot of Mount Tomaros. I made the journey, as I have often done, on the 6:00 A.M. bus from Ioannina. I was alone with the driver. We talked for a while; then, tired of the push and pull of the mountain curves, I drifted into sleep.

The radio was playing a sentimental song, music full of sadness and longing, the words only a haze around the noise of the engine. It sounded like a thousand other songs. Then, some phrase, strange, yet distantly familiar, reached down into my sleep and I woke up to listen.

The words were from a poem by Odysseas Elytis, a Greek who won the Nobel Prize for Literature almost twenty years ago. A moment later and the bus was climbing steeply. The words faded; but the bouzouki clattered on, sustaining this love affair between the high art of poetry and the world of popular song. It is a collaboration that is distinctively Greek, with a long tradition behind it, but to an outsider it always comes as a surprise; as if, on the bus into Nashville, the torrent of country music suddenly revealed the voice of T. S. Eliot.

As Hobhouse says, the amphitheater at Dodona is very fine. It once accommodated eighteen thousand spectators and has been marvelously restored in recent times. The stone seats overlook a green valley of goats and donkeys and tinkling bells.

Theaters are always an attractive part of a Greek site, since a theater is a place where we can most completely imagine ourselves at home. It is a building whose functions we clearly understand, whereas it is less obvious what we might be doing in a stoa, a nymphaion, or the opisthodomos of a temple. Not that the continuities here are entirely secure. The Romans often converted the theaters they inherited and turned them to less happy purposes. Here, in the arena at Dodona, men once fought with bulls and wild boar, for the casual enjoyment of spectators.

Nevertheless, a sense of wonder survives at Dodona, in this still remote corner of the Greek world. Over the past thirty years the site has been used once again as a venue for ancient theater. People sit on the stone seats, watching the same plays, the same movement of the clouds over the mountains, as they did more than two thousand years ago. The Greek theater at Epidauros in the Peloponnese is justly famous for its acoustics and its fine condition, but the setting of Dodona is without a rival.

I spent a cold mountain night near the ruins. For the first time since I had arrived in Greece there were no crickets to share the hours of darkness. In the morning, the sun was slow to burn off the heavy dew. By afternoon, the sky was full of autumn and days of heavy rain to come. I returned to Ioannina and prepared to go south again to Arta, to wait out the weather.

Before I left, however, I crossed over, one Sunday afternoon, to the island of Nissi, on the Lake of Ioannina. It was the last really hot day of the year and the boats on the lake were crowded with families enjoying a final excursion. The island is a good place to escape from the summer heat. It isn't very large and the few streets are narrow, but the breeze from off the lake is a mercy in the heat of August. There are restaurants serving fresh fish from the polluted water, nets strung out on poles to dry, mountains of seaside junk in the shops. There is also a group of monasteries, in one of which, the Monastery of Pandelimonos, Ali Pasha met his end.

The Monastery of Pandelimonos is guarded by a single rusting cannon. Part shrine, part museum of horrors, part place of entertainment, it was full of people on that Sunday afternoon. Children running, shouting to each other across the courtyard, their parents telling and retelling the story of Ali's final moments. Fragments of a past half familiar, half lost in legend.

When Byron met Ali in 1809, the old man's fate had probably already been sealed. A new sultan had recently appeared in Constantinople, Mahmoud II. He had decided to eliminate the semi-independent feudal lords like Ali, who were draining power away from the Turkish Empire. It was not until 1820, however, when Ali was seventy-six years old, that the pressures began to threaten him seriously.

Ali twisted and turned, using all the experience of a lifetime to try to delay the inevitable. He even appealed to the British, asking the government to intervene at the Turkish capital on his behalf. As the year went on, however, he found his empire attacked by land and sea, and he fell back on Ioannina to make his final resistance.

By August 1821, he had lost most of the city. He set Ioannina ablaze when he saw that he could no longer hold it, and the Turks entered triumphantly on a smoldering ruin. Confined from then on to his fortified positions by the lake, he continued the struggle, while his sons Veli and Moukhtar surrendered Prevesa and Gjirokastra, before passing over to their father's enemy. Only Ali's grandson, Mahmoud, Byron's favorite, the boy "with large black eyes as big as pigeon's eggs"—only he held on until Ali's death, defending the town of Tepelena.

In April 1821, while the Turkish forces were besieging what was left of Ioannina, the Greeks in the Peloponnese launched the War of Independence. By the summer they were achieving their first military successes. Still Ali held on, now grown thin and thoughtful, while his garrison began to melt away around him from desertion and disease. Then, in January 1822, he was persuaded to cross over to the island of Nissi, to try to barter his future with the Turkish authorities.

He arrived at the Monastery of Pandelimonos, bringing a few

faithful companions and his favorite wife, Vasiliki. The Turkish commander sent him supplies and a band of musicians and, for nine days, kept him waiting and wondering. Finally, on 24 January, Ali received word that a pardon had arrived from Constantinople. On his orders, the great castle of Ioannina then surrendered.

That day he waited for a Turkish official to come and read out the pardon formally in his presence. He spent most of the time lying on a sofa, in a room on the second floor of the monastery. Toward evening, thirty armed men arrived by boat. Ali went to the head of the stairs to greet them, just at the place where today you buy your ticket for the museum. He saw at once that all talk of pardon had been pretense, drew his pistols, and opened fire. He was a man with many failings, but he never lacked courage.

Wounded in the left arm, he was taken back into the monastery and lay down on the sofa again. Then a group of men entered the room immediately below and fired upward through the ceiling. Ali received a terrible wound in the lower abdomen, and died soon after.

His last words were for the comfort of his wife. He ordered one of his closest followers to put her to death, so that she should not fall into the hands of his enemies. This was, however, never done, for all resistance ended with the death of Ali. His body was dragged out to the top of the stairs and decapitated. The head was placed on a silver salver and, after, exposed for three days in the city, so that everyone should know the Old Lion of Ioannina was dead. He was buried with great ceremony on 25 January; and his head, embalmed, began its long journey to Constantinople, where it arrived before the sultan on 23 February.

His riches were loaded onto fifty horses and they, too, made the journey to Constantinople. But much of his wealth had vanished; some into banks in Malta and Corfu, some to support the Greek insurgents in the Peloponnese. Vasiliki, his wife, was interrogated for several days. But neither she, nor anyone else, ever told the secret of Ali's treasures. Vasiliki survived. She was young. Despite numerous offers, she never remarried. In the course of her long retirement, she used to say that there was no man left in the world for the widow of Ali Pasha. She died, prematurely, near Mesolongi, in 1835.

Something of this remarkable man is still present in the tiny cells of Pandelimonos. Most popular with visitors are the bullet holes that mark the floor where Ali lay in the last moments of his life. Around the walls are prints and paintings. Ali's head served up to the sultan in Constantinople; Ali with a long, pointed beard, reclining in the stern of a boat on Lake Butrinto in Albania. The visitors that afternoon were all Greeks; and, from their conversations, it was clear that people are still not sure what to make of Ali Pasha.

A "remorseless tyrant, guilty of the most horrible cruelties," as Byron said. Duplicitous beyond words, right until the end. For, if he chose, in the last months of his life, to aid the Greek insurgents, it was only in the hope of salvaging his own dreams. By stimulating havoc in the Peloponnese, he planned to force the Turkish authorities to turn to him for the restoration of order there. Yet he was a man with immense ambitions, in an age when most ambitions were petty. The powerful chieftains in the Balkans at that time were concerned with little more than the opportunity for localized plunder. For Ali, the dying weight of the Ottoman Empire contained the promise of change, whereas, for most, it seemed the condemnation to eternal sleep.

In a letter of 1821, Byron wrote: "I never judge from manners—for—I once had my pocket picked by the civilest gentleman I ever met with; and one of the mildest persons I ever saw was Ali Pacha." Byron must have heard, at some point, of Ali's death. It is a shame no record survives of his reaction.

I returned to Arta the long way around, driving over the mountains to the west of Ioannina, then south, to cross the River Acheron at Gliki. It rained without ceasing and the small towns and villages went by, monotonous in the mist. Nothing catches the eye to distinguish one from another. In Greece, more than anywhere I know, your memories depend on the weather and the time of day. There are few things more dismal than a small Greek town at four o'clock in the afternoon on a day of rain. Yet that same town, empty and desolate when you passed by at four, might have been one of your best moments if you had come a few hours later. Then the shops begin to open, the cafés begin to fill up, and people show themselves on the streets. The towns and villages here are nothing without their people and, whatever their destiny, they will never add anything memorable to the long history of this country of ruins.

Four

When one subtracts from life infancy (which is vegetation),—sleep, eating, and swilling—buttoning and unbuttoning—how much remains of downright existence? The summer of a dormouse.

—Byron's Journal, 7 December 1813

Byron and Hobhouse moved out from Ioannina on 3 November 1809. They traveled back to Arta and the Ambracian Gulf, along the same road they had taken in early October. From Salaora, the port of Arta, they planned to cross the gulf, then continue their journey overland, through the province of Akarnania. Having reached the sea again, somewhere near Mesolongi, they would turn eastward toward Athens, their final destination.

But Akarnania, they discovered, was "up in arms," troubled by bandits, and unsafe. They were invited to accompany one of Ali's Albanian commanders, who was about to set off in pursuit of the bandits. The prospect of adventure, however, failed to appeal and instead they decided to return to Prevesa on the west coast. From there they could travel safely by ship down to Patras and pick up the road to Athens along the northern coast of the Peloponnese.

At Prevesa, they lodged badly, as they had on the way out. It was, said Hobhouse, a "little dirty house." Leake was in town, but he had already done his duty and he "did not ask us to dinner." With no incentive to prolong their stay, they embarked the next morning, courtesy of Ali Pasha, on a fifty-ton ship, crewed by forty sailors. It was the beginning of a minor adventure, one that could easily have ended in tragedy, like Shelley at Viareggio, but which both Byron and Hobhouse survived to remember as farce.

It turned out that only four of their forty sailors knew how to sail. These four were Greeks. The rest were Turks, who were notorious for their dislike of the sea. There appeared to be several captains on board, first among whom was a mild-mannered man of fatalistic temperament, who spent most of the time smoking or playing with his worry beads.

They ran aground trying to get out of Prevesa harbor and the chief captain was all for going home. They tried again and eventually reached open sea at one o'clock in the afternoon. With a fair breeze, they should have been able to round the headland of Lefkadha easily, and, for a time, all seemed well. By four o'clock, however, they were in danger. The wind was blowing harder and the mizzen sail had split. The captain had put away his worry beads and nearly all the sailors had gone below, miserably sick.

They gave up trying to head south and turned north instead, hoping to make Corfu. By nightfall, they were rolling in heavy seas. The captain wept. The main yard snapped in two; and the ship, said Hobhouse, "lay like a log on the water." The captain, having volunteered to surrender his command to anyone who wanted it, happily gave it up to the Greek sailors. After which, things improved. The Greeks got the boat under control and brought it back inshore. At one in the morning, they dropped anchor at the entrance to a bay.

Byron's account of the incident is swiftly told in a letter of 31 July 1810, where he casts himself, not too seriously, as the hero: "Masts by the board, sails split, captain crying, crew below, wind blowing, Fletcher groaning, Hobhouse despairing, and myself with my upper garments ready thrown open, to swim to a spar in case of accidents."

In the afternoon, they landed on the west coast, opposite the island of Paxi, not far from the modern resort of Parga. They sent to the nearest village for horses and spent the next few days riding back down the coast to Prevesa, where they arrived at sunset on 11 November.

Byron was in a happy mood following his adventure, and, on 12 November, sitting in the house of the British consul at Prevesa, with the doors wide open to the sun, he wrote a long letter home to his mother. It was full of enthusiasm for his escape from England. He talked of going to Athens to learn modern Greek and then, dreamily, of going to Asia in a year or two. In the meantime, Greece and, maybe, Africa, or, at least, Egypt. "I have no one to be remembered to in England," he concluded, "& wish to hear nothing from it but that you are well."

The next day, 13 November, they left Prevesa. Now they decided to do what had seemed too dangerous before: to cross the Ambracian Gulf and try their luck through the wilds of Akarnania. They were given an armed guard of forty soldiers and embarked on a rowing galley, commanded, if that was the word, by the same captain who had nearly drowned them a few days before.

All went well, for there are no dangers in the gulf. With scarcely a breath of wind, they were rowed eastward all afternoon and, by sunset, had reached the fortress of Vonitsa, a distance of perhaps ten miles. The next day they traveled on and, at four in the afternoon, landed in the bay of Loutraki, in the southeastern corner of the gulf.

At Loutraki there was a customs house and a military command post, both defended by a high wall. Five days before, bandits had come down from the woods and seized two men. Then, in sight of the guards, they had shot one and stoned the other to death. Byron and Hobhouse went swimming, but did not dare walk up into the thickly wooded hills that rise behind the village.

In *Childe Harold*, Byron remembered the site with a romantic tenderness:

Where lone Utraikey forms its circling cove,
And weary waves retire to gleam at rest,
How brown the foliage of the green hill's grove,
Nodding at midnight o'er the calm bay's breast,
As winds come lightly whispering from the west,
Kissing, not ruffling, the blue deep's serene. . . .

Ever since, Byron's biographers have handed down a tradition that there really was a village in Greece called Utraikey or Utraikee. In fact, it was simply Byron's mishearing of the name. "Loutraki" means a place where there are mineral springs. There is a famous Loutraki to the east, not far from Corinth: the discarded wrappings from its bottled water are one of the most ubiquitous sights in modern Greece.

Byron's memory of the night they spent here was one of the most vivid of his travels, a poet's dream of the exotic. The guards killed a goat and roasted it whole. Then the company sat down around the fire to eat and drink. It was a moonless night and the fire played on water, rocks, and forest, and on the faces of the Albanian soldiers. When they had finished eating, the men danced, "man link'd to man," and sang their own songs; or, as Byron thought, "half sang, half scream'd." Songs of warfare and of women, of political events, past and contemporary. The kind of songs, the kind of evening, that were still common in Greece thirty years ago.

They sang the song of Ali's destruction of Prevesa:

Remember the moment when Previsa fell,
The shrieks of the conquer'd, the conquerors' yell;
The roofs that we fir'd, and the plunder we shar'd,
The wealthy we slaughter'd, the lovely we spar'd.

I talk not of mercy, I talk not of fear;
He neither must know who would serve the Vizier:
Since the days of our prophet the Crescent ne'er saw
A chief ever glorious like Ali Pashaw.

Exactly what they sang is, of course, irrecoverable. Byron says that the versions he gives in *Childe Harold* were attempts to convey the original Albanian in English, via hazy translations through modern Greek and Italian. But whatever the poetic license, the emotional power of the music and the dance is completely convincing. Byron had rarely felt such energy in Greece as on that calm night by the shores of the gulf. It was an enormous contrast to the apathy he had encountered in much of the country.

Of course, the soldiers who sang were Ali's Albanians, not Greeks. The problem remained; and in *Childe Harold*, the songs lead directly on to the famous question about the people for whom one day he would give his life:

> *Fair Greece! sad relic of departed worth!*
> *Immortal, though no more! though fallen, great!*
> *Who now shall lead thy scatter'd children forth,*
> *And long accustom'd bondage uncreate?*

At half-past eight the next morning, they left Loutraki and the shores of the gulf and set off through the bandit country to the south. The bandits are long gone, but this is still a route worth taking. The main road now lies some way to the east: it takes almost all southbound traffic across the dull plain that extends beyond the town of Amfilokhia. The way Byron and Hobhouse came is through higher country, as deserted now as it was for them.

I walked it in a glorious few days of sunshine at the beginning of December, coming down from Arta after weeks of rain. The sky was wide open, without a cloud, the unnatural blue of cheap postcards. The climb out of Loutraki is the only hard part of the walk. For hours, at your back, you have the unbelievable calm of the gulf. Then, at a turn of the road near the village of Trifos, the sea vanishes. The long inland road through the hills of Akarnania begins, and you find the sea again only on the approach to the lagoon of Mesolongi.

By midday, Byron and Hobhouse had reached Katouna. It was a village of twenty houses then, but prosperous, as were the other villages they passed through on their way south. It's a little bigger today, still a quiet, solid sort of place. The countryside, though, is empty, little cultivated; marked by a few plowed fields, endlessly stony, and the ravages of flocks of sheep. The great mountain mass of Boumistos closes the view toward the west.

Much of the Greek countryside is as unpromising as this, a fact that accounts for a great deal in the history of Greece. Words such as "rugged" and "austere" mask the heartbreak for the farmer or the shepherd. Once you've spent a few weeks here you begin to understand why almost anywhere else seems more tempting, the car factories of Germany, the garment warehouses of London, the overcrowded spaces of modern Athens.

For an outsider, though, it is easy to imagine a kind of eternity in this scarred earth, these heaps of stones; as if nothing could have changed since the first farmers began to scratch the soil of Greece, more than eight thousand years ago. A romantic fiction, of course, as any traveler will discover sooner or later.

I know a shepherd, from the village of Prosilio, to the west of Delphi. I have met many Greek shepherds, but never one who looks more like a Greek shepherd than he does. His face and clothes are the very mirror of an ancient past. Twice a year he moves his flock up or down the mountains, in a pattern that goes back to Neolithic times.

It used to give me pleasure, each autumn and spring, to think of him setting out on the age-old journey. Until one afternoon, as we sat watching the sun over Mount Parnassus, he told me that for years he'd moved his sheep in a pickup truck borrowed from his brother in Athens.

· · · ·

There have been many changes in the Greek countryside. The old isolation, however, remains.

I once set out to cross the mountains of central Greece, from the town of Karpenisi to Amfissa. In fine weather, this is a week's walking, by Mount Vardousia, Mount Ghiona, and the Reka Ravine. If you come this way, you reenter the old communication system of the Greek mountains, with its mule tracks, sheepfolds, and tiny villages, a world now suddenly dying after thousands of years of life.

It was late spring, the paths were already as dry as summer. The snow line dazzled the eyes, but looked far out of reach. Then, one evening, as I pitched my tent in a corrie seven thousand feet up on Mount Ghiona, a blizzard came down. It lasted all that night and the next day and most of the following night. I lay in my tent as the snow piled up around me. But there was no danger. Only the monotony of the howling wind. I was secure, content to wait out the storm.

In the early morning, before dawn, there was a moment when the wind blew less strongly and the snow almost stopped. I went outside. The view had opened out onto the plain below, and far away, to the northeast, I saw the lights of a village. Then, after a few minutes, the wind blew up again and the lights vanished into the snow.

In that moment of illumination solitude shifts into loneliness, a familiar moment for the traveler, when the world outside reasserts itself, and all the illusions of self-sufficiency are undone. Down there, in the village square, people carry on eating and drinking, pursuing the tiny routines in which you have no place. It's the kind of loneliness you feel when you walk through a strange town and hear the clash of plates and laughter around the dinner table. It's the sight of old furniture in softly lighted rooms from which you are forever excluded.

In this, at least, the traveler and the old mountain dweller have something in common. In the early 1960s, there were still people

in the Greek interior who could claim they had never seen a foreigner. A decade later the outside world had turned on the lights
almost everywhere. Suddenly the old ways of survival began to
look absurd to the survivors themselves. Many left. They went
down into the cities, where I sometimes met them, in Athens and
elsewhere. There they were learning, often in bitterness, to deal
with a new kind of isolation, and the loneliness that is born from
the inescapable presence of others.

From Katouna, Byron and his party went on to a village that
Hobhouse called Makala, about four hours on horseback. My
map showed nowhere of that name. I climbed up to the village of
Fities. Set on a small plateau, with a steep drop on both its eastern
and western sides, Fities is a big, bustling village, with one of
the ugliest churches in Greece and a fine view of the western
mountains.

I asked an old man if he'd ever heard of a place called Makala.
He gave me one of those huge wide smiles that are the preroga-
tive of country people in the presence of strangers. "This town
was called Makala in my grandfather's time," he said, his eyes
full of the politeness of unasked questions. "Lord Byron spent the
night here once," I said. "He did?" the old man said and smiled
again. Patted me on the back, half in friendship, half, I suppose,
because he thought me just a little, quite harmlessly, mad.

There are still some fine old houses in Fities, with red-tiled
roofs and peeling gray stonework. Nothing prepares you, however, for the extraordinary description Hobhouse gives of the
place where they stayed the night in November 1809. The house,
he wrote, "had very much the appearance of one of those old
mansions which are to be met with in the bottoms of the Wiltshire
Downs." It had a courtyard in front and another behind, enclosed
by a raised terrace. The whole property, he noted in his diary, was
surrounded by "a strong, high wall, which shuts out the prospect, it is true, but shuts out the thieves likewise, who always
infest this country."

On 18 November, they left Makala. The way south is easy, but one of their horses fell and died by the roadside. In a couple of hours they reached the village of Prodromos. The name means "forerunner," an epithet of John the Baptist. It lies on a hillside, with a view over rolling country that might, in the sunshine, almost be English. The slopes are green and wooded and the aridity of the Greek countryside has retreated to the bald crags of the mountains in the west.

Prodromos, wrote Hobhouse, was "a village of a few huts." No one comes this way who doesn't live here. It is on a road that comes to a sudden end a few miles farther on. As you pass by, the curiosity is friendly, unobtrusive—except for the dogs, one of the few hazards of the Greek countryside.

Byron and Hobhouse followed a path that went in a south-easterly direction beyond the village. They traveled for five hours through dense forests of oak. Today the great forests have gone, but, in the half-light of early evening, I lost my way, coming down, as they did, toward the River Akheloös. One of the principal rivers of Greece, the Akheloös rises in the Pindus Mountains and flows into the Ionian Sea. You approach it here across gentle, open country, ringing with sheep bells.

Byron and Hobhouse crossed the river at sunset and spent the night in the village of Gouria. They had taken fourteen and a half hours in all to make the journey from Loutraki and they had seen no one on the road. The whole of Akarnania, Hobhouse wrote, "appeared to us a wilderness of forests and unpeopled plains."

In December, as I came toward Gouria, the road was lined with ripening oranges, waving bamboo, and the yellowing leaves of trees that had finally surrendered to the changing season. From Gouria it is not far to the sea, and the land is flat all the way. Byron's party took three hours to reach the town of Etoliko, which sits on a tiny island in a motionless lagoon. Another three hours and they were in Mesolongi.

It is part of the romance that attaches to the name of Mesolongi that the place itself should be terribly unromantic; a model of backwardness, wretched, poor, inhospitable. The kind of town no famous man would ever die in, except through rotten luck or gross misjudgment. Pouqueville, in the early nineteenth century, set the tone for almost all who have subsequently written about the town. The Greeks of his time called it Little Venice. But what a difference, he wrote, between Venice, queen of the Adriatic, and Mesolongi, cesspool of the province of Aetolia. For him it was a place of evil-smelling, stagnant waters. An altogether insignificant fishing village that had been ruined by the extortions of Ali Pasha; the poverty-stricken end of the world.

One of the best of modern guidebooks suggests that things have not changed much over the years: Mesolongi, we read, is "a pretty miserable and desperately unromantic place—wet through autumn and spring, and comprised of drab modern buildings." Critics, too, have added their weight to the myth. William St. Clair, in *Trelawny: The Incurable Romancer*, called Mesolongi "a miserable mean place in which to spend eternity."

Pouqueville was a notoriously bad judge of places, often writing authoritatively about towns he had never seen. Neither he nor the writers of the late twentieth century have been fair to Mesolongi. When the wind drives the winter rains from off the sea, it can be a depressing town. In the height of summer, the heat and the mosquitoes at night can make life miserable. But this can be said of so many places.

Only for a few years, in the aftermath of the War of Independence, has Mesolongi truly been a model of wretchedness. Though it may seem to have been condemned by its geography to insignificance, it has played its part in Greek history. It was the western center of resistance to the Turks at the time of the Independence struggle and the home of five future prime ministers of an independent Greece.

Hobhouse didn't have much to say about the town. Mesolongi had no particular distinction for him, but it was a decent enough, prosperous enough, place. On a dull and rainy day, he wandered up and down, saw a few "tolerable shops," went into a mosque, and noted that the streets were paved, which was unusual in Greek towns of that size. He met a man who told him that there were no rich inhabitants in the town, but a good many who made five thousand piastres a year, a solid basis for an average family of the time.

By Greek standards, Mesolongi is a recent settlement. Its origins go back only as far as the sixteenth century. It was built as a tiny collection of huts over three small islands in the lagoon; and its early function as a fishing village is confirmed by the fact that it was known for some time in the sailing handbooks simply by the Italian name of Porto Peschiere (Fishing Harbor). The name Mesolongi first appears in the late sixteenth century. Though there have been attempts to derive it from the Greek word *longos,* meaning "thicket," thereby giving it the sense of "in the middle of the forest," it almost certainly comes from two Italian words, *mezzo* and *laghi,* and would mean something like "place in the midst of the lakes." To this day, fishermen in Mesolongi talk of going down "to the lake" rather than "to the sea" or "to the lagoon."

By the time Byron and Hobhouse came here, it was a town of about five thousand inhabitants. A mixed settlement, partly Greek and partly Turkish, its houses were mainly of wood and it still lived on the value of its fisheries. It was quiet, undistinguished, more than a decade away from its fame as the heroic town of the Independence War.

If you approach today the way Byron did, from the northwest, your worst suspicions of Mesolongi would be confirmed. The town of Etoliko, eight miles away, is visibly poor. Some of its houses are ruined or in decay. I saw old women bringing back armfuls of firewood at evening and young children, barefoot, in the warm rain of early December. Past Etoliko, you come to some ancient industrial buildings that are like an echo of Albania. Beyond that, the deep poverty of a gypsy camp and ragged children. The salt marsh, which stretches a long way out toward the open sea and the Gulf of Patras, looks empty and forlorn.

In fact, the marsh is full of birdlife. It is a protected area of international importance. And the saltworks, which you reach a little farther down the road, have their own presence: great white pyramids, each the size of two or three houses, a monstrous snowfall that all the bulldozers and cranes will never clear away. André Maurois, one of Byron's biographers, called Mesolongi "cet étrange royaume de l'eau et du sel" (that strange kingdom of water and salt); and, when you first catch sight of the city, a long promontory of white buildings stretching out into the sea, the arid mountains behind, and the peace of the vast lagoon, it is not hard to feel that this has been a place that is different from others.

The first time I came here was at the end of summer. I stood by the water's edge in the gray heat of an overcast afternoon and watched two women, fully dressed, with large hats, swimming in the sea. A sea that was so shallow it seemed you could walk out into it forever. I remember a few small fishing boats drawn up on the pebbles and some ruined huts on the shoreline. A town of long, straight streets, just big enough to get lost in on a first visit, but intimate. People wandered through the streets, without fear of traffic; they whitewashed their houses; they sat out in the ongoing heat of early evening at small café tables.

Barefooted children ran everywhere. In some houses there were life-size portraits of a strange-looking man who could only have been Lord Byron, though they were nothing like any pictures of him I'd ever seen before. Everyone knew who he was, of course, though what they spoke about most often was his beauty and his love affairs, rather than his politics. In the old days in Mesolongi, they said, his picture was in every house and any handsome man might find himself nicknamed Byron.

But I was not so interested in him in those days. After a sleepless night, struggling with Mesolongi's insects, I left early the next morning and it was years before I returned.

Byron and Hobhouse spent just two days in Mesolongi in November 1809. They would have spent less had bad weather not prevented their getting out of the harbor. They sailed, in the end, for Patras on 23 November, happy at the thought of finding letters there from home.

I followed them down in the second week of December. When they were in Patras, the mountains behind the city were covered in snow. When I was there, in the middle of the mildest winter for years, there were only the faintest white traces on the higher peaks. On the whole, Hobhouse liked Patras. It was a city long used to foreigners and had had a British consul as early as the sixteenth century. It was comfortable, after the weeks of travel; and the landscape all around it was beautiful.

Hobhouse writes of the plantations of oranges and lemons, the vineyards and olive groves; and of the currant grounds that furnished the staple of English trade with the Levant. Contemporary prints and drawings confirm that it was once a lovely place. It has long ceased to be that, though it still has some magnificently tall palm trees. The Turks burned Patras to the ground in 1821. Now the third city in Greece, after Athens and Thessaloniki, it is somewhere to come only if you have friends or want to catch the ferry to Italy.

The sea is much polluted, but otherwise the area is healthier than in Byron's time. Then it was damp and fever-ridden in autumn. In September 1810, Byron was touring the Peloponnese with the teenage boy Nicolo Giraud. He was so violently ill at Patras that he wrote later: "I was in great pain & looked upon death as in that respect a relief."

They left the city on 4 December, heading for Athens. If the weather is fine, this is the best time of year to travel in Greece. The days are still drenched in light, the evenings cool. Even at noon, metal and stone are cold to the touch, but the sun has not lost its power to remind you of those summer mornings when, in the words of Pouqueville, it rises "like an angry god." In the villages, old couples sit out under the orange trees and talk through the day, as if summer had never gone; and the black dress of women in mourning, so brutal in the heat of August, now seems at last almost gentle, comforting.

·　　·　　·

Old country people I knew as a child were hardened to the changes in the seasons. They made arbitrary divisions, deciding on a particular day, for no reason, that summer had ended and autumn had begun. Clothes and food, even tone of voice, changed abruptly overnight. But for us as children, autumn was a dismal time, so we hung on to summer to the bitter end, into those days when arms and legs turned blue in the sea, teeth chattered in the wind along cliff-top paths, and even the most optimistic had to admit that the best season of the year had finally gone.

Byron adored the Greek climate, the apparent escape from this inexorably turning world. Well into December, there are days when you can do all the things you did in summer; and then, by the end of the year, it seems only a moment before spring is back. For Byron, the climate was a mirror of his desire for an unending youth, and the undying sun was its ever potent symbol.

Only once, in the surviving correspondence, is there any hint that Byron was ever troubled by the tyranny of the Greek summer, that season of monotony which, by a strange inversion, is the true companion to the winters of the north. In a letter from London, in December 1811, he writes to his correspondent William Harness: "In the present *frost* I sincerely sympathise with you, it is the first I have felt these three years, though I longed for one in the Oriental Summer."

The depression of summer is a cliché among the psychiatrists of Athens: the sadness of those first days of real heat when there is only the heat to look forward to, the same blue sky, by day, and stifling, cloudless nights, month after month. That is why the warm days of autumn can feel like Greece liberated, when the dry roasted countryside of summer, the heady smells of rosemary and basil, the cacophony of the night's insects, have all retreated. That is a good time to travel.

Byron and Hobhouse had by now seen the rugged mountains of the north and the lonely forests of Akarnania. In comparison, the road east from Patras had little more than hard work to offer them. Much rain had fallen and the paths were in a poor state. On their first day out, they saw only a single village, at Rio; beyond that, nothing more than a solitary house, before they came to a *han* at Lambiri. Sometimes they were able to ride by the water's edge; at others they were forced into the thick woods that reached down the lower slopes of the mountains almost into the sea.

If they had taken the fastest route to Athens, riding all the way along the coast as far as the Isthmus of Corinth, the journey would have taken them forty hours or so. This route still gives the quickest approach, by road or rail. It takes advantage of a long, narrow strip of flat land by the sea, one of the few extended stretches of level ground in Greece.

If you come this way today, you cross the isthmus over the Corinth Canal. The journey would be worth it for that alone. Few engineering projects in history have been so long meditated as the canal, which was first conceived in the sixth century B.C. and finally completed in A.D. 1893. The Greek capital lies about fifty miles beyond it, along the old road by the shores of the Saronic Gulf.

There is, however, a slower route to Athens, over much rougher country. It begins along the same stretch of coast, then crosses over the Gulf of Corinth onto its northern shore. This way, you approach the capital via the town of Thebes. The advantage is that you can visit the site of Delphi along the way; and that is what Byron and Hobhouse decided to do.

From the *han* at Lambiri, they traveled the few miles to the port of Vostitsa. This, the ancient city of Aigion, has, in recent times, taken back its old name; and it is still, as it must have been for millennia, a natural point for the crossing of the gulf.

I took the bus to Aigion from the ferry terminal in Patras. It was a fine December day. Men and women passed by, luxuriously over-dressed, in thick padded jackets, against a sun that would have brought people out in shirtsleeves in northern Europe. There is something sensuous in this excess, this determination to live a winter season in the absence of winter. The Christmas decorations, strung half-heartedly across the road, vanished into the glare of light as the morning went on.

I watched a black cat lying in the sun until, toward noon, she slid gracefully into the cool of shadows. After which, every now and then, there was a flicker of a tail back into the sunlight, in a lazy dream of mice and birds.

When traveling, it is always better to listen than to talk. This is something I learned a long time ago and it is a rule I have seldom broken without regret. The approach favors observation over engagement, of course, and it has its limitations. You no doubt miss some interesting moments; but then you escape some of the worst moments, too.

I sat at the back of the bus, on the way to Aigion. On one side of me was a woman who might have been English; on the other, a Greek Orthodox priest. It was several weeks since I had spoken English with anyone and several days, on the road through Akarnania, since I had had any real conversation at all. The woman next to me was reading from a large volume of Byron's poetry. In English. So I said:

"Are you interested in Byron?" The futility of the question returned to me at once in her raised eyebrows.

"I teach Byron," she said, as if that were something else altogether. "As a Special Subject."

Then, if ever, was the moment to withdraw. But if there is one thing I find harder than initiating a conversation, it is terminating one; and so, driven by some misplaced civility or desire for appearances, I said: "I have just been in Albania."

"Oh, Albania," she said. "When I was last in Albania . . ." My spirits sank further.

"When I was last in Albania, it was a dreadful place. Full of day-trippers from Greece, gawking at all the poverty. It was a marvelous country ten years ago. . . ."

As I thought this over, she asked me, without curiosity, "Do you find Byron a sympathetic figure?"

I knew already that the right answer was no. But I wasn't sure at the time what I thought about Byron; and so it must have been out of simple perversity that I said yes.

"His attitude to women was absurd," she replied. "His attitude to young boys was outrageous. And his attitude to the Greeks . . ."

I caught the eye of the priest on my right and in gratitude exchanged greetings with him.

"What are you doing here?" he asked, in English.

"I'm interested in Byron," I said, with a kind of desperation.

"Do you speak French?"

"Yes."

"Then we must speak French together," he said, and gave a twirl of his long black gown.

We did, and the teacher of Byron returned to her book. I suppose she understood everything we said, though her motionless face no doubt would have been the same if she hadn't.

"He had a great passion for Greece," said the priest.

"Yes," I said.

"And for the Greeks also . . ."

"Yes."

He patted my hand, told me to call him Cyril. "Oui, il aimait la Grèce à la passion. . . . And all those young boys," he said, cheerfully. "Et tous ces petits garçons . . ."

Then suddenly we had reached Byron's Vostitsa and the marvelous anonymity of the port. I got off the bus. Another priest appeared from the crowd. "You were talking to Cyril?" he asked me. "He isn't happy here, you know. He's a very Athens man, very Athens man."

Byron and Hobhouse spent nine days at Vostitsa, something you might still do in a good season, for near here are some of the best beaches of the north coast. They were entertained by the local governor, Andreas Londos, a wealthy Greek; and, as their stay with him lengthened, while they waited for an easterly wind to turn, they had the fortune to discover a remarkable man.

Though a high servant of the Turkish Empire, Londos was a Greek patriot. He was later to become a general and political leader during the War of Independence. Young, just a little younger than Byron, he was the first Greek they had ever met who had authority in all its senses. Under five feet tall, with, as Byron later recalled, "the face and figure of a chimpanzee," Londos gradually relaxed in their company, to reveal what Hobhouse described as "his real character of a merry playful boy."

Byron's attachment to Londos was instantaneous. The mix of high seriousness and childlike playfulness was entirely to his taste. Just a month before Byron died, he wrote a letter to his banker, Samuel Barff, in which he remembered Londos as "my old friend and acquaintance since we were lads in Greece together." To Londos himself, Byron wrote a letter in Italian, from Mesolongi in January 1824. In it, he opened his heart both to memories of the past and to his hopes for the future: "I have towards you the duties of friendship," he wrote, "and of gratitude for your hospitality during my stay in [Greece], of which you are [now] become one of the defenders and adornments. . . . To see you again, and to serve your country by your side and under your eyes—will be for me one of the happiest moments of my life." The opportunity never came.

Londos in Vostitsa had shown himself the kind of Greek who

belied the stereotype of a fawning, submissive people. He was an example Byron never forgot.

On 14 December, they set out across the Gulf of Corinth in a large boat crewed by fourteen men. In three hours, they landed in a bay on the north side of the gulf and had lunch on the beach. Then they rowed on, following the coastline eastward, until, after dark, they passed Galaxidhi, now one of the few resorts on what is one of Greece's most inhospitable shores. By midnight, they had reached to the head of the Bay of Salona, now called the Gulf of Itea, the landing place for the excursion to Delphi.

There was a miserable *han* in the port, so full that they had no choice but to bed down for the night in a room full of onions. The next morning, they sent for horses and rode up to the village of Chrisso, where they spent the night of 15 December. The next day, they moved on upward to the "small mud town" of Kastri, site of ancient Delphi.

Delphi is a huge climb from the sea. At first the road is lined with olive groves, then you reach a scrubby countryside of red rock and low trees; unproductive, except for the grazing of sheep.

The site of the Sanctuary of Apollo at Delphi is among the most famous in the Greek world, second only to the Temple of the Virgin Athena on the Acropolis at Athens. The Homeric Hymn to Apollo describes how the god traveled the length and breadth of Greece, looking for a place to build his temple; and here, in a landscape of cliffs and chasms, with the foothills of Parnassus rising another thousand feet above, he found what he was looking for: a site so remote that neither the rattle of chariots nor the pounding of horses' hooves would ever disturb its sanctity.

Yet the sanctuary became, in its golden age between the sixth and fourth centuries B.C., the religious and moral center of the Greek world. Its geographical center, too. For Delphi was the *omphalos*, the navel of the earth.

Here was the site of the most famous oracle in the world,

the source of guidance to individuals and city-states for a thousand years. Everyone came to Delphi, to find out whether to get married, make a business deal, or start a war. Even the Romans consulted the oracle, after the Carthaginian general Hannibal had inflicted on them the worst defeat they had ever known, at Cannae, in 216 B.C. Nearly three centuries later, Nero took five hundred bronze statues from the god to decorate his new house in Rome, in a rage, some said, because the oracle had condemned him for murdering his mother.

In the fourth century A.D., there was still a priest of Apollo at Delphi, though the sanctuary had long been in decline. In the fifth century, it was revitalized and became prosperous again as the seat of a Christian bishop. Churches were built here among the old buildings. Then, sometime in the sixth or seventh century, Delphi was devastated by unknown hands and never recovered.

The ruins were gradually buried under soil and stones washed down by the rains and, by the seventeenth century, no one knew for sure where the sanctuary had been. The village of Kastri grew up over the debris. It was one of those small, dusty settlements that were the despair of European travelers in Greece, a place that seemed to symbolize the absolute decline from a glorious past to a dismal present.

It was, then, almost inevitable that Hobhouse should have been disappointed with his excursion. It was not until 1891 that French money led to the expropriation of Kastri and its rebuilding on the site of the modern village of Delphi. Which, in turn, led to the long excavations that uncovered the marvelous ruins the visitor sees today. When Hobhouse was there, simply too little existed to excite the interest of an amateur antiquarian. "And Delphi now, however rich of old, / Discovers little silver, and less gold," as Byron succinctly put it.

They saw the outline of the stadium, and, in the dark room of a hovel, a piece of old wall covered in illegible inscriptions. They went into the Monastery of the Holy Virgin and scratched their names on a marble column. The monastery no longer exists, but the French novelist Flaubert found Byron's signature still intact in 1851.

It was a desultory pilgrimage. But if Hobhouse's disappointment was understandable, given his fascination for ancient monuments, it is no less in keeping with Byron's temperament that he should have fallen in love with the natural beauties of the site. For him there was pleasure in simply being there, at the foot of Mount Parnassus, home not only of Apollo, but of Dionysus and the Muses.

For centuries, Parnassus—even Greece itself—had been hardly more than a geographical expression or a figure of speech to most English writers. When Chaucer, in the late fourteenth century, called on the Muses "that on Parnaso dwell" to help him write a poem, he was already following a ritual long established, and with no physical referent. Parnassus could almost as easily have been on the moon.

Byron, however, sitting in the village of Kastri and gazing up at the snows on the real Parnassus, could claim a new legitimacy. His excitement still depended on all that had gone before, on the memory of those who had worshiped Parnassus from afar. But his relationship with the landscape was new, personal, and direct. The Muses, he knew, had long since departed. Something, however, remained in the air. A sensation more physical than literary, deeply connected with the past, yet not confined by it. In *Childe Harold*, he explained how it felt; as, pausing in the middle of some flabby lines about Spanish women, he wrote:

> *Oh, thou Parnassus! whom I now survey,*
> *Not in the phrenzy of a dreamer's eye,*
> *Not in the fabled landscape of a lay,*
> *But soaring snow-clad through thy native sky,*
> *In the wild pomp of mountain majesty!*
> *What marvel if I thus essay to sing?*

And Delphi survives, still arouses, in the words of one modern guidebook, "universal awe and long remembrance." The natural setting retains its ancient contrasts: the blue sea of the Itean Gulf, the snow on the mountains. The dry earth of Delphi itself, suspended between the two. Birdsong in the pine trees, the sound of sheep's bells, and cats stalking the roofs.

It survives its endless reduplication in the modern world, the reduction of its myths: the Hotel Oracle, the Cafeteria Zeus, Apollo Street, the Omphalos Taverna. In Greece it is the destiny of myths to end as advertisements, retaining in this way an echo of their former power. Even the most dedicated of sun followers prefer a Greece that is classical.

The continuities, of course, are long gone. The old gods and heroes are become, like Ulysses in Tennyson's poem, simply names, detached from the stories that once gave them life. How else to explain the existence in Greece of Ikaros Air-Lines, named in honor of the wild boy who flew too high into the sun, lost his wings, and came crashing to his death in the Aegean Sea.

Any visitor to Delphi today can only feel grateful for the labors of the archaeologists. There was so little a hundred years ago, so much today. The magnificently ravaged Temple of Apollo, the dusty climb up the Sacred Way, the idealized stillness of the Charioteer in Delphi's museum. In comparison with all that, everything else is marginal. The swarms of coaches, the noise of guides, the incongruities of modern pilgrims ("It is forbidden to enter the archaeological site in bathing suit"). Delphi is no longer the center of the world, but the whole world still comes to Delphi, all through the year, in all weathers.

Byron and Hobhouse had no reason to linger and they were now anxious to reach Athens. They left Delphi on 17 December for Arahova, six miles away. Looking down from Arahova, you can see clearly the way they came. The descent from Delphi into a narrow valley, the passage along the valley floor, and then the final huge climb to over three thousand feet. Day or night, Arahova is a spectacular place to break a journey.

The town takes a lot of heavy traffic, but away from the road it still has the rhythms of a mountain village. Very old men, silent, unmoving, warm themselves on the terraces of the cafés, with the calm of infinite survivors. The houses are raked back severely into the mountainside behind them, as in a giant theater.

At the upper end of the town I sat by the church, on a night of new moon. Traces of cloud wandered across the streetlights, and from way below a smell of wood smoke rose up to mix with the scent of incense. The lights of the town trace a curve at your feet, against absolute darkness beyond, as if this were a Greek island village fronting the sea. It's only in the light of morning, when you wake up with the air sharp on your lungs, that you find yourself overlooking the deep gorge of the Pleistos River.

The road east from Arahova is a continuous fall through gray, scrubby mountains. By the time you reach Livadhia, twenty miles away, the mountains have gone. The land opens out into a wide plain and the slopes that border it are now green. When Byron and Hobhouse came to Livadhia, it was one of the most prosperous towns in Greece, later reduced, at the outset of the War of Independence, to what Hobhouse called "a heap of deserted ruins." The modern town is prosperous once again— still, as in the late Middle Ages and under the Turks, more important than Thebes farther east, which has retained from the past only its famous name.

Livadhia is one of those Greek towns where, away from the center, people still sit and call to one another from their balconies. On the south side of the town, a great cliff rises and at its base the River Herkina surfaces in a series of rushing springs. Near here, in classical times, was the Oracle of the god Trophonios.

Pausanias, the inexhaustible traveler, was here in the second century A.D., and he left a record of how a man went down to consult the god. On the chosen night, the man was taken to the springs, anointed with oil, and washed by two teenage boys. Then, from one spring, he drank the water of Forgetfulness, so that his mind would be cleared; and afterward, from another spring, the water of Memory, so that he would remember everything that happened in the presence of the god.

Above the springs is a fourteenth-century castle. It is a pleasant place to sit for an hour, with the smell of fir trees around you and the sounds of a Greek town rising from below. For Hobhouse, though, it was simply "a ruin that forcibly reminds one of the latter miseries and degradation of Greece."

They stayed for three days in Livadhia, and from there they made an excursion a few miles to the north, to visit the site of one of history's most famous and influential battles, at Chaironeia.

There is almost nothing to see at Chaironeia. Just a fertile plain and rolling hills, with a few traces of the ancient city that was once the beloved home of the biographer Plutarch. These battle sites depend entirely on the power of the historical imagination to separate them from a dozen others that are geographically almost identical. It is the same with the other famous plains Byron saw on his travels: Troy, still, in his day, unexcavated; Waterloo; Marathon, which he celebrated in some of his best-known lines.

If Marathon is the symbol of Greek freedom, scene of the first Greek victory over the Persians, Chaironeia is the image of final Greek defeat. "The tragedy at Chaironeia," wrote Pausanias, "was the beginning of catastrophe for the whole of Greece." Here, in 338 B.C., Philip II of Macedon, with help from his son, the future Alexander the Great, defeated a Greek coalition of Athenians, Thebans, and Corinthians. The old city-states lost their independence forever and Greece entered on the long period of foreign domination that would end, with some assistance from Byron, 2,168 years later.

The Thebans buried their dead after Chaironeia in a common tomb. Above it was placed a large lion in gray Boeotian marble, as a testimony to their courage. Hobhouse knew of its existence from Pausanias, but it had vanished in his time. Today, as you pass by on the main road to Lamia, you suddenly come across it, sheltering in a grove of trees.

The lion squats on its haunches, a little under thirty feet high, and rests on a huge and ancient plinth. There's no sign to say what it is or why it's there. There never was any memorial inscription to the Theban dead. "I suppose nothing was inscribed," says Pausanias, "because the fortune that rewarded them was so much worse than their courage deserved." The lion is very large, but not very frightening. The statue has obviously been resurrected from bits and pieces; now, with its front paws uncertainly patched, it looks almost domestic, like an overgrown Saint Bernard.

The monument was apparently smashed sometime in the early nineteenth century, in the hope that it contained treasure. Perhaps by Ali Pasha, perhaps by the Independence war leader Odysseus Androutsos. It was found almost completely buried by some passing Englishmen in 1818. In the early twentieth century, it was restored and now sits, memorably, by the wayside.

When Byron and Hobhouse returned to Livadhia from their excursion to Chaironeia, they made preparations for the journey to Thebes, about thirty miles to the east. They sent their heavy baggage by the direct road, while they themselves made a detour to the northeast, to see what remained of Orchomenos, an ancient city that Homer compared for its riches to Thebes in Egypt.

This area makes for dull traveling. Flat, arable land, which in Byron's time, before the draining of Lake Kopaïs, was often drenched in water. The villages are drab, some only reached by dirt tracks, a few falling before your eyes into final ruin. Then, in Orchomenos, a drab village like all the others, you come across a beautiful Byzantine church with, opposite, the remains of a classical theater.

Hobhouse was, predictably, uninterested in the church, while the theater had yet to be excavated. He redeemed the excursion by a moment of rare lightness: he went to pay a visit to the Fat Man of Orchomenos. This man, a shepherd, was the fattest human being Hobhouse had ever seen. So large, that he was forced to spend the hot summer days up to his neck in the nearest river.

From Orchomenos, they struggled through mist and swamps toward the main road for Thebes. After dark, they finally caught up with their luggage, lost, along with their servants, in some low hills. They spent the night in Mazee, then a miserably poor village inhabited mainly by Albanians. On the next day, 22 December, they galloped into Thebes at half past four in the afternoon, through driving rain.

Thebes was already a ruined memorial to its past greatness at the time of the coming of Christ. The legendary home of Dionysus, Herakles, and the Greek alphabet, it was once, for a few years, the leader of all Greece. It had renewed fame, in the Middle Ages, as a center of the silk trade, but by 1500 it had long fallen back into degeneration. Under the Turks, it was never more than the miserable village of five hundred wooden houses that Hobhouse saw. "There is nothing worthy of notice in this place," he wrote; and the same is true today, apart from a fine museum.

I stood, one icy morning in late December, shivering above a hole in the ground. Part of a Mycenaean palace, said a sign. There were some loose stones, a few more solid blocks, now decorated with a heap of Coca-Cola cans. Almost all the visible remains of Theban history.

Sooner or later, it is the fate of every traveler in Greece to be overcome by what Greece was, by the sheer length of that receding line that joins us, however tenuously, to the past.

Sometimes the extravagant profusion of Greek history is delightful, a sensual indulgence, like eating a fine meal on a fine day. I have a memory of sitting in the December sun in Old Corinth, reading the poem by Elytis that begins:

> Drinking the sun of Corinth
> Reading the marble ruins . . .

In front of me, against blue sky and the blue waters of the Corinthian Gulf, the seven columns of the Temple of Apollo, the oldest standing columns in Greece. All around, the vast ruins of Roman Corinth. Beyond, the simple modern monument that commemorates Paul's letter to the Corinthians . . . "Love bears all things, believes all things, hopes all things, endures all things." Somewhere to the northwest, Delphi, in the haze across the gulf; and, high above, the citadel of Acrocorinth that guards the road to Argos and Mycenae. I read, in the perfect heat of noon, and watched children coming home from school, the past as wondrously alive as the present.

But there are times in Greece when history is only the deadweight that bears down unfairly on the modern world. Sometimes, as you pass through a sleepy village that still bears a name out of antiquity, you feel the way you do when you read in a newspaper that someone famous is finally dying after a long illness. There's the same surprise that they were still alive at all, after so many years of silence; and the same sorrow at the unrecorded space, all that time when they had really ceased to be and had just gone on and on, doing nothing but dying.

Once, driving south from the Ambracian Gulf, I stopped at the village of Stratos. Here was the ancient capital of Akarnania. The guidebook called it "a melancholy village," which was curious, for it was no different from dozens of others. I saw a donkey, bent under a tree, in that uncomplaining, forlorn way they have. There was a cream-colored church, with red-tiled domes; and a woman with a large hat, ankle deep in drying corn.

As I read on, I realized that the guidebook's melancholia was all about the past. Stratos, it said, was important in the fifth century B.C., "but before our era began it had lost all importance."

I walked over the ruins of the famous city. I saw the walls ("particularly well preserved") and the theater, which was then being excavated. The site was surrounded by prickly pears and abandoned houses. It was near the end of siesta time and there was still no one about.

Then a woman came out onto the veranda of one of the ruined houses. She was dressed only in faded blue jeans. She looked at me casually, disappeared, reappeared, slowly drawing on a T-shirt. We spoke. An archaeologist from Finland, she said. Sunworn, tired at the end of a long season with the past. After a while she set to work. On hands and knees, inch by inch, the endless brushing back and forth of centuries of yellow dust.

I watched for a time; then, full of melancholy, I returned to the car and drove on.

The modern road from Thebes to Athens goes at first due north, then makes a loop to the east. This avoids the mass of Mount Parnes that blocks the entrance to the Attic plains. An older road goes due south toward the sea, making for a pass at the western end of Mount Parnes. But the oldest route of all takes an almost direct line between the two cities and lies across the very center of the mountains. This was the way Byron and Hobhouse came. It remains by far the finest approach to the capital and is today the only one that can still give pleasure.

Leaving Thebes, you follow the fertile plain toward a solid mountain wall. In the early morning mist, the mountains rise straight out of the flat land, a relief after much drabness. I crossed the Asopos River and began a long climb through the fir trees. The country was just as Hobhouse described it, but I went too far to the south and lost my way. I met three farmers who gave me bread and icy wine and drew a map for me in the red earth. After a long time, I got onto the Skourta plateau, a stony moonscape that then showed tiny patches of old snow in the shadows by the roadside.

Hobhouse and Byron spent Christmas Eve, 1809, in a stable in the village of Skourta. It was, Hobhouse wrote, "a miserable deserted village, where half the houses were shut up." They shared the night with cows and pigs and choked on the smoke from the fire. It was, said Hobhouse, "the worst hovel of which we had ever been inmates."

Today, Skourta is an ordinary, friendly village in a bleak setting on the plateau. A narrow dirt road leads into the mountains. The road is first white, then red. There was no traffic and I walked the fifteen miles to the next village. For a long time, I had the mountain road to myself. Then I passed an old woman with her daughter. Two children followed them, trying to play snowballs with the few scattered flakes that had survived the late morning sun. Later the road improves and a few cars came by. The scenery is magnificent: high mountains, deep gorges, fir trees topped with snow, like Christmas, rugged outcrops of rock.

Then, at over two thousand feet, you pass the ruins of the fifth-century B.C. fort of Phyle. This was one of a number of outlying forts that guarded the approaches to Athens in classical times. In *Childe Harold*, Byron recalled how Thrasybulus, the Athenian general and statesman, held Phyle, on his way to rescue Athens from dictatorship. The historical memory prompted some thoughts on what Greece was then and what she had become, now, in the early nineteenth century:

> *Spirit of freedom! when on Phyle's brow*
> *Thou sat'st with Thrasybulus and his train,*
> *Couldst thou forebode the dismal hour which now*
> *Dims the green beauties of thine Attic plain?*

In former times, heroic resistance. But now only defeat, as the sons of Greece lie

> *Trembling beneath the scourge of Turkish hand,*
> *From birth till death enslav'd; in word, in deed unmann'd.*

It was from Phyle, on Christmas Day, that they had the first sight of their destination: the plain of Athens, the Aegean Sea, the Acropolis. Suddenly, all the relics of an English public-school education were at their feet. It was "a more glorious prospect," Byron wrote, than anything they ever saw on their travels. He thought it more glorious even than the approach to Constantinople.

At Phyle, the traveler is less than twenty miles from Athens, and, miraculously, still at peace in the mountains. But, though the scenery is as beautiful as it ever was, it is a struggle today to see very far. The sea, the Acropolis, everything is hidden now in the brown haze of polluted Athens.

Straight ahead, and far below, is the village of Fili, called Khasia in Byron's time. A few moments after you enter it today, by a transformation that seems improbable even as it happens, you find yourself in a world that is the absolute contrast with all that has gone before. Suddenly, the past is only last week, or last month. The air, like a sickness, rasps on eyes and throat. You're surrounded by belching, screaming cars, and the dusty, concrete mass of always moving, always half-finished, modern Athens.

Five

There is no freedom—even for Masters—in the midst of slaves.

—Byron, "Detached Thoughts," 1821

Hobhouse approached Athens in his mind as many do for the first time. A city on the edge of Europe, remote, Eastern, far from home, it seems to offer the final promise of the unfamiliar. Yet, by the depth of historical association, this is a city that provokes the illusion of an eternal homecoming. For, however irrelevant or contested the clichés now seem, Athens remains, for the Westerner, the place where everything in the West began: politics, democracy, literature, science, architecture, the pursuit of the beautiful. And the first sight of the rock of the Acropolis with its ruined temple, rising three hundred feet above the city, has, for generations, been a plausible symbol of everything that other nations owe to the Greek past.

Hobhouse's account of the final descent from Phyle toward the city they had for so long anticipated shares the same mix of the expectant and the knowing. If the road became "every moment more romantic," the Attic plain yet "appeared more like England than anything we had for some time seen." If they saw in the distance a mosque "tipp'd with the last rays of the sun"—the very image of Eastern difference—it still reminded Hobhouse of an

English provincial church. The woods they passed through took him back home in memory to Lord Ludlow's seat at Cople Hall, in the county of Bedfordshire.

For hundreds of years, Athens had seemed familiar to western writers. Many had written about it as if they had seen it for themselves. The poet Milton, frustrated in his desire to visit Greece by the onset of the English Civil War, still felt confident enough to express the conventional praises of the ancient city:

> behold
> *Where on the Aegean shore a city stands*
> *Built nobly, pure the air, and light the soil,*
> *Athens, the eye of Greece . . .*

Through repetitions like this, the city of Pericles and Socrates survived, as a compelling anachronism, into the modern world.

In the Greek tradition, on the other hand, writers had long since recognized the passing of time. Here is Michael Choniates, who became metropolitan of Athens in A.D. 1182:

> *Though I live in Athens, I see Athens nowhere,*
> *Only dust, sorrowful and empty, blessed.*
> *Where is your magnificence, wretched city?*
> *All vanished, as if become a myth . . .*

Byron and Hobhouse soon had the opportunity to measure the truth for themselves.

They came down into Athens across the immense belt of olive groves that was then, as it had long been, one of the dominant features of the Attic plain. An English visitor in the late seventeenth century, Bernard Randolph, wrote that "the olive-trees stand so thick to the West of the City that they seem to be a Wood, reaching Six Miles in Length and Two in Breadth."

It was evening and they passed long lines of men returning from work in the fields. Some time after eight o'clock, they entered through a gate in the low wall that surrounded the city. Finally, the journey they had begun three months earlier in Prevesa was over. Byron would never travel so extensively again.

Curiously, both Byron and Hobhouse came to like Athens. Hobhouse because, though the city was far fallen from its prime, it still offered the promise of many fine old things to see. Athens remained, he said, "venerable from the recollection of her former renown, and still possessed of many objects worthy of admiration." Byron, for his part, because he was soon in love with three young Greek girls. The same ruins that intrigued Hobhouse became the most romantic of stages, the backdrop to an easy, giddy social life, free from the constraints of home.

Many others who came at this time were disappointed— principally, by the failure of Athens to be the Athens of the past, but also because there was a real harshness to life in the city.

When Bernard Randolph lived in Athens, in the 1670s, he found it a happy place. The Greeks, he reported, lived better there than in almost any other part of Turkey, forming what he called "a small Common-wealth amongst themselves." The city was unwalled then, and the main problem was not the behavior of the Turkish overlords, but the frequent incursions of pirates.

In 1760, however, changes in Turkish legislation brought oppressive increases in taxation. There was greater hardship and repression in Athens; and, for a period of twenty years after 1770, the city lived through the darkest moments of the long Turkish occupation. Many Athenians fled, or quietly disappeared.

It was then that a wall was built to encircle the city. A wall ostensibly defensive, but that served to control those within. The building work was done with forced labor and the whole circuit completed within three months. It rapidly came to symbolize the horror of alien power and it would be demolished with the liberation of Greece after the War of Independence.

The Athens of the early nineteenth century had still not recovered from these depredations. John Galt, who had been with

Byron and Hobhouse on their way from Gibraltar to Malta, arrived in the city in February 1810. He found nothing positive to write about in his letters home: "How wretched, how solitary, how empty is Athens!" Byron and Hobhouse were almost his only source of consolation; and when they left the city, he noted: "Their society occasionally served to vary the monotony of my solitude, in a way that I must always think of with satisfaction."

The two travelers lived for the next ten weeks with the widow of a former British vice-consul in Athens, Theodora Makri. The house was on today's street of Ayias Theklas. This narrow street runs off Odhos Ermou (Hermes Street), the long east-west thoroughfare that now bisects the old city of Athens. In their day, Hobhouse writes, the house could be easily seen at a distance, "as there is a tall flag-staff rising from the yard; and on this the English ensign, in the time of the late Vice-Consul, used to be displayed."

Here, they were in the center of things. This was where the wealthy lived, where the chief administrative buildings were, and the coffeehouses, public baths, and shops. A famous city, yet one that was in many ways a backwater. In all its long history, it had never been the capital of anywhere, and it would become the capital of an independent Greece, by courtesy of a German king, only in 1834.

Theodora Makri had three daughters under the age of fifteen. Byron said he was in love with all of them, but especially with the youngest, Theresa. She was twelve years old and made such an impression that her mother believed she might, with a little intrigue, end as Byron's wife. She did not, of course; but she achieved greater fame, as Byron's "Maid of Athens," the subject of a sentimental song that has given her an unshakable place in the poet's biography:

> Maid of Athens, ere we part,
> Give, oh, give me back my heart!

So the song began. It was to be Byron's farewell to Theresa, as he prepared to leave Athens, in February 1810, for a four-month tour of western Turkey.

Theresa, or one of the girls, had taught him a few words of modern Greek, the sort of Greek any romantic tourist would be happy to bring home among the souvenirs: "Zoi mou, sas agapo" (My life, I love you). Byron fitted these words into his song. They appear as the last line of each of the four verses, in a simple rhyme. In verse one:

> *Hear my vow before I go,*
> *Zoi mou, sas agapo.*

And at the end:

> *Can I cease to love thee? No!*
> *Zoi mou, sas agapo.*

The effect is charming, innocent; a little strange to the modern Greek ear, since *Zoi mou* is the intimate language of lovers, while *sas* is the French *vous* or the Spanish *usted*, the formal form of "you."

In 1822, Byron remembered the three Makri girls in Canto VI of his long satiric poem *Don Juan*. There the enclosed, heady jealousies, the young eroticism focused on a visiting stranger, are transferred to the Turkish Sultan's seraglio in Constantinople. The Makri sisters have become concubines: Theresa, under her pet name Lolah; Katinka; and Mariana, nicknamed Dudù:

> *Lolah was dusk as India and as warm;*
> *Katinka was a Georgian, white and red,*
> *With great blue eyes, a lovely hand and arm,*
> *And feet so small they scarce seemed made to tread,*
> *But rather skim the earth; while Dudù's form*
> *Looked more adapted to be put to bed,*

> *Being somewhat large and languishing and lazy,*
> *Yet of a beauty that would drive you crazy.*

In the seraglio, the hero Don Juan appears in disguise, dressed as the woman Juanna. All three Makri girls volunteer to share his bed. But, in the end, it is Dudù who succeeds; and Juanna watches as Dudù slowly undresses, in a scene that mingles all the fantasies of Eastern eroticism with Byron's own cross-sexual longings.

Athens in Byron's time centered, as it had for centuries, on the area around the square that is today called Monastiraki (Little Monastery). Many illustrations survive to give an idea of what it looked like then, even if visiting artists had a tendency to improve on nature, often adding rivers, lakes, and forests to an aridity that seemed unacceptably pervasive.

In the early nineteenth century, Western visitors were quickly turning the place into a city of monuments. The historian Gibbon, in a famous passage from *The Decline and Fall of the Roman Empire*, had poured all his elegant scorn on the Athenians for their failure to appreciate the monuments that educated Westerners loved so well. The Athenians, he wrote, "walk with supine indifference among the glorious ruins of antiquity; and such is the debasement of their character that they are incapable of admiring the genius of their predecessors."

This way of putting it legitimized a fashion. Lord Elgin's removal of the Parthenon sculptures was part of that fashion. For, if the Greeks could not see the monuments around them, then the glories of the past needed to be removed elsewhere for safekeeping.

It is true that many Athenians of the time saw no monuments. They simply lived in a familiar world that was the accumulation of the debris of centuries. They lived among the old stones, pitched their tents there, parked their camels, built houses; hacked off bits and pieces of the past, according to necessity or convenience. They called them "old things," "old columns," with a mixture of condescension and awe and an almost complete ignorance of chronology.

Even so, Gibbon's view was only a partial truth about the state of Greece. Some there always were who could see things differently. In 1759, the governor of Athens, Tzistaraki, blew up the seventeenth column of the Temple of Olympian Zeus while he was building the mosque that stands in Monastiraki Square. This provoked such anger among Turks and Greeks alike that he was exiled from the city as a vandal.

Hobhouse tells of meeting a man from Ioannina—then the cultural capital of Greece—who said to him: "You English are carrying off the works of *the Greeks*, our forefathers—preserve them well—we Greeks will come and redemand them!" A prophecy that still echoes around the Duveen Gallery at the British Museum in London, where Lord Elgin's marbles are so lovingly displayed.

Naturally, the differences between Byron's Athens and the Athens of today are great. The place he knew would emerge from the War of Independence as a shattered ruin of perhaps six thousand inhabitants. It had to be rebuilt as the new capital city for a new country. Of all the things that were lost in that transition, it is the easy commerce with the past that a visitor today might most regret—more even than the modern invasions of pollution and the motorcar. The old Athens of Byron's time was not yet a museum, but a place intimately, confusedly, in touch with its past.

A building like the Tower of the Winds, which stands to the south of Monastiraki, had evolved over eighteen hundred years. First a Roman water clock, weather vane, and sundial. Then a Christian baptistery. Then, in Turkish times, a sanctuary of the whirling dervishes, whose performances, by 1810, had made it one of the great tourist attractions of the city. Now it's simply there, its white Pentelic marble long graying in the sooty air, looking out over the stunted columns of the Roman Market, the perfect monument.

•   •   •

When Byron and Hobhouse arrived, they immediately became part of an intimate expatriate group of French, Italians, Germans, and others. One of the first to call on them was Giovanni Lusieri, a Neapolitan painter. Lord Elgin had employed him to make drawings of the city's antiquities and to supervise the removal of the sculptures from the Parthenon. In the notes to *Childe Harold*, Byron called Lusieri "the agent of devastation." Through him, he met Nicolo Giraud, Lusieri's brother-in-law, a Greek-born French national, who later became Byron's Italian teacher and lover.

They also quickly met the French consul, Fauvel, one of the most popular Europeans in the Levant and a long-time resident of Athens. In the notes to *Childe Harold*, Byron wrote off Fauvel as easily as he dismissed Lusieri, though he acknowledged his "talents as an artist and manners as a gentleman." A decade later, in 1822, Fauvel was to show his deeper qualities, as he worked to save the Turks from the massacre that followed the surrender of Athens in the second year of the Independence War.

Byron fell naturally into this circle of cultivated foreigners, but he never felt completely at home there. He was unhappy with the truth that he was merely a passerby in the company of men who had long been settled in Athens. But, as an outsider, he was also conscious of the facile superiority that characterized this expatriate group. Even as, inevitably, he shared some of its assumptions.

Reading the notes to *Childe Harold*, and the accounts of conversations in Athens, is to rediscover a familiar model. There is a hostility or condescension toward Greece that still survives; a pervasive mistrust and frustration. You can hear the same conversations today, as foreigners struggle to thread the labyrinths of Greek bureaucracy, or simply find a place to park their car.

In 1810, the focal point of much discussion in Athens was whether the Greeks deserved to be free from their Turkish masters. The general view among the resident foreigners was that they did not, and most of the visitors who passed through ended by sharing the same opinion.

Fauvel, according to Byron, talked openly of the Greeks' "national and individual depravity." Behind such remarks lay a weight of tradition. Terence Spencer, in his *Fair Greece Sad Relic*, recalls that the word "Greek" signified "crook" in the English of the early 1500s, and that this sense was common for the next three hundred years. There was nothing eccentric or even unusual about Fauvel's views.

Byron himself never idealized the Greeks. Writing from the Dardanelles in May 1810, while he was on his way to Constantinople, he records his earliest impressions: "I like the Greeks, who are plausible rascals, with all the Turkish vices without their courage.—However some are brave and all are beautiful . . . the women not quite so handsome."

To the end of his life, Byron could be as hostile to the Greeks as anyone. Julius Millingen, who served as surgeon to the Byron Brigade at Mesolongi, quotes him as saying that "the Greeks are perhaps the most depraved and degraded people under the sun." Another doctor, James Kennedy, who also knew Byron in the last year of his life, remembered him saying: "I despise the present race of the Greeks, even while I pity them, I do not believe they are better than the Turks, nay, I believe that in many respects the Turks surpass them."

Yet, Byron also, and regularly, made the mental effort to understand why things should be as they were. If the Greeks presented a wretched picture to outsiders, this was not in their nature as Greeks, but in their condition as a people without freedom. Where so many Europeans simply despised the Greeks, dismissed them as lazy, cringing, and duplicitous, Byron looked further.

His most famous remarks on the subject are, once again, in the notes to *Childe Harold*:

At present, like the Catholics of Ireland and the Jews throughout the world . . . , [the Greeks] suffer all the moral and physical ills that can afflict humanity. Their life is a struggle against truth; they are vicious in their own defence. They are so unused to kindness, that when they occasionally meet with it they look upon it with suspicion, as a dog often beaten snaps at your fingers if you attempt to caress him. "They are ungrateful, notoriously, abominably ungrateful!"—this is the general cry. Now, in the name of Nemesis! for what are they to be grateful? Where is the human being that ever conferred a benefit on Greek or Greeks?

This is Byron at his humane best, talking of the Greeks in a way that was not common in his time. Change the circumstances of oppression, he argued, and the nature of the people will change with it. It was a faith that would be ruthlessly tested in Mesolongi.

Not that Byron had the slightest idea in 1810 that Greek independence might be either possible or desirable. "The Greeks will never be independent; they will never be sovereigns as heretofore, and God forbid they ever should!" he wrote. The best chance for Greece, he believed at the time, lay in acquiring the virtues of modern statehood, under the benevolent supervision of a foreign power, preferably Britain. In this political assessment, at least, his views were entirely those of his age.

Byron and Hobhouse soon settled to a routine of socializing and sightseeing. Hobhouse was lost in "the contemplation of the noble monuments of Grecian genius," Byron in sustained flirtation with his young girls in flower. Life for both of them was easy and comfortable. Athens was a city you could hold in the palm of your hand. Hobhouse said he had walked all around the walls in forty-seven minutes. You could go anywhere in half an hour.

The city covered the land that lies between the lovely Doric Temple of Hephaistos in the west—still known as the Theseion—and the present Vouli Street in the east, no more than a mile and a half from point to point. If a traveler approached across the open land to the west, the city with its little cluster of houses was almost completely hidden by the high rock of the Acropolis. This approach was still unchanged in the 1850s, when Edward Lear celebrated the view in a famous painting.

But if Athens was small, it was also cosmopolitan. There were Albanians, many of whom lived as farmers out on the plain; gypsy ironmongers, who congregated in the swampy, stagnant land to the west of Monastiraki; Greeks, Turks, and Ethiopians. It was a city that lived on trade, and so on movement and cooperation. Almost everyone, including the Turks, spoke Greek, and people lived side by side, unsegregated.

The best place to recover some sense of what this trading world was like is still Monastiraki and its surrounding streets. On Sunday mornings you can buy a lot of what you need in life, and even more of what you don't, by just wandering a few hundred yards up and down. The area feels like what it is: the natural successor to the Turkish bazaar of Byron's time.

The old center of the bazaar lay around today's Pandrosos Street, a narrow lane that runs east out of Monastiraki toward the Cathedral. Now it belongs to tourism and sets a crushing uniformity of taste: perfumes and gold, and all the tawdry inventions of Greek popular art. T-shirts with the opening lines of Homer's *Odyssey*, or the oath of Hippocrates, in proud Greek script. Glittering icons and heavy furs, which, in the height of summer, are an endless challenge to the imagination.

Sometimes, on Pandrosos, however, you come across real continuities. This was always the place for buying shoes, for example. Until the First World War, shepherds and peasant-farmers came here to buy the old turned-up country shoes that in Greek are called *tsaroukhia*. Later, when the *tsaroukhia* had passed into tradition, tourists and schoolchildren still came looking for them in the same street. Now, when they are long gone, people come to buy sandals instead. At number 89 Pandrosos is Stavros Melissinos, a poet–sandal maker who, in the days when sandals were fashionable, sold them to the Beatles and Jackie Onassis.

.   .   .

Soon after their arrival, Byron and Hobhouse climbed up through the narrow streets of what is now the Plaka district and headed for the central prize of Athens: the Acropolis, with its Temple of Athena. In Turkish times the Acropolis was a military zone and, nominally, Christians were forbidden to set foot on it. The Parthenon had been converted into a mosque and the lovely Ionic temple of the Erechtheion served as a harem for the military commander.

The two travelers had sent up a present of tea and sugar in advance, without which there was no hope of entry. As Hobhouse reported, repeated demands for presents were making the Acropolis an expensive place to visit in their time.

From their house on the street of Ayias Theklas, they would have passed the Byzantine Church of the Pandanassa. This was once a part of the Great Monastery of the All-Holy Mother of God and Mistress of the Universe. It was famous in Turkish times and had grown rich on a trade in homespun cloth. It survived the War of Independence, only to fall victim to modernization and the building of the Athens-Piraeus railroad. In 1810, it was still one of the landmarks of the city and covered a large area, gradually reduced in the post-Independence period, until, by 1868, it was called simply Monastiraki, or Little Monastery.

From here, the old Turkish path to the northern slopes of the Acropolis lies buried under the modern Odhos Adrianou (Hadrian Street). It passes by the ruins of the vast Library of Hadrian. Higher up are the ruins of the Islamic Seminary, the Medrese. Here, Turkish leaders met in 1821 to discuss the news that a Greek revolt had broken out in the Peloponnese. After the liberation of Greece, the Medrese was converted into a prison; men were hanged from the branches of the plane tree in its courtyard. Today, only the entrance gate remains, almost unnoticed, facing the Tower of the Winds across a little square.

High above is one of the most famous sights in the world: the arid limestone rock of the Acropolis, setting for a thousand sun-bleached, moon-drenched postcards; and, looking up toward the summit of the rock, you see the ruin of one of the most successful buildings of all time. The Parthenon, the temple designed as a home for Athena, goddess of Athens, has been the unrivaled symbol of the city from the moment of its construction until now. A visit there is no longer an act of piety, but it is still not exactly free from the weight of ritual.

Not that everyone comes to the Acropolis and goes away satisfied. On one August afternoon, a time for sleeping as the city simmers in its own exhalations, I stood with the immense crowds that flowed through the entrance. A quiet Texan, from Odessa, he said, looked at it all for the first time. The ancient wreckage, now propped up by scaffolding and covered in sheets of gently flapping plastic. "You mean," he said to me, "that I've come all this way just for *that*?" And, for a second, seeing what he saw, the Acropolis and its temple looked like miserable survivors, after all.

For over two thousand years after its foundation, in the fifth century B.C., the Parthenon remained largely as it was. As late as 1630, the French ambassador to Constantinople described it as "so undamaged and so little affected by the hand of time that it seems to have been only just constructed." Then, on 26 September 1687, while the Parthenon was being used by the Turks as a storehouse for their gunpowder, a besieging Venetian army cut the building in two with a well-aimed shell. Columns, interior walls, sculptures: all collapsed, to become the fodder for later souvenir hunters.

In 1810, Hobhouse predicted: "If the progress of decay should continue to be as rapid as it has been for something more than a century past, there will, in a few years, be not one marble standing upon another on the site of the Parthenon." The looting of the eighteenth and nineteenth centuries has since given way to the pollution of the twentieth, and Hobhouse's prediction seems almost as plausible now as it did then. This truly is a monument to disaster.

Even so, the Parthenon and its surrounding buildings have remained a center of pilgrimage. Plutarch, when the temples were already half a millennium old, wrote that they had been "created in a short time for all time. . . . A perpetual newness blooms upon them untouched by the years, as if they held within them some everlasting breath of life and an ageless spirit intermingled in their composition."

So, generation after generation of travelers have come to wonder and to find words for their wonderment. George Guillet de Saint-George, one of the last foreigners to visit the Parthenon before it was blown to pieces, wrote on seeing it for the first time: "And here I cannot but acknowledge my own weakness, you may call it folly if you please: At the first sight . . . I started immediately, and was taken with an universal shivering all over my Body." All those with him, he says, opened their eyes so wide that, dazzled, they saw nothing.

Even Hobhouse, the ever attentive chronicler of detail, found a space to register his own feelings: "The portion of the Parthenon yet standing," he wrote, "cannot fail to fill the mind of the most indifferent spectator with sentiments of astonishment and awe."

With Byron, naturally, things were a little different. A poet could hardly indulge in the superlatives accumulated over two thousand years. "Very like the Mansion House," is what he is supposed to have said, as he stood before the Parthenon. The Mansion House, official residence of the Lord Mayor of London, was a new building in Byron's time. Its famous giant Corinthian columns were only a few decades older than he was. So the joke was topical, no doubt long prepared; and, of course, it implies its own tribute, even in the moment of apparent dismissal.

The Acropolis today represents the climax of a remaking of the classical past. In Byron's time, the whole hill was crowded with houses and the rearrangements of all the years of medieval and Turkish occupation. But once Greece became an independent state, the authorities began to sweep away everything that did not belong to the very ancient past. By the end of the nineteenth century, the Acropolis had been cleared down to bedrock, and the mark of centuries had been precisely erased.

From the air you can see clearly how empty the rock of the Acropolis is now. Splendid monuments are all that remain; and in the spaces around them an entirely new vision of ancient Athens has been created. Greece was a backward country in the post-Independence period, and its governing class tried to give it an identity that drew on westernized images of a brilliant past. Everything was sacrificed to the ideal of clarity and purity of line, which is what influential Westerners most passionately wanted to see. The Greece of white temples standing alone against immaculate blue skies.

In the Royal Ontario Museum, Toronto, there is a reconstruction of the gold and ivory statue of Athena that originally stood in the Parthenon. It comes as a shock. Athena's statue stood forty feet high and was gilded with 220 pounds of gold. It isn't at all in the ideal mold; it recalls, rather, the remarks of the original protesters in the time of Pericles, who complained of their leader "gilding their city and ornamenting it with statues . . . , as a proud and vain woman decks herself out in jewels." Yet it was this statue that most excited ancient authors; and they have little to say about the buildings that so move us today.

On their way up to the Acropolis, the two travelers were accosted by a man Hobhouse calls "a renegade Spaniard." It was a trivial incident, but the English gentlemen complained to the Turkish governor, and with instant results. The Spaniard was strung up in the presence of Byron's valet, Fletcher, and beaten fifty times on the soles of his feet, the traditional punishment of the bastinado. "Whatever I may think of it at home," Hobhouse noted dryly, "abroad autocracy has its advantages."

Turkish Athens was a place where rough justice was common. A Christian who threatened a Moslem might have his hand amputated. Christians were forbidden to ride a horse or to build a house higher than a Moslem neighbor's.

But it was in sexual matters that contemporary codes most shocked visiting Europeans. Illicit heterosexual acts were punished in a variety of ways, according to the status of the woman involved. A married woman who was a Christian and who was found guilty of adultery might be merely fined; or else publicly humiliated by being paraded through the streets on a donkey, tied with her face to the donkey's tail. An unmarried Christian woman who fell under suspicion could be sold into slavery, unless she was able to prove her virginity under formal examination.

The ultimate horror, though, was reserved for the Moslem woman caught in adultery. By custom, she was tied up in a sack and drowned at sea.

Of this last tradition, Byron had some personal knowledge. How personal, how deep his involvement, no biographer has ever been able to discover. But an incident of some kind took place, in September 1810, one which Byron was to transform later into his poem, *The Giaour, A Fragment of a Turkish Tale*. Lord Sligo, who had been with Byron at Cambridge, arrived in Athens a few days after the incident. He later wrote out a version of the story he had heard, an account that Byron agreed was "not very far from the truth."

According to Sligo, Byron was returning from a swim at Piraeus when he came across a procession. An adulterous woman was being taken down to die in the sea. He intervened, drew a pistol, and threatened the leader of the escort with death. Then he went to the governor's house, where he obtained pardon for the woman, by a combination of threats and bribery. Finally, he got her away safely into exile at Thebes.

That is about all that is known. It has long been suspected, however, that there was more to it than meets the eye. Though, just possibly, there might have been less, since the story cries out for embellishment and for Byron to be given some central and guilty role. Byron's friend Thomas Medwin said that he heard from Byron himself that the woman taken in adultery had been his lover; and that, having been sent to Thebes, she died a few days later from fever, or, just possibly, from love.

Hobhouse, however, says that the woman was the lover of Byron's Turkish servant. That was also Fletcher's view. Both, naturally, may have wanted to protect Byron's reputation. Hobhouse, in any case, had returned to England by the time of the incident. The melancholy John Galt has a third possibility: the woman was a prostitute, convicted for her general liaisons with passing travelers. Byron himself equivocates. The passionate violence of *The Giaour* perhaps says something; as does a journal entry he made in 1813: "To describe the *feelings* of *that situation* were impossible—it is *icy* even to recollect them." But the concealment is, in the end, impenetrable.

Byron and Hobhouse were both intensely alive to the ordinary visual pleasures of Athens, to the common sights that lay outside or within the conventional round of ruined monuments. Life in this city was inherently rural and remained so until recent times. In the 1940s, the busiest streets still looked out onto fields. Shepherds still drove their flocks in to market. Hobhouse remembered the luxury of warm winter days, with the corn standing a foot high in the middle of February. Dancing and guitars. Mothers and children walking out with their pet lambs. The frequent sight of sacrificial rams, their horns decked with flowers.

Just outside the city there was fine riding country. To the west they rode out to the scattered stones that are all that remains of the legendary city of Eleusis. To the east, they climbed Mount Hymettus, the dying spurs of which are the modern traveler's first view on arriving at Athens airport. "Neither a high nor a picturesque mountain," as Hobhouse observed; and still less picturesque today, disfigured by a radar station.

To the northeast, they went up into the mountain range of Pendeli, now also crowned by radar. From there it is estimated that twenty-two thousand tons of marble were quarried and brought down for the building of the Acropolis. "Poor mad Galt," as Hobhouse calls him, went with them to see the ancient quarries. He cannot have been an easy companion. In a letter of 28 February 1810, recording the excursion, he wrote: "Of all the miseries of travelling, I do think that one of the greatest is to be obliged to visit those things which other travellers have happened to visit and describe." The quarry, he reported, "is a large hole in the side of the hill." There was nothing more to see and he regretted his three hours riding "over a vile break-neck road."

Of all the excursions Byron made in Greece, the most productive for his poetry were those that took him to the plain of Marathon, beyond Pendeli, and to Sounion, fifty miles to the south of Athens. The memory of these two places, and the thinking they inspired, coalesced in the famous lines from Canto III of *Don Juan*, which begin:

> *The isles of Greece, the isles of Greece!*

These two very different sites come to stand, in the end, for a set of opposing values that lie at the heart of Byron's Greece.

It is a tribute to the romance of history that so many people still make the journey over the mountains to the plain of Marathon. For Marathon, simply a long plain lying beside a deep bay of the sea, has little to show the visitor. The name probably means "place overgrown with fennel." Here a force of ten thousand Greeks once threw back two divisions of Persian infantry, who were, until then, the terror of the world.

History is ruthlessly, unfairly selective. So the great Athenian runner Pheidippides is now remembered only for something he almost certainly never did: the marathon run of twenty-six miles, from the site of the battle back to Athens, where, according to a late and dubious source, he uttered the dying words: "Greetings, we win."

It is almost forgotten that, not long before the events at Marathon, Pheidippides had done something even more extraordinary. He had run from Athens to Sparta in forty-eight hours through the heat of late summer. The distance is close to 150 miles and, even if he caught a boat or a passing cart for some of the way, it is an amazing achievement. Not the distance simply. But the time of year, and the landscape of the Peloponnese, where there is hardly an acre of level ground to be found anywhere. . . .

> *The mountains look on Marathon—*
> *And Marathon looks on the sea. . . .*

Byron registers the simplicity of the site. The Greeks formed up in the foothills, the Persians by the sea. The battle was fought out in the plain and along the beach. In the notes to *Childe Harold*, Byron recalled that the owner of Marathon in his time offered him the site for £900, which he took to be further evidence of the degeneracy of modern Greece.

The Persians left thousands dead on the plain; the Athenians just 192 warriors, who were buried where they fell, in special recognition of their courage. Through the gloriously unexpected outcome of their sacrifice, the Athenian dead became godlike in the imagination. The Parthenon would later be their memorial and a thanks-offering to the goddess Athena. Pausanias reported that every night on the Marathon plain you could still hear the whinnying of horses and the sounds of battle, and that it "has never done any man good to wait there."

> *The mountains look on Marathon—*
> *And Marathon looks on the sea;*
> *And musing there an hour alone,*
> *I dream'd that Greece might still be free;*
> *For standing on the Persians' grave,*
> *I could not deem myself a slave.*

What Greece had once achieved, against impossible odds, now becomes, in Byron's song, a celebration of what Greece might be again. This is strengthened in the following verse of the song, when the scene shifts south to the Saronic Gulf, and the poet recalls the destruction of the great Persian fleet at the Battle of Salamis. He imagines the Persian king Xerxes:

> *A king sate on the rocky brow*
> *   Which looks o'er sea-born Salamis;*
> *And ships, by thousands, lay below,*
> *   And men in nations;—all were his!*
> *He counted them at break of day—*
> *And when the sun set where were they?*

By the end of Byron's song in *Don Juan*, we have come still farther south, to Sounion. If there is little to see at Marathon, the Temple of Poseidon at Sounion stands as one of the marvels of the fifth century B.C., and the site is rightly one of the most famous in Greece.

Hobhouse and Byron went there early in their stay. They left Athens on 19 January 1810, in the company of Dimitrios Zograffo, who was later to be one of Byron's servants in England and, later still, a leader in the Independence War. At a leisurely pace, slowed by bad weather, they reached Sounion on 23 January.

They took the inland route, which soon leaves the rocky plain of Athens behind and crosses the *mesoghia*—the middle land—the only part of Attica from which you cannot see the sea. This middle land, now decaying into an unplanned industrial park, is still famous for its vineyards, and its fertility is still surprising after the dust of Athens.

Cape Sounion is the southernmost promontory of Attica. Homer, in the *Odyssey*, calls it "the sacred promontory of Athens." It rises nearly two hundred feet above the sea, with the Temple of Poseidon almost at the cliff's edge. For thousands of years,

Sounion has been a sanctuary. Once sailors rounded the cape, they were safe from the prevailing north winds of summer or the winter gales from the south. The temple was there to offer thanks to the god of the sea for a journey done, or supplication for the voyage ahead.

The temple is built of local marble: white, interlaid with a pale gray-blue. It stands isolated in a bare landscape. Remote, until recently, it inspired generations of travelers in the eighteenth and nineteenth centuries. They wrote of it or drew it according to their experience of its dual nature: its classical calm on soft summer days; its romantic defiance in times of storm.

Byron left his signature on one of the marble columns. It is still there, surrounded by a hundred others, part of a tradition the authorities are struggling to end. Visitors are now kept far away and you need binoculars to read the five sea-worn letters of the famous name.

From Sounion, more than anywhere, the isles of Greece appear as magical as Byron's poem requires. Most often blurred on the horizon, even in the sharpest light of winter, they stretch in a long arc over the blue sea: Kea, closest at hand; and then the other islands of the Cyclades: Kithnos, Serifos, Milos. To the right, the islands of the Argo-Saronic: Hydra, Poros, Aegina.

This is the natural place for Byron's song to end, as he celebrates the privilege of a shared intimacy:

> *Place me on Sunium's marbled steep,*
> *Where nothing, save the waves and I,*
> *May hear our mutual murmurs sweep. . . .*

"Nothing, save the waves and I": of all the Byronic memories, few are harder to recapture now than this. For Sounion swarms with visitors most of the year. Only if you go in winter can you still feel the romance of Byron's poem.

I was living in Athens when I first went to Sounion. I made the excursion only by chance. Someone lent me a car for the weekend and I set off down the immensity of Singros Avenue, the great escape route that leads out of central Athens and down to the sea at the Bay of Phaleron. I failed to find the road for wherever it was I wanted to go. Instead, I drove south down the coast. It was a warm midwinter day. I passed the airport, then the long succession of resorts that serve Athens. Some full of life, even in January, with people playing on the beach; others shuttered and mournful.

The coast road is slow. It twists and turns around a difficult shoreline, taking a path that was impossible to follow in Byron's time, when all this was rough country. I almost turned back, as it was getting dark. But suddenly, the land comes to an end, and you've reached Sounion.

I had always imagined I would never come. I'd seen the Temple of Poseidon often from the sea, on my way to and from Athens. But it was always crowded, and while some sites, like Delphi, are fine that way, all the charm of Sounion is in its solitude. The Theseion, in the heart of Athens, was probably built by the same architect as Sounion. It is much better preserved, but it will never draw the crowds as Sounion does.

I spent the night there, in the only hotel still open. After weeks in the polluted air of Athens, the smell of the sea was a reawakening. I opened the doors and windows and slept with the sound of the waves hardly breaking in the shelter of the bay. The next morning I climbed up to the temple through a fine drizzle. The sea on the eastern side of the promontory was running high and white. I had the Temple of Poseidon to myself. And for a few moments I felt Byron's presence more strongly than anywhere else in Greece.

Byron's song of the isles of Greece contains some of the most famous lines he ever wrote. Read on its own, in an anthology, it looks simple enough. A poet's journey through the past and present of Greece. From Marathon to Sounion, via Salamis and Suli.

It is only when the poem is traced back to its context in *Don Juan* that it looks more complex. For there Byron makes clear that the man who sings the song is not himself. On the contrary, the singer is described as a paid flatterer and entertainer. He has a good deal in common with the English poet laureate Robert Southey (1774–1843); and Southey was a man toward whom Byron felt nothing but derision, both for his poetry and for his deeply conservative politics.

So the song turns out to be a self-critical look at the value of poets and poetry in the modern age; and the journey from Marathon to Sounion turns out to be symbolic. Marathon is the world of public duty, heroic action, and self-sacrifice. Sounion, the place of romantic indulgence, escape, and love. Poetry can sing of both, testimony to Byron's long struggle to find a resolution in the conflict that is central to his life. His return to Greece in 1823 is a final phase in the debate, a final attempt to leave Sounion for Marathon, the tangled uncertainties of the self for the bright, hard world of action.

Six

Since now thou put'st thyself and work to Sea
And leav'st all Greece to Fletcher *and to me . . .*

—Byron, "Farewell Petition to
J[ohn] C[am] H[obhouse] Esq."

 In the Athens of 1810, Byron and Hobhouse found themselves inevitably caught up in the great controversy of the day. When Thomas Bruce, seventh earl of Elgin, became British ambassador at Constantinople in 1799, he had set in motion plans to remove the sculptures from the Parthenon. The work of removal had begun in 1801. This led to a debate that has seen no end, a debate about the morality of the act and the rightful resting place of what, even in modern Greek, are called the Elgin Marbles.

The Parthenon sculptures once ran for 525 feet in a long ribbon around the temple. In Elgin's time, they were fast disappearing. Souvenir hunters frequently hacked off small pieces to carry away in their luggage, while the sculptures were also threatened by an older, indigenous practice of pounding marble into whitewash. This practice had already led to the complete destruction of the Stadium of ancient Athens.

One side of the argument, then, is that the removal of the sculptures was an act of rescue and preservation. This view is now represented by the British Museum, which holds about half the Parthenon frieze, mostly acquired from Elgin. Among the modern defenders of Elgin, one of the most persuasive is William St. Clair. Elgin's aims, he says, were honorable from the beginning. He obtained "as much legal authority for his operations as it was possible to do in the disordered circumstances of the time." Most important of all, the sculptures "would be in a far worse state today if he, or someone else, had not removed them."

There is a logic to this, and the final point, at least, is undeniably true. For Elgin's opponents, however, the logic was—and is—simply too cool. In their eyes, the removal of the sculptures was an act of mercenary destruction, something that arrogantly confirmed the helpless position of a poor country in the face of the most powerful state on earth. In this way, the Elgin Marbles became an unshakable symbol of Greek national pride, and they have remained so ever since.

The removal of so large a piece of the Parthenon caused damage, not simply to the sculptures themselves, but to the rest of the building as well. This loss was very fresh when Byron and Hobhouse were in Athens. Wherever foreigners met, the issue was a subject for discussion, and it was colored by old European rivalries, since it was no secret that the French had designs on the Marbles also.

Hobhouse reviewed the main arguments in a footnote to his book. "We heard, I suppose, everything that could be alleged by either party on both sides of the question," he wrote. He concluded, in his reasonable way, that the sculptures were safer out of Turkish Athens and that, when they were displayed in a major European museum, they would be of great benefit to young Western sculptors and architects.

Byron, on the other hand, was radically opposed to the actions of Elgin. Even before he went to Greece, he had already made up his mind on the issue. In an early satire called *English Bards and Scotch Reviewers*, he had written of the "maimed antiques," and of how men like Elgin

> . . . *make their grand saloons a general mart*
> *For all the mutilated blocks of art. . . .*

He was especially contemptuous of the fact that Elgin, having taken the Marbles, then tried to sell them to the British government, a sale he finally achieved in 1816. Byron also rejected the argument that, by bringing the sculptures to London, Elgin was doing something for the benefit of young artists. "I opposed—and will ever oppose—," Byron wrote in 1821, "the robbery of ruins—from Athens to instruct the English in Sculpture—(who are as capable of Sculpture—as the Egyptians are of skating). . . ."

There was another side to this. The artist Benjamin Robert Haydon spoke for many in London who were dazzled by the arrival of the sculptures: "I felt as if a divine truth had blazed inwardly upon my mind, and I knew that they would at last rouse the art of Europe from its slumber of darkness." Elgin's efforts to sell the Marbles can be seen as the desperate act of a man who had spent a fortune acquiring them and who had then fallen deeply into debt. Elgin's finances, indeed, never recovered and he was to die in France in 1841, in exile from his creditors.

Elgin's character has suffered continual assault over the years, and there was clearly something provocative about him. St. Clair suggests that Byron's own contempt was motivated by Elgin's Toryism, by his "apparently typical British contempt for foreigners." It is hard otherwise to understand the weight of personal abuse heaped on a man whose life was, in almost every way, a failure. Elgin remains to this day the model of the patrician vandal and it is generally forgotten that, when the Greek War of Independence broke out, he sided immediately with the forces of liberation.

His reputation has suffered as a result of the sheer monumentality of his raid on the Parthenon. But he was also unlucky. When the second consignment of the Marbles reached England in May 1812, the event coincided with the instant popularity of Byron's *Childe Harold*. Byron was merciless toward Elgin, both in the second canto of *Childe Harold* and in *The Curse of Minerva*, a poem he began in Athens and finished late in 1811. Byron spared Elgin neither the misfortune of an epileptic son, nor the humiliation of an adulterous wife and a messy divorce.

No matter that he had carved his own name on a column at Sounion or at Delphi, the discovery of the names of Elgin and his wife on one of the columns of the Parthenon drove Byron to fury:

> *That all may learn from whence the plunderer came*
> *The insulted wall sustains his hated name. . . .*

As St. Clair suggests, Byron's cruel opposition "dealt a blow at Elgin's reputation from which it has never recovered." There is no sign that Byron ever regretted it.

After ten weeks in Athens, Byron and Hobhouse left for western Turkey. They landed at Izmir, visited Ephesus, saw the plains of the Troad, and spent two months in Constantinople. They then returned to Greece.

The Turkish venture was of limited success. Its highlight was Byron's repetition of Hero's legendary swim across the Dardanelles. Byron did it in May, in a sea icy from the melting of winter snows. In general, though, he felt cramped in Turkey, reduced to the activities of a simple tourist. He had almost no knowledge of the language and, since Turks were in any case segregated from foreigners, he found himself thrown into the company of English diplomats and naval officers. In Constantinople, they were forced, like other foreigners, to live outside the old city. It was all very different from the easy life in "dearly beloved Greece."

From the middle of July 1810 until April 1811, Byron was in Greece again. This time he was on his own, for Hobhouse immediately returned to England once they got back from Turkey. They parted on the island of Kea, otherwise known as Tzia or

Zea. In his diary, Hobhouse revealed something of the emotion that in his published writing was so often held under control:

> Arrived at the port of Zea. Went on board with Lord Byron and suite. Took leave, *non sine lacrymis* [not without tears], of this singular young person, on a little stone terrace at the end of the bay, dividing with him a little nosegay of flowers; the last thing perhaps that I shall ever divide with him.

The relationship between Byron and Hobhouse was always an unequal one. In a letter written three years after his friend's death, Hobhouse talked of "the nature and character of my long association with Byron," and he summed it all up with an extraordinary bitterness: "He had all the praise, I all the abuse. . . ."

There is no doubt that Byron cared much for him. And Hobhouse, for his part, was just old enough, and more than happy enough, to play the elder brother. Hobhouse was never the prim moralizer he sometimes appears. One glance at his diaries or his letters to Byron will show the range of his interests and emotions. He was, for a time, a Radical in politics and in 1819 his principles landed him in Newgate Prison. But he remained a man with a strong sense of the importance of boundaries and a survivor's instinct for those limits it is too dangerous to transgress.

The steadying hand, which was so much a part of their relationship, was also what set up barriers between them. Even from the time of their earliest letters in 1808, it is clear that Hobhouse had already taken on the role of protector and defender. First, trying indulgently to save his friend from the consequences of life's ordinary vices. Later, when Byron had become one of England's most famous men, seeking to be the guardian of his reputation beyond the grave.

Lord Rosebery wrote that Hobhouse "loved Byron with a jealous affection and admiration which never degenerated into flattery." He lived on for forty-five years after Byron's death, enjoyed a long political career, and ended as a peer of the realm. During those years, he was, as Rosebery put it, "the high priest of the Byron mystery.... Those who saw him in his old age ... regarded him with unspeakable interest as one who knew all and could tell all if he chose. But he did not choose to tell. Much of Byron, of the secrets of that brilliant, unhappy life, died with him. Perhaps it is as well."

A protector, brotherly or otherwise, was just what Byron did not want in Greece. If Hobhouse was sensibly aware of the importance of limits, especially in sexual matters, Byron had almost certainly come to Greece in order to find out what life was like beyond them. His ambiguous feelings toward his traveling companion are well caught in a moment of humor: "You cannot conceive what a delightful companion you are now you are gone," he wrote to Hobhouse, twelve days after they separated at Kea.

There is, however, a darker side to Byron's feelings for his traveling companion. It emerges in a letter written from Patras, in July 1810, to one of his closest friends, Scrope Berdmore Davies. This letter, along with a number of others to Davies, was discovered only in 1976. "I determined after one years purgatory," Byron wrote, "to part with that amiable soul [Hobhouse], for though I like him, and always shall, though I give him almost as much credit for his good qualities as he does himself, there is something in his manner &c. in short he will never be any thing but the *'Sow's Ear.'* "

The judgment is savage. Yet there was indeed "something in his manner" and even now it is possible to feel it. An hour in Hobhouse's company, among the pages of his *Travels in Albania*, is enough. He is one of those whose many good qualities are fatally undermined by the trivial weakness of being a little dull. His bitterness, as he found himself face to face with Byron's memory, is not surprising.

Still, while they both lived, Hobhouse remembered their time in Greece with affection, recalling, in a letter of January 1814, what a marvelous companion Byron had been: "a friend by my side in the dull monotony of locomotion." For Byron, on the other hand, the departure of Hobhouse was simply liberation. "I feel happier, I feel free," he wrote to Davies; and he would be freer still from January 1811, when he sent his valet, Fletcher, home to England.

The course of Byron's life in Greece during these nine months of freedom in 1810 to 1811 is a classic biographer's challenge. There is very little evidence. Few letters, almost no observers; Byron is, as he wanted to be, almost out of sight. Yet the suspicion remains that this was one of the most significant periods of his adult life.

In the journal that he kept from November 1813 to April 1814, Byron made an entry, looking back on the months when he was alone in Greece. Always on the edge of revelation, the entry remains, in the end, fundamentally elusive. He talks of Hobhouse: "People sometimes hit near the truth; but never the whole truth. H. don't know what I was about the year after he left the Levant; nor does any one—nor—nor—nor—however, it is a lie—but. . . ." Then he adds a quotation from one of his favorite Shakespearean moments, Act 5, scene 5, of *Macbeth*: " 'I doubt the equivocation of the fiend that lies like truth!' "

Here Byron identifies with the monstrous course of Macbeth's life, a life that is about to end in blood and guilt. Macbeth discovers that what cannot possibly happen in the real world is nevertheless happening to him: Birnam wood is marching on Dunsinane and the conditions for his fall are being fulfilled. There is without doubt a sexual allegory to be read here; how to read it is another matter. Even in his private journal, Byron seeks to disclose at the very moment that he most fears disclosure.

A voyeur in search of the more intimate scenery of Byron's Greece can make a pilgrimage to the Monastery of Pendeli, ten miles from Athens. This is, in any case, a trip worth making and it is a fine escape from the capital in the heat of summer.

Soon after leaving the center of Athens, the road begins to rise into the mountains that divide the city from the Marathon plain. After a long climb you come to the village of Pendeli, where Athenians gather to breathe the air and eat out, on evenings when the capital lies suffocating far below.

The Monastery of Pendeli was founded in 1578 and is dedicated to the Assumption of the Virgin Mary. In origin a traditional Byzantine complex, it has lost much of its past through generations of restoration. It was, however, one of the important places in seventeenth- and eighteenth-century Greece and its influence on Athenian life was cultural and social, as much as religious. It is now one of the richest foundations in the country. Embedded in trees and flowers, it is as luxuriant as anywhere could be in this waterless landscape.

The monastery is a celebration of the relations between Greece and its Church. Monks from Pendeli struggled, throughout the latter years of the Turkish occupation, to keep alive an idea of Greekness and they later fought in the War of Independence.

You can visit the Clandestine School, where once Greek children were secretly taught their own language. There's a life-size model of a priest with long white beard, holding forth to some overgrown children. A plaque on the wall reads "Our language is the most powerful element of our identity," voicing a confidence that connects this room to all the Greek communities of the Diaspora, from Melbourne to Chicago. You walk through a succession of dimly lit cells, heady with incense; a contrast to the even headier world outside of blue sky and whitewashed walls.

Though the spirit of the Greek Revolution is still alive in the Monastery of Pendeli, the connection with Byron has not primarily to do with that. It was simply here, according to a letter Byron wrote to Hobhouse in October 1810, that his homosexual experiences in Greece began: "I have obtained above two hundred pl & opt Cs and am almost tired of them," he wrote. "You know the monastery of Mendele, it was there I made myself master of the first."

Mendele is Pendeli, as Byron confirmed in a note to *Childe*

Harold. But the phrase "pl & opt Cs," and thus the whole sense of this passage, long remained enigmatic to those outside Byron's circle. Then, in 1957, Professor Gilbert Highet saw that the key to understanding what Byron was talking about lay in the text of one of Europe's earliest novels, the *Satyricon* of Petronius.

The *Satyricon*, written in the first century A.D., survives only in fragments. It is the loose narrative of a bisexual adventurer called Encolpius, who, in a lost episode of the book, elopes with Giton, the boyfriend of his mistress. The book has long been notorious, though modern attitudes have brought it into the literary mainstream. Michael Heseltine, who translated the *Satyricon* for the Loeb series in 1913, gives a good idea of its reputation at that time: the "book is befouled with obscenity," he wrote; and, in an interesting aside, he continued: "like obscenity itself, [it] is ceasing by degrees to be part of a gentleman's education."

In the passage that is the key to Byron's activities, a homosexual friend of Encolpius tells a story of how he seduced a handsome youth when he was out in Asia Minor, at Pergamum. On the first night, he kisses the boy; on the second, he goes further. On the third, he reaches the "full satisfaction" of his desires: in Latin, *coitum plenum et optabilem* (full sexual intercourse to the heart's desire).

At once Byron's code, "pl & opt Cs," was clear, the cover for his sexual interest in young boys. He had already used the Latin phrase in a letter written from Falmouth in June 1809, as he prepared to set sail from England. The port, he wrote, was a "delectable region," with unrivaled opportunities for "the 'Plen. and optabil.—Coit.'" He uses the phrase again, in a letter to Hobhouse from Athens in November 1810, where he says: "I am tired of pl. & opt Cs, the last thing I could be tired of."

All this suggests that, once Hobhouse had left Greece, Byron embarked on a long-repressed orgy of homosexual adventure; and that, within three months, he was already satiated by his efforts and the extent of his successes. What is strange, though, is the apparent discrepancy between his revelations to Hobhouse in the letters of 1810 and his statement in his journal a few years later that "H. don't know what I was about the year after he left the Levant."

It is not likely that in the intervening years Byron forgot what he had told Hobhouse in 1810. And Hobhouse, for his part, was well aware all along of the dangers his friend was running. In a letter to Byron of July 1811, he reminded him of an earlier letter, now lost, in which he had said: "I told you to keep the Mendeli Monastery story and every thing entirely to yourself." It takes imagination to guess what other kind of secret life Byron could have had in Athens. What else could there be that Hobhouse didn't know? Perhaps it was simply the scale of his activities that he hid from Hobhouse, rather than their nature; but the journal entry suggests something different, and darker still. So far, no biographer has given a plausible account.

Byron's homosexuality was directed exclusively toward the young. It was rooted in a cult of the beautiful youth and shares, at a great distance, something of the erotic inequality that flowered so famously in classical Athens. There, as Eva Keuls describes it in *The Reign of the Phallus*, "the archetypal relationship was between a mature man at the height of his sexual power and need and a young, erotically undeveloped boy." The three boys to whom Byron was most attached in life—Edleston at Cambridge, Giraud in Athens, Chalandritsanos in Mesolongi—were, as Louis Crompton points out, all fifteen years old when he first became involved with them.

The Greeks of the fifth century B.C. lived free from religious interference in their sexual behavior. In the Christian era, too, the Orthodox Church, which still has the nominal allegiance of most Greeks, has been less interested in sexual morality than the Catholic or Protestant churches of western Europe. This dual inheritance, from antiquity and Byzantium, has made Greek attitudes toward homosexuality very different from those of England in the early nineteenth century—or, indeed, in the late twentieth.

In Greece, Byron encountered a society in which, as he put it in a note to *Childe Harold*, Greeks, Turks, and Albanians were all "addicted to Pederasty." If they were so addicted, it was with an apparent detachment from the guilt and all the other complex sexual baggage that Byron brought with him from home. Greek sexuality for Byron was, in the simplest kind of way, a revelation of freedom.

The isles of Greece, in the song from *Don Juan*, were the place

> *Where burning Sappho loved and sung. . . .*

In that poem, Byron moves easily from the lyrical praise of Lesbian Sappho to the thought of Greek political freedom in the modern world, the one effortlessly foreshadowing the other. But Byron's homosexual experiences in Greece were also, and perhaps more negatively, a desire simply to transgress, to go beyond the accepted limits of his own culture. In that sense, the homosexual orgy of Athens shared a good deal with the heterosexual orgies that followed later in Italy. Both ended in world-weariness, the sadness of that labor-intensive existence so memorably preserved in Byron's poem:

> *So, we'll go no more a roving*
> *So late into the night,*
> *Though the heart be still as loving,*
> *And the moon be still as bright.*
>
> *For the sword outwears its sheath,*
> *And the soul wears out the breast,*
> *And the heart must pause to breathe,*
> *And love itself have rest.*

The fascination with life beyond the boundary is general in Byron. His sexuality was just one of a number of ways in which it was expressed. Creatively, it takes him into a world apart, as he suggests in Canto X of *Don Juan*:

> But at the least I have shunned the common shore,
>   And leaving land far out of sight, would skim
> The Ocean of Eternity. . . .

The other side of this creative ambition was a deep self-destructiveness, one that often yielded to simple nihilism, but which drove him on in the end toward a kind of tragic crisis. Byron's life is constantly poised between these two alternatives: the indolence of despair, or the wild flight into action. His poetry often seems to be the only refuge from the struggle, the place where some creative negotiation remained possible.

In one of the series of "Detached Thoughts" that Byron set down between October 1821 and May 1822, he turned to the great Athenian general and statesman, Alcibiades: "It may be doubted whether there be a name in Antiquity which comes down with such a general charm as that of *Alcibiades—Why?*—I cannot answer—who can?"

The obvious answer is that Alcibiades was one of those historical figures who most clearly responds to Byron's vision of the flawed hero. One who fascinates by his faults, in the middle of an extraordinary brilliance. Outstanding both as a politician and a military leader, the close friend of the philosopher Socrates, young, noble, beautiful, and rich: Alcibiades had so many talents he must have seemed destined for immortality.

He appears memorably in Plato's *Symposium*, the record of a great all-night drinking and discussion party, where the guests, adrift on what Plato calls "the wide sea of the beautiful," talk endlessly of love. Alcibiades turns up late, so drunk he has to be helped into the room. He stands, the perfectly feminized man of action, crowned with a wreath of violets and ivy, a bunch of ribbons in his hair. He, like Byron, knew the seduction of the precipice; later he broke the most sacred laws of his tribe, turned traitor, and died in the obscurity of exile.

Inevitably, then, Byron's time alone in Athens was a rough mix of emotions and experience. The elation of freedom, the tyranny of sexual abandon. There were excursions with pretty boys; "a variety of fooleries" with women, both Greek and Turkish; dinner parties and balls. The delights of riding in the countryside. Or swimming down at Piraeus, once—and now again—the busy port of Athens, but in Byron's time no more than a few ruined huts by the sea. Above all, Athens was a return to the self-conscious world of adolescent games, a flight from maturity in the face of the darkening world of experience.

After the return from Turkey, Byron did not go back to live in the house of the widow Makri and her three more than nubile daughters. Relations had become strained by the mother's desire to marry off her Maid of Athens; or, failing that, to secure thirty thousand piastres for her daughter's virginity. Either way, things had become too serious.

Instead, from August 1810, Byron took lodgings in the Capuchin Monastery, which had been built by the French mission to Athens in 1669. The monastery—Byron called it the convent—was well known as a hostel for visiting foreigners and it was also a school for the sons of prominent Greeks and expatriate Europeans.

When the French bought the land for their monastery, they inherited a white marble monument dating from the fourth century B.C. This is known today, with opaque exactitude, as the Choregic Monument of Lysikrates. In Byron's day, it was called, as it had been since the Middle Ages, the Lantern of Demosthenes, a name that lingered on until recent times. The name derived from the belief that the great Athenian orator had once used it for the preparation of his speeches.

The French incorporated the monument into their monastery, which protected it for 150 years and accounts for its fine state of preservation today. It was used as a reading room and library, and it was there that Byron studied and wrote his letters home. A simple inscription in Greek today records Byron's time here. To Hobhouse, late in August 1810, he wrote: "I am most auspiciously settled in the Convent, which is more commodious than any tenement I have yet occupied."

The Capuchin Monastery burned down during the Independence War and today only the Lantern of Demosthenes survives. It stands at the junction of what are now Byron Street and Shelley Street. Byron loved the situation. "I am living in the Capuchin Convent," he wrote to a friend in January 1811. "Hymettus before me, the Acropolis behind, the temple of Jove to my right, the Stadium in front, the town to the left, eh, Sir, there's a situation, there's your picturesque! nothing like that, Sir, in Lunnun, no not even the Mansion House."

Today the marvelous prospect has been closed off by encroaching development. This is still, however, a picturesque place for an evening out, backed by the awesome southern face of the Acropolis, its bare rock rising to massive walls high above. There's a clear view down to the Arch of Hadrian, which, in Roman times, marked the boundary between old Athens and the new suburbs and which, in Byron's day, served as one of the gates into the city.

But you can no longer see the Temple of Olympian Zeus (Byron's "temple of Jove"), the building Livy called "the only temple on earth of a size adequate to the greatness of the god." The Stadium is also now out of sight. Long stripped of its marble in Byron's day, it has been meticulously restored, and was home to the first modern Olympic Games in 1896.

For Byron, life in the monastery, as he said himself, was like being back at school. He had six young boys for company or flirtation. He began to learn Italian from Nicolo Giraud, who would soon be his lover. "My lessons," he wrote to Hobhouse, "though very long are sadly interrupted by scamperings and eating fruit and peltings and playings." This restored innocence, the helter-skelter world of childish amusement, was the perfect foil to the reality of departing youth. It is no surprise to find him writing openly: "I am vastly happy."

Byron traveled a good deal during these months. Almost immediately after saying farewell to Hobhouse, he left for the Peloponnese. There he found again a young boy he had met at

Vostitsa in 1809. His name was Eustathios Georgiou. Byron referred to him as "my dearly-beloved" and said the boy was "ready to follow me not only to England, but to Terra Incognita, if so be my compass pointed that way." Eustathios was exquisitely feminine, with "ambrosial curls hanging down his amiable back," and he outraged Byron's valet, Fletcher, by riding with a parasol, to protect his complexion from the sun.

They rode from Vostitsa along the coast to Patras, quarreled in the way of adolescent lovers, then made up. When they parted, Byron wrote, it was with "as many kisses as would have sufficed for a boarding school, and embraces enough to have ruined the character of a county in England."

Byron visited Veli Pasha, one of Ali's sons, at Tripolitza, in the heart of the Peloponnese. Veli gave him a horse, flirted with him as openly as his father had done, embarrassed Byron by his public shows of affection: "He has an awkward manner," Byron reported, "of throwing his arm round one's waist, and squeezing one's hand in *public*. . . ."

On another excursion, Byron returned to Sounion, where, with a group of armed companions, he faced down a band of pirates. Most important of all, however, was the second tour he made of the Peloponnese with Nicolo Giraud, in September 1810. They both fell ill with fever in the marshes of the west and were nursed by their two Albanian servants. In a comment, which the manner of his death in Mesolongi makes darkly ironic, Byron attributed his recovery not simply to the skills of the servants, but to their assistance in frightening away the doctor. The malarial fever remained with Byron for the rest of his life.

As for his relationship with Giraud, it is hard to make much of the little that is said. But in a document headed "Directions for the Contents of a Will to be Drawn up Immediately," dated 12 August 1811, Byron gave to "Nicolo Giraud of Athens" the sum of £7,000, to be handed over when he reached twenty-one years of age. That is an immense amount. Louis Crompton, in his book *Byron and Greek Love*, published in 1985, estimated it as the equivalent of around $200,000. So, at least, it was no ordinary relationship.

Athens in 1810 to 1811 was undoubtedly one of the best periods of Byron's life. He was freer than he had ever been before. Fit and bronzed, a kind of sun-beaten idol to himself. Above all, young again in his imagination. But it was a partial refuge all the same. He was troubled by lack of news about his finances at home, and then devastated when news finally reached him in November 1810, advising him that the ancestral home at Newstead would have to be sold.

He tired quickly of promiscuity: "I have spent my little all," he wrote to Hobhouse. "I have tasted of all sorts of pleasure . . . I have nothing more to hope." But he continued to find Athens immensely sociable: "Here be many English," he wrote to Hobhouse in January 1811, "and there have been more, with all of whom I have been and *am* on dining terms." Even so, he remained isolated, strangely unchallenged. Even at those moments of highest enthusiasm, as he surveyed the magical city from the Capuchin Monastery where he was most at home, a note of tedium intrudes; the dullness of expatriate life in a small foreign town: "I wish to be sure I had a few books, one's own works for instance, any damned nonsense on a long Evening."

So, wearying of a life of social and sexual adventure, and troubled by his finances, Byron threw a final party for the foreign community in Athens. Then, on 22 April 1811, he left for Malta, on a ship carrying the final installment of Lord Elgin's Marbles. Nicolo Giraud went with him. His reward was to be a decent schooling in Malta, at Byron's expense.

It is not easy to recover Byron in Athens today. It's mainly a problem of scale. He loved the intimacy of a place which, even in 1835, was lit simply by fifteen oil lamps, and then only on moonless nights. Hadrian Street, the finest thoroughfare of his day, is now given over completely to tourism, like Pandrossos and

Hephaistos Streets, which once marked the commercial center of Athenian life. Now the small winding streets of the old town give way toward the east to the huge, car-choked boulevards that run from Sindagma Square up toward Omonia.

The famous pollution, the *nefos* (cloud), can be seen from miles around. Whatever the direction of your approach, it hangs before you on the horizon. Orange, yellow, or brown, according to the light and the time of day. It's almost tactile. The smell, at night, when you wake up from sweated midsummer dreams, pours in at the open window, half familiar, half malevolent.

Modern Athens is a shackled city, struggling for mobility. Hemmed in by the geography of the Attic mountains and the unplanned sprawl of the postwar years. The atmosphere is frenetic, the pace slow. Journey times are often enormous, rivaling those of Third World cities, as people shuffle toward the twenty-first century at the speed of the nineteenth. The paradox is resolved in impatience, the energy of the modern city continually dispersed in frustration.

There is an unromantic shortage of green in Athens. It's a place so recently rural that it has been taken quite unaware by the ugliness of its transformation. Luckily, there is a refuge in the center: the old Royal Garden, which, long ago, became the National Garden and was opened to the public. "A lot of its original trees live until day and constitute monumental plants," says a faded English sign at the entrance; though many of the seven thousand trees are wilting in the polluted air.

More serious than the lack of greenery is its cause: the lack of water. As you walk through this driest of cities, you can only regret that it has no river. The sight and sound of water would change everything. Athens has few public fountains and the once famous River Ilissos, where Socrates and Phaedrus dabbled their feet, has now vanished. It disappointed generations of travelers—Byron dismissed it as a dry ditch—and finally ended its career in 1960, when it became a covered drain.

On one side of the National Garden, the picturesque *evzones* perform the changing of the guard in their kilted skirts, long-tasseled caps, and overgrown bedroom slippers. For a long time they stand motionless, then suddenly thrust out along the pavement, with great high-kicking steps, an arm raised in time with each laborious raising of the thigh. After, they return to their lonely contemplation of the middle distance, while the traffic roars by. A decorative oddity, tied to an empty ritual.

Not love, certainly—which late-twentieth-century cities are lovable? But a kind of intimacy nonetheless. Athens is still a city that would fill you with regret if you knew you were leaving it for the last time. It has more drab streets and fewer memorable ones than any western European capital. It is deadly in the heat of summer, with bitter winters that often continue well into March. But, if it is rarely a comfortable place to be, it never quite fails its famous name. Athens reveals itself, not suddenly, or on the grand scale, but in fragments, accumulated over time.

Some of the best moments come when you have been there long enough to take its ancient past for granted. In the middle of an ordinary day, thinking of ordinary things, then suddenly catching sight of the Parthenon up there on its rock, surviving, or just about, after all these years. Or watching lizards playing among the old stones of the Agora. Or the approach by sea on a fine winter's morning, when it seems as if half the world's ships are lying at anchor in the roadstead; Athens ahead, renewing the old cliché of where east meets west.

One of the problems for the visitor is that Athens seems to have only a very ancient past, or else one so recent it hardly deserves the name. There is the great weight of classical times, on the one hand; and, on the other, a world that seems to go back no further than the 1960s, a sad encroachment of concrete and dust. In between, it looks as if nothing has ever happened.

It takes effort to reach back into this empty space, not least because this is a city in which so many are recent arrivals from the rest of Greece; as cut off, in their way, as any casual visitor.

But there are still plenty of people who can talk of the terrible winter of 1941–42. Thousands died then of famine under the German occupation. Through that winter the poor of Athens tried to survive on wild grass gathered in the countryside; they begged outside restaurants, suffered in the great sprawl of tenements around Piraeus, which had grown up to receive the refugees after the Asia Minor disaster of 1922. After that, after the horrors of defeat, famine, and occupation, came the civil war of 1944–49, a subject about which many younger Greeks know almost nothing and about which it is still prudent for the foreigner to have no opinion.

Athens for me has always been a political city. This is simply chance: for when I first went there, I expected, like most others, to spend a few days in antiquity and then move on.

I arrived on a boat from Venice in the summer of 1965. It was the first time in my life that I had been far from home and in a place where I couldn't speak the language. All of Athens was marvelously strange, with that vividness that is intensified by one's complete lack of understanding. I had almost no money in the beginning and slept out at night on waste ground by the airport, commuting in each morning to what seemed the most exciting place on earth.

I imagined at the time that Athens must always be the way I had found it that summer. All through July there were demonstrations on the streets, an uncountable succession of rallies and speeches. Burning buildings and cars, riot police. What was happening I couldn't tell. There was no doubt, however, that the crowds hated the king of Greece, and that they adored the prime minister, the elder Papandreou, then nearly eighty years of age. King Constantine was away from Athens—people said he was spending his days playing soccer in Corfu. The city was given over to the crowds and the heat. Almost the first modern Greek I ever learned was the slogan: "The king reigns and the people rule."

In mid-July, Constantine removed his prime minister from office and returned to Athens. I heard the ousted Papandreou speak at a vast afternoon rally in the sun. Even his enemies agreed that he was one of Europe's great orators and, though I understood nothing of what he said, it was then that I began to develop a habit I have never quite been able to abandon. Standing and waiting in dusty squares, listening to the voices of the powerful. Straining to catch the very smell of history.

On 16 July, I was in Sindagma Square at midnight when the police fired tear gas on the crowd. We fled past the great hotels on the square. I remember the faces of those inside, behind the barred doors, looking out, curious and afraid, at the chaos on the streets. A few days later, I joined the vast funeral procession for a student killed, no one knew how, in the course of the disturbances. And, with everyone else, I learned the magic of the numbers 114.

Everywhere, on the streets of Athens, people chanted 114, *ena, ena, tessera*. For a time, nothing was more seductive, more incomprehensibly Greek. It was only when I returned to England and read the newspapers that I found out what the numbers meant, and then they seemed even more magical than before. For the reference was to the last article of the Greek constitution, which placed the responsibility for its proper functioning on the patriotism of the Greek people.

That was my first view of Athens, in which the Acropolis and all the rest were nothing more than minor intrusions into the excitement of the present. By chance, I was in Athens again in April 1967. It was the time of the military coup, and the revelation of a darker side of Greece. During the following seven years of dictatorship, Greece seemed to have become another country entirely. I became involved in solidarity work, through a one-armed Greek sculptor I knew in Paris. Through him I met a wide circle of discordant exiles and followed an increasingly disabused education in Greek politics.

Finally—this time by design—I returned to Athens in the summer of 1974. The military junta had fallen, the prisoners were being released from the island concentration camps, and the talk of Greek freedom resumed its endless course.

Byron has left few relics in Athens for the casual eye. There is nothing to see on the street of Ayias Theklas, where once he lived with the young girls of the widow Makri. When I last went down this dingy street, in a dull quarter off Monastiraki Square, someone had scrawled his name in gray English letters across a concrete pillar. But it was only in honor of the football team from the Byron district beyond the Stadium. A distant enough tribute, after all.

In the National Historical Museum, there is Byron's helmet and sword. In the Benaki Museum, the traveling desk he used in Greece. In the Gennadius Library, a lock of his hair, which Fletcher cut at the moment of death, and the crown of Greek laurel placed on Byron's coffin when it lay in state in London.

If you cross the National Garden to its southern edge, on Avenue Vasilissis Olgas, not far from the huge standing columns of the Temple of Olympian Zeus, you come to the best memorial of all: the statue of Byron and a personified Greece. Or, rather, since the Greeks have never called their country Greece, the statue of Byron and Hellas. They gaze into each other's eyes, eternal lovers, overlooking one of the busiest intersections of the city. The bus stop nearby is called *aghalma Bironos*, "Byron's statue." So he has a place, after all, in modern Athens; and it will be years yet before anyone needs to ask why he is there, lovingly clasped in the arms of Hellas.

Seven

There is no life of a man, faithfully recorded, but is a heroic poem of its sort, rhymed or unrhymed.

—Thomas Carlyle

When Byron left England for the first time in 1809, it was under the cloud of his own dark thoughts. He was already committed, in fantasy or reality, to a lifestyle he knew could have no place in his society, except at the margins or in shadow. The prospect of escape, which was finally realized in that summer of 1809, was a promise of lightness, almost of innocence. Byron and Hobhouse could have been any two college students in search of experience: a little bored with life at home, a little self-conscious of their ability to impress on the wider stage.

Travel was fun, a break even from the lax routines of a privileged English life; and, in the best traditions of traveling, the more uncomfortable it was, the more authentic it seemed. In some lines written just before his departure for Lisbon, Byron captured the right note of carelessness:

> Now at length we're off for Turkey,
> Lord knows when we shall come back.
> Breezes foul, and tempests murkey,

May unship us in a crack.
But since life at most a jest is,
As Philosophers allow,
Still to laugh by far the best is,
Then laugh on—as I do now.
Laugh at all things,
Great and small things,
Sick or well, at sea or shore,
While we're quaffing
Let's have laughing,
Who the Devil cares for more?

This sense of easy abandonment does not survive Byron's experiences of travel. When he came home again in 1811, the fun had gone; and the naive hope that the tedium or pain of one world could be redeemed by shifting to another had also been fatally challenged.

In Malta, on 22 May 1811, he wrote himself a memorandum, a kind of statement of the dead end he believed he had reached. It is a world-weary catalog, but behind the youthful, dramatic pose, there is a large measure of self-knowledge. "At twenty three," he began, "the best of life is over and its bitters double." Then, he went on, with reference to his recent travels: "I have seen mankind in various Countries and find them equally despicable, if anything the Balance is rather in favour of the Turks."

His third point is simply: "I am sick at heart." And it is the crucial point. To these brief words, Byron added three lines of Latin poetry taken from the fourth book of Horace's *Odes*. The full sense of what Horace wrote is: "Now neither woman nor boy delights me, nor the credulous hope of finding my love returned." Byron, in his quotation, however, omits the phrase *nec puer* (nor boy). The omission conceals Horace's bisexual reference for anyone who does not know the lines, but draws attention to it for anyone who does.

The whole context of the Horatian poem is interesting.

He writes as a man nearing fifty years of age, tormented by the fear of ridicule and self-betrayal that comes with the sudden onset of love. Through most of the ode he claims to be free of sensual longings—nothing anymore delights me, neither woman nor boy—only to surrender, by the end, to a sentimental vision of an inaccessible youth who means everything to him.

Byron quotes the three lines as a kind of shorthand, a way of thinking about his own moral dilemmas: about sexual practice, sexual identity, and the ever-present possibilities of self-betrayal. At twenty-three, he must have believed he had a lifetime's sexual experience behind him, with his more than two hundred "pl & opt Cs." But the poem insists that neither age nor experience is a guarantee against a revival of desire. Though he was tired of promiscuity, passion could always return, and, in the England he was going home to, the desire for young boys placed him beyond society.

Horace's poem is also a strange forecast of Byron's own position at the end of his life. The humiliations of the aging lover, the self-betrayal in pursuit of the young: these Byron would know in the final months with Loukas Chalandritsanos.

The concluding points of Byron's Malta memorandum talk about his health, his temperament, his financial affairs, and his ambitions: "4thly A man who is lame of one leg is in a state of bodily inferiority which increases with years and must render his old age more peevish & intolerable. . . . 5thly I grow selfish & misanthropical. . . . 6thly My affairs at home and abroad are gloomy enough. 7thly I have outlived all my appetites and most of my vanities aye even the vanity of authorship."

Here in outline is the image of the misanthropy and melancholia which have been inseparable from Byron's name ever since. It is, perhaps, presumptuous to say that at twenty-three the best of life is over, particularly if you are only twenty-three. But the presumption does not necessarily make the prediction untrue.

•   •   •

Byron had particular reasons to be miserable in the spring of 1811. Malta, two years before, had been the site of his first foreign romance. Now he could only lament over the difference between what he had been on the journey out and what he felt he had become. Besides, his health was poor. He was returning home with a wretched trio of afflictions: malaria, hemorrhoids, and gonorrhea. He believed there was nothing to come back to, except the prospect of trying to adjust what he called "my inadjustable affairs."

For the longer term, Byron's gloomy prognosis was accurate enough. The moments of protected pleasure he had known in Greece would never return, those times when the illusion of an extended boyhood could be sustained in innocence and fun. Eight months after coming home, Byron would be suddenly famous with the publication of *Childe Harold*. From then on, he would be demanded at every turn, as lover, dinner guest, or adornment of great houses.

Life became serious. He entered a man's world, with a man's decisions to make. So he married, and, with the failure of that marriage in 1816, he finally went beyond hope of innocence or recovery. He then left England, never to return. Travel now had lost the quality of enticing escape. It had become instead the sad consequence of rejection. Byron searched for a new home in a series of moves across the Italian peninsula: Venice, Ravenna, Pisa, Genoa. And after that, Greece again.

Byron's life, in the twelve years that separated his two visits to Greece, was so marked by events that it would be fruitless to search for the defining moments. More obviously than with most biographies, Byron's is a succession of forking paths, resisting the comfortable straight lines of inevitability. There are so many moments when, if something had been different, the whole future course would have changed beyond recognition. If he hadn't married, if he hadn't married Annabella Milbanke. If he hadn't loved his half-sister, Augusta. If he hadn't met Count Gamba. If he had followed his inclinations and left for South America with his natural daughter, Allegra. Any of these, or a dozen others, might have led to a quiet old age, a career of respectable fame, which would have made the return to Greece unlikely or unnecessary.

All this underlines one of the most curious paradoxes of Byron's life. Simply told, the biography seems to be a record of spontaneity, of constantly shifting perspectives; yet Byron was one of the least spontaneous of men, slow to reach decisions, even slower to act.

Spontaneity is there all through the poetry, of course. "When I take pen in hand," he wrote to his publisher, "I *must* say what comes uppermost—or fling it away"; and to the same correspondent: "I am like the tyger (in poesy) if I miss my first Spring—I go growling back to my Jungle.—There is no second.—I can't correct."

Those who were on intimate terms with him often recorded the magic of his company. "Lord Byron was nothing in conversation," wrote his friend Trelawny, "unless you were alone with him, but then he was rich as a gold mine, in every direction you bored into him you could extract wealth, and he was never exhausted."

This mobility, however, was almost entirely in the mind. Try as he would, action eluded him. It is a measure of the enduring power of Byron's sacrifice for Greece that its inevitability should still appear so natural. That it was not is something Byron never doubted for a moment. He had no romantic, idealizing passion for Greece. "Trust not the *Greeks*," he wrote in a letter of 1812; and in a journal entry of 1823 he remained of the same opinion: "The worst of them [the Greeks] is—that . . . they are such d——d liars; —there never was such an incapacity for veracity shown since Eve lived in Paradise."

There is never a time in Byron's life when the Greek cause becomes the single and obvious choice for him to make. Though he was long fascinated by the dream of self-realization through action, he never achieved it. That is why his return to Greece has sometimes appeared a merely helpless gesture. Perhaps, in the end, it is among the dull spaces between events, rather than in events themselves, that the explanations lie. He was a man of powerful habits, and, like many such men, given to the frustrations of a self-created boredom. "Alas! I have been but idle—and have the prospect of early decay," he wrote to Hobhouse in August 1819. "This is a bitter thought. . . . Philosophy would be in vain—let us try action."

All through May 1811, Byron remained in Malta. He said good-bye to his boy lover, Nicolo Giraud, sent him to school, gave him a large sum of money, and asked him to write once a month. He blustered and shrugged his way to the end of his romance with Mrs. Spencer Smith, who, to his dismay, was still waiting for him, and still, apparently, in love. He rescued some Greek sculptures that Hobhouse had taken from Athens and mislaid on his way home. "I have succeeded in the discovery and embarkation of your memorable marbles," Byron later wrote to him in mockery.

Then, on 2 June 1811, he sailed for England. Though he brought home no fashionable lumps of Greek sculpture himself, he did not return empty-handed. The details of his souvenirs are given in the letters he wrote on the long journey home, letters to pass the time amid "the gentle dullness of a Summer voyage." He carried a three-volume Greek-Italian dictionary; a vial of Attic hemlock, which he later gave to his publisher in London; a shawl, as a present for his mother; four Athenian skulls, presumed ancient, later to be presented to the novelist Walter Scott; "two live Greek Servants"; four live tortoises; and a greyhound, which soon succumbed to the pressures of life at sea.

The tortoises and greyhound are not surprising, for Byron had a lifelong fascination with the company of animals. When he was at Cambridge, he kept a tame bear, which he walked on a chain, like a dog; while later, in Ravenna, he supported an entire menagerie: cats and dogs, monkeys and peacocks and guinea hens, a badger, a falcon, an eagle, a tame crow, an Egyptian crane, and a fox.

The hemlock was presumably in memory of the plant that had caused the death of Socrates. And the "two live Greek Servants" might be interesting, if we knew more about them. One of them, the Athenian Dimitrios Zograffo, was later to play a prominent part in the War of Independence. When Byron discovered his rise to fame from the newspapers in 1821, he wrote in his journal: "He was my Servant in 1809—1810—1811—1812—at different intervals in those years . . . and accompanied me to England in 1811— he returned to Greece—Spring 1812.—He was a clever but not *apparently* an enterprizing man—but Circumstances make men." That is about all we know of Byron's attitude toward him.

Byron was a convinced vegetarian at this stage of his life. To his mother, while still at sea on the way home from Malta, he wrote, a little haughtily: "I must . . . inform you that for a long time I have been restricted to an entire vegetable diet neither fish or flesh coming within my regimen, so I expect a powerful stock of potatoes, greens, & biscuit, I drink no wine. . . ."

He was also at this time lighter than he would ever be. Byron had constant weight problems throughout his life. In 1806, he weighed 202 pounds, an un-Byronic, massively unflattering size for someone who was just a little over five feet eight inches tall. By ferocious dieting and the effects of his various illnesses, he was now, in the summer of 1811, down to 137 pounds.

When, over the next few months, he looked back at his two years abroad, it was generally with nostalgia for the imagined simplicity of life in Greece. At times he affected a disabused worldliness, as in this letter to his half-sister, Augusta, in September 1811: "I don't know that I have acquired any thing by my travels but a smattering of two languages & a habit of chewing Tobacco." More often, though, Greece returns as a physical and emotional point of reference, to counter the depression of an English winter or his increasing confrontation with feelings of loss.

Greece was a memory of warm seas and blue skies. It was "dearly beloved Greece." When, after the success of *Childe Harold*, he was encouraged to write further cantos, he wrote: "to do that, I must return to Greece and Asia; I must have a warm sun and a blue sky; I cannot describe scenes so dear to me by a sea-coal fire." He hated the English climate, the rain and mist of a "beef eating & beer drinking Country." In early April of 1813, he wrote: "The snows of an English *Spring* now falling around me add one more inducement to reconcile me to expatriation."

The clarity of the Greek skies was also, for Byron, the mirror of another kind of clarity. Greece was a land where things were simpler than at home. This, of course, is a classic illusion of the traveler, but Byron felt it deeply. To one of his most intimate correspondents, Lady Melbourne, he wrote of his regret at leaving Greece: "I wish I had never left a country with more quiet & fewer clouds—Everything is so roundabout here." This sense of the roundabout nature of English society would later flower into the great comic attack on hypocrisy in *Don Juan*. For the present, it simply complicated the problems of coming home.

The supposed simplicity of life in the Levant was most compelling in terms of the relations between men and women. While Byron was one of the most successful of heterosexual lovers, he remained forever suspicious of women's sexual attraction. "A mistress," he wrote in his journal, "never is nor can be a friend. While you agree, you are lovers; and, when it is over, any thing but friends."

The thrill of Ali Pasha's Tepelena had been in the absolute separation of the sexes. Ali's court was like an exotic boarding school, only with fewer restraints. Women there were a group apart, silenced, and veiled. For the bisexual adventurer, this inevitably simplified things, seemed to normalize the passion of man for man, or man for boy. As far as Byron could see, women in Eastern society were clearly limited by their function. They were either whores, or else marriageable commodities for the fathering of heirs. Either way, negotiations were straightforward.

This, to the modern eye, is one of Byron's least interesting sides. He was, however, always happier when sexually attractive women were marginalized. This was obviously true in the East; while later, in Pisa, he found something of the same security in the almost exclusively male world of the Casa Lanfranchi. An entry in Byron's journal for 6 January 1821 represents his views at their most extravagantly perverse:

> Thought of the state of women under the ancient Greeks— convenient enough. Present state ... —artificial and unnatural. They ought to mind home—and be well fed and clothed—but not mixed in society. Well educated, too, in religion—but to read neither poetry nor politics— nothing but books of piety and cookery. Music—drawing— dancing—also a little gardening and ploughing now and then. I have seen them mending the roads in Epirus with good success. Why not, as well as hay-making and milking?

The entry overstates, of course, and, in that, disguises Byron's problem. In fact, he found great pleasure in the company of educated and talented women, just as he found pleasure in the beds of those who were sexually available in his time: prostitutes, servants, and the wives of friends. He could not, however, easily imagine how these two forms of pleasure might meet. The prospect was always disconcerting and made his serious relationships with women famously difficult.

To his future wife, Byron wrote in September 1813: "[Women] are all better than us—& their faults such as they are must originate with ourselves." While there was no doubt a measure of flattery in the remark, it perhaps contained a fair measure of what he believed. By their active presence in Western society, women challenged the directness of male desire, insisted on the existence of other, complex forms of relationship. The rituals of Western life made for a messy world, where sex was traded against commitment and the long-term stability of marriage. In the West, as he said, women had to be "cared for, or fought for, or danced after."

In the East, it had all been so much easier. This nostalgia affected his whole sense of belonging, so that Greece remained latent within him as a possibility of return; while England, with its turmoil, its social and political hypocrisy, was progressively erased from his thoughts as a future theater of action.

Byron landed in England on 14 July 1811. Once back, he felt adrift, as anyone might who had returned from two years abroad with nothing in particular to come home for.

Almost immediately, the blows began to fall. His mother died on 1 August, while he was still in London, so that he never saw her again. On the following day, his close friend Charles Matthews was drowned in waterweeds on the River Cam at Cambridge. By October, he had learned of the death of John Edleston, the great romantic attachment of his university days. Edleston, Byron wrote in February 1812, was "the only human being, that ever loved me in truth and entirely."

Hobhouse, the solid, reliable companion, had joined the army and was garrisoned out of reach at Dover. It was a wretched time. In a letter of August 1811, Byron wrote: "At three and twenty I am left alone. . . . It is true, I am young enough to begin again, but with whom can I retrace the laughing part of life?" Early in the same month, Hobhouse had written to him saying: "I can not bear to read such melancholy letters from you. . . ." While in a letter of early January 1814, Hobhouse refers at length to a rumor that Byron had committed suicide.

In the midst of the evaporation of the laughing part of life, the personal tragedies, the lack of direction, Byron had nowhere to turn. There was no refuge for him in orthodox faith. To a friend who was nagging anxiously after the salvation of his soul, he wrote: "There is something Pagan in me that I cannot shake off. . . . I deny nothing, but doubt everything."

His family had now dwindled to a single close relative,

his half-sister, Augusta. They had first met some time before 1804, when Byron was in his teens. His later relationship with her, which dates perhaps from the summer of 1813, would be one of the great passions of his life and its greatest tragedy.

As far as the world was concerned, the outlet for his energies was limited. A nobleman couldn't be a poet in any serious way, could only dabble in verses as an affectation to pass an hour of boredom. The only other possibility was politics. Here Byron was unlucky. From his days at Harrow, he had dreamed of becoming an orator and statesman. But two things barred his way, and they were both insuperable.

In the first place, the general political climate in England was massively hostile to Byron's natural leanings. Until 1815, the country was on a war footing. With the final defeat of Napoleon in that year, the old European conservative order first basked in its triumph, then wondered desperately how to make sure revolution would never come again. There followed in most countries a period of dull, occasionally savage, reaction. In England, the first generation of the Romantics—Wordsworth, Southey, Coleridge—had, by 1815, all followed the same path, which had led them from early excitement in the face of the French Revolution to the safe harbor of tradition, religion, and the Tories.

Byron had no sympathy with any of this. At heart, he was a moderate reformer in an age when even the most moderate reforms threatened the stability of the governing class. He loathed the static carelessness of Toryism, which held that economic depression and social distress were beyond politics, phenomena that had to be endured, like the weather, because there was no human remedy. He was also, and genuinely, disturbed by the viciousness that was often the establishment's only response to opposition. Through the dull postwar years, the Conservatives went on and on. As he wrote in Canto XI of *Don Juan*:

Nought's permanent among the human race,
Except the Whigs not *getting into place.*

At another moment, in a humorous act of faith, he wrote: "God will not be always a Tory"; but the Tories held power almost continuously for seventy years and he never, in his short life, knew anything else.

The second problem for Byron, in political terms, was that he belonged, by inheritance, inescapably, to the House of Lords. Though it was certainly less irrelevant then than it may seem today, the Lords was still no theater for Byron's ambitions. It was, he wrote, "a hopeless & lethargic den of dullness & drawling." Neither House of Parliament, he said, "ever struck me with more awe or respect than the same number of Turks in a Divan—or of Methodists in a barn would have done"; but at least the Commons had its moments of drama or animation. It was a place, however, to which he could never descend.

So, in a state where he longed to do something, but where all obvious routes were blocked, he did what he could. He proceeded with the publication of *Childe Harold*, the poem he had begun in Ioannina in October 1809. Its appearance in March 1812 made him famous overnight. This gave him ever greater means to indulge his large appetites, while all along he turned over and over in his mind the problem that England gave him: to stay or to leave, to belong or to desert. Each option apparently sealed a future, a sexuality, a way of life. England meant marriage, family, orthodoxy. Beyond England, there was the uncertain and ambiguous freedom of the outlaw. Ironically, by choosing the first of these options, he soon found himself obliged to take refuge in the second.

Byron's letters from 1811 onward are full of indecision and restlessness. He talks of shipping off again for Greece, of the horrors of the English climate. Then of settling down, making the most of things. "*I* shall marry," he wrote to Augusta with forced cynicism, "if I can find any thing inclined to barter money for rank." For at least a dazzling marriage might redeem the failing fortunes of the Byrons, if it did nothing else.

Two years later, it appeared that he had resolved his dilemma, but it is only an illusion. "Without occupation of some kind I cannot exist," he wrote in March 1813, "travel therefore is the only pursuit left me." And to Augusta, the same month: "For marriage I have neither the talent nor the inclination—I cannot fortune-hunt nor afford to marry without a fortune." The dejection is palpable in both letters and it is not surprising to find that the alternative solution imposes itself with his engagement to Annabella Milbanke the following year.

Meanwhile, he enjoyed his fame, which had spread not only across England, but, increasingly, to other countries as well. When he heard that his poetry had become popular in the United States, he wrote in his journal: "These are the first tidings that have ever sounded like *Fame* to my ears—to be redde on the banks of the Ohio!"

He went to parties with the cream of the Whig aristocracy, his natural political and social allies. Carriages pressed about his house, bearing invitations to dinners and balls, holding up the traffic in their desire to claim one of the glittering stars of the day. Long divorced from the centers of political power, the Whigs had withdrawn into the brilliance of their own society, stimulating the arts of conversation, adultery, and scorn for the Tories. In this aimless, superficially agreeable world, Byron was, for a time, at home.

In 1821, from exile in Ravenna, he remembered those days with a rare nostalgia. Listening to the sounds of a street organ outside, he noted: "They are playing a waltz which I have heard ten thousand times at the balls in London, between 1812 and 1815. Music is a strange thing." In London during those years he was endlessly in demand as fashionable poet and conversationalist. Even in the leaden, patrician prose of his most celebrated host, Lord Holland, he is "that extraordinary young man."

He was also, of course, in the manner of the age, a very public lover. Most famously, he began, in the spring of 1812, a relationship with Lady Caroline Lamb, which will be remembered always for her judgment on seeing Byron for the first time: "I looked earnestly at him, and turned on my heel. My opinion, in my journal was, 'mad—bad—and dangerous to know.' " This judgment, so sexually potent, could have applied equally to herself, and the relationship charted a predictable course through passion, possession, and jealousy, to end in mutual antagonism and hatred.

"I know not whom I may love," Byron wrote in 1813, "but to the latest hour of my life I shall hate that woman." In 1824, when that latest hour had passed, Caroline watched, still haunted by "that beautiful pale face," as Byron's body passed by her home on the way to burial in Nottingham.

Those years between 1812 and 1815 have a tawdry glamour in retrospect and convey a false sense of freedom or abandon. For the constant, outrageous rule-breaking of that aristocratic society was all, in the end, contained within unmovable boundaries.

This Byron was to discover for himself, after the breakdown of his marriage and the scandals that surrounded it. At a party given by Lady Jersey, the only London hostess who dared receive him in the company of his fallen sister, he was comprehensively and finally snubbed. The excitement of that world, its self-conscious aloofness from prevailing moral standards, clothed a succession of broken lives. Bitterness concealed beneath stylish innuendo. It was a society so closed, so enveloping, that exclusion from it could only seem like a form of death.

In February 1812, just before the fame of *Childe Harold* carried him headlong into this society, Byron made the first of three speeches in the House of Lords. He had originally thought of speaking about the Irish Catholics, a group he associated with the Greeks and Jews as being prey to "all the moral and physical ills that can afflict humanity." In the end, however, he came closer to home for his maiden speech and took as a subject one of the most pressing issues of local life in the county of Nottinghamshire.

The details of his Frame Work Bill speech have by now long lost their urgency, but the language continues to say much about

Byron's attitude to suffering, his anger on behalf of the oppressed. At that time, England and France had been at war, with some intermissions, since 1793. Large numbers of working people had fallen into poverty over these years, and by 1812 almost half the population of Nottingham was on poor relief.

The Nottinghamshire weavers were a visible symbol of the general problem. This group of workers suddenly found themselves confronting a changed world, as new technology led to demands for less labor and, perhaps more importantly, for less skilled labor. The weavers turned to violent protest and the smashing of machinery. The government's response was to send in troops; and then to propose that crimes against property should be punished not merely by transportation, but by death.

Byron opposed this intransigence. He saw it as morally wrong and politically short-sighted, and he made his stand a personal one, in a way that characterizes much of what is best and most problematic about his politics. He understood the issues. Much of the violence was taking place near his home at Newstead. As he wrote to Lord Holland: "I have seen the state of these miserable men, & it is a disgrace to a civilized country."

This passion is at the heart of his speech to the Lords. I have seen these men, he repeats, "meagre with famine sullen with despair." You may call them a mob, he went on, but "it is the Mob, that labour in your fields & serve in your houses, that man your navy & recruit your army, that have enabled you to defy all the world."

It was a passion that never left him, an anger that was always ready to flame in the face of injustice. At the same time, the intensity of the personal commitment limited his political effectiveness. Powerful as his words still seem, they were never likely to carry the Lords and scarcely even moved some of the most influential of the Whigs. Lord Holland looked down from Olympus and decided that Byron would never succeed in this most rarefied of societies: "His speech," he wrote, "was full of fancy, wit, and invective, but not exempt from affectation nor well reasoned,

nor at all suited to our common notions of Parliamentary elo-
quence. His fastidious and artificial taste and his over-irritable
temper would, I think, have prevented him from ever excelling in
Parliament."

The judgment would have stung anyone, Byron not least, but
it was almost certainly correct. "I have been in some of the most
oppressed provinces of Turkey," Byron had said, "but never
under the most despotic of infidel governments, did I behold
such squalid wretchedness as I have seen since my return in the
very heart of a Christian country." His approach, his language,
were too dramatic, too personal, and, before long, Byron came to
share the view that he would never have a place in English political life.

He would not, could not, learn the appropriate language, or
the arts of alliance building. So he has been charged ever since
with quixotic, gesture politics. Not only as far as England is concerned, but in his activities in Italy, after 1820, and, finally, of
course, in Greece.

Whatever the justice of the criticism, however, it is not clear
that he could have furthered his own aims in politics, no matter
what he had done. The climate was simply against him. By the
end of the 1820s, the political situation was changing in favor of
reform, and not just in England. But by then Byron was long
dead. The years when he might have given himself wholeheartedly to politics were a time of reaction, savagely unheroic.

The failure of his political hopes depressed Byron. It took away
all chance of a commitment that might combine passion with
action, indignation with the means of its transcendence.

Love, inevitably, was the primary means of escape. Two
relationships dominated his final years in England. Both, in their
different ways, created unbearable pressures, both brought lifelong pain.

By August 1813, Byron was deeply involved with his half-sister,
Augusta. If they hadn't been related by blood, this might have

been the most successful relationship of his life—though what they shared, through blood, was partly what made the relationship so compelling. Both were only children who had inherited a vast family history through a common father. With Augusta, more than any woman, Byron could "retrace the laughing part of life."

There was passion, but also fondness; love, but also friendship. They could be happily childish together. Above all, it was a relationship free from the complex negotiations of ordinary affairs, the constant search for definition, the play of sexual power. "I am much afraid that that perverse passion was my deepest after all," Byron wrote to his confidante, Lady Melbourne, and there is every reason to believe it.

In the summer of 1813, he planned to elope with Augusta and go to Sicily. The step into exile was, however, too great to make voluntarily. Augusta was married and there could have been no disguising the nature of the journey, nor could there have been any hope of return. With that failure to take the decisive step, the relationship was doomed.

Of all the places associated with Byron, the one that today most easily evokes a memory of Augusta is Newstead Abbey. Especially Newstead in winter. In January 1814, Byron and Augusta traveled together up the snowbound Great North Road from London to Nottingham. The day before they left, Byron had written to Lady Melbourne: "What I want is a companion—a friend. . . . I have seen enough of love matches—& of all matches."

They spent three weeks alone together at Newstead, closed in by the harshest winter of a generation. The abbey under snow, surrounded by its vast acres, the gentle fall toward the lake: Newstead is no less romantic today. Augusta was pregnant. The roads were impassable, giving them every excuse to remain.

The servants lit huge fires and they sat and talked or read. They celebrated Byron's twenty-sixth birthday, "a very pretty age if it would always last," he wrote. "We never yawn nor disagree—and laugh much more than is suitable to so solid a mansion—and the family shyness makes us more amusing companions to each other—than we could be to any one else."

Still, Byron thought of marriage. And this relationship, when it came, would be the single greatest disaster of his life.

In October 1812, Byron had proposed to Annabella Milbanke, in a roundabout way, and had been rejected. Annabella was the daughter of Sir Ralph Milbanke, the brother of Byron's confidante, Lady Melbourne. Byron proposed to Annabella again, tentatively, in September 1814, and this time, after thinking it over for a while, she accepted. They married on 2 January 1815.

Vultures still hover over the carcass of this marriage, about which we know rather a lot, though very little about the things that truly matter. Biographers, over the years, have taken sides, passionate about who was right and wrong. Mario Praz, in *The Romantic Agony*, first published in 1933, echoes the extreme anti-Byron position: "His conduct towards his wife," he wrote, "seems to have been of a moral cruelty so exceptional as to make one for a moment doubt the reliability of the historical evidence."

It is easy to say the marriage was made for catastrophe. Annabella was what used to be called a self-possessed woman. When Lady Melbourne asked her what she wanted in a husband, she replied: "He must have consistent principles of Duty governing strong and *generous* feelings, and reducing them under the command of Reason."

She was clearly attracted to Byron, but chose to rationalize her feelings as a Christian attempt to redeem a lost soul. Byron, for his part, seems to have persuaded himself that this was his last chance to belong to English society.

Underlying it all, however, was an inflammatory dynamic. Byron had been through numerous homosexual affairs in Athens, followed, most recently, by an incestuous relationship with his half-sister. The more Annabella opposed her Christian standards to him, the more he found an erotic satisfaction in trying to initiate her into sin. "There is *no* Vice," wrote Annabella after they had separated, "with which he has not endeavoured . . . to familiarize me." For all its dramatic tone, her statement is entirely plausible.

In Byron's letters of 1814, we can already see him struggling toward marriage, while old doubts and hesitations become ever sharper. There is the familiar nostalgia for life in the East as an escape from it all: "There I was always in action or at least in motion— —and except during Night—always on or in the sea—& on horse-back—I am sadly sick of my present sluggishness—and I hate civilization." The references to his future wife are already ambiguous: "I do admire her as a very superior woman a little encumbered with Virtue." While to Annabella herself, he wrote: "All contemplative existence is bad—one should *do* something."

The restlessness, the indecision are part of an internal war. He knew his experiences, his desires, were a problematic background to an orthodox marriage. It was fine for a young gentleman to indulge in whoring, gambling, and laudanum—all of which Byron had done; none of that prevented the glittering marriage. But the love of boys, the love for a sister, even if she was only a half-sister—that was beyond recovery.

As the autumn of 1814 came on and marriage loomed inevitable, Byron whiled away the hours at Newstead, fishing, swimming, and boating. To one correspondent, he confessed that he had taken to shooting at soda water bottles with his pistols. From London, in October, he wrote to the countess of Jersey: "I wish it was well over—for I do hate bustle—and there is no marrying without some."

Perhaps most significant of all is a postscript to another letter of same month: "By the way, my wife elect is perfection, and I hear of nothing but her merits and her wonders, and that she is 'very pretty'. . . ." Then the addition: "I have not seen her these ten months." A week later, to a friend, he wrote, shrugging it all off: "I am about to be married—and am of course in all the misery of a man in pursuit of happiness."

The faithful Hobhouse accompanied Byron on the journey to be married. They left Cambridge together on 26 December 1814, arriving at Annabella's home in the evening of 30 December.

"Never was lover less in haste," Hobhouse noted in his diary. "Miss Milbanke," he wrote, "was silent and modest, but very sensible and quiet, and inspiring an interest which it is easy to mistake for love."

The marriage, in the end, was a small family affair. Trying to brazen it out with Lady Melbourne the day after, Byron wrote: "We were married yesterday . . . so there's an end of that matter and the beginning of many others . . . the kneeling was rather tedious—and the cushions hard—but upon the whole it did vastly well." Hobhouse recorded his own feelings in his diary: "I felt as if I had buried a friend."

So began a marriage that was to last a few days over a year and left, for both parties, the bitterness of a lifetime. Byron's attitude toward his wife seems to have been set very early on, leading to a pattern of sexual play that was self-consciously shocking. According to Hobhouse, Byron claimed, in his now lost memoirs, that he "*had* Lady B. on the sofa before dinner on the day of their marriage." This may—who knows—have appealed to them both; but Annabella was subsequently drawn into the full range of Byron's sexuality, through hints, innuendo, and perhaps, also, practice. For a woman of twenty-three, with no sexual experience, the revelations can hardly have been tolerable.

Byron, she claimed, when it was all over, used to try to convince her that all morality was merely conventional; that it was "one thing at Constantinople, another in London." It is not clear how much of it all she understood at the time. At the age of forty, she declared that "*not to see things as they are* is . . . my great intellectual defect." But to Byron's moral relativism she tried to oppose what she called "one Immutable Standard." The circle of mutual conflict was quickly closed and the marriage progressively undermined by Byron's erratic behavior, heavy drinking, and descent into debt.

Curiously, it did not end in one vast conflagration. Perhaps it would have made for a less obsessive aftermath if it had. Annabella simply left one morning in January 1816, with their five-week-old baby, Ada, and went to see her parents. Byron seems to have believed without doubt that they would soon meet again, but they never did. Amid the ensuing recriminations, and the legal moves by Annabella to secure an amicable separation, Byron's reputation in England suffered irreparably. Not least from a mountain of insinuations about things that were, after all, mainly true.

By April, he had sold his books, said farewell to Augusta, whom he would also never see again, and planned his departure for Europe. He signed the deed of separation from his wife on 21 April and left London for the port of Dover two days later.

In two poems, written in March and April, Byron voiced the turmoil of his life during the final weeks in England. The first of these, entitled "Fare Thee Well," he sent to Annabella, in the hope of a reconciliation. After the power in the movement of the opening lines:

> *Fare thee well! and if for ever—*
> *Still for ever, fare thee well—*

the poem is, by turns, bitter and sentimental, but always manipulative. The kind of outpouring Annabella had already scorned in a letter of 7 February: "It is unhappily your disposition to consider what you *have* as worthless—what you have *lost* as invaluable."

The second poem, written in mid-April, was a farewell to his sister, Augusta, a testimony of his love and of his gratitude to her in standing by him to the end, through what he called "that deep midnight of the mind":

> *When fortune changed—and love fled far,*
> *And hatred's shafts flew thick and fast,*
> *Thou wert the solitary star*
> *Which rose and set not to the last. . . .*
>
> *Still may thy spirit dwell on mine,*
> *And teach it what to brave or brook—*

> *There's more in one soft word of thine,*
> *Than in the world's defied rebuke.*

The bitterness and the gratitude both stayed with Byron for the remaining years of his life, which were spent entirely abroad. "You must not talk to me of England," he wrote to Hobhouse in October 1819. "I had a house—and lands—and a wife and child— and a name there—once." While in Canto XIV of *Don Juan*, written a year before his death, he remembered the "female *friends*"

> *Who did not quit me when Oppression trod*
> *Upon me; whom no scandal could remove;*
> *Who fought, and fight, in absence too, my battles,*
> *Despite the snake Society's loud rattles.*

Byron set out for the port of Dover in his coach. He had had it specially built along the lines of one that once belonged to Napoleon. Ten minutes after he left London, the bailiffs descended on his house in search of reparation for his debts. Hobhouse reported that even his pet birds and squirrel were taken into custody. Of course, Hobhouse was there at Dover for the sailing of Byron's ship on 25 April. Ever willing, like one of those characters at the end of Shakespearean tragedies whom no one ever remembers, there to say a few words when the catastrophe is over, the hero dead, and to sweep up the stage.

Large crowds had gathered to watch Byron's departure. It was reported to Lady Byron that "the curiosity to see him was so great that many ladies accoutred themselves as chambermaids for the purpose of obtaining under that disguise a nearer inspection." Byron and his friends walked down to the ship through the crowds. The ship moved out and Hobhouse ran to the end of the wooden pier to watch it pass by in rough seas. Byron pulled off his cap and waved. "I gazed until I could not distinguish him any longer," Hobhouse wrote. "God bless him for a gallant spirit and a kind one."

Eight

All tragedies are finish'd by a death,
All comedies are ended by a marriage. . . .

—*Don Juan*, Canto III

After the short sea crossing from Dover, Byron landed at Ostend. He was accompanied by his valet, Fletcher, his personal physician, Polidori, and a Swiss guide. According to a letter he sent a few years later to Annabella, his first thoughts on leaving England in 1816 were to go back to the East. The Napoleonic Wars were over, and it was now possible to travel overland across Europe again. Characteristically, Byron took his time. He reached Switzerland in May 1816 and Italy in October. There he stayed for seven years, finally returning to Greece in 1823.

From Ostend, they passed through the Belgian towns of Bruges, Ghent, and Antwerp, arriving in Brussels at the beginning of May. There Byron began a new canto of *Childe Harold* and visited the site of the Battle of Waterloo. It was not much, he wrote to Hobhouse, after the plains of Marathon, Troy, and Chaironeia. But then, as he said, there was, no doubt, prejudice in his antipathy. For he had admired Napoleon, and of Waterloo he could say quite openly: "I detest the cause & the victors—& the victory." England's victorious and much celebrated commander he called: "that disgrace to his country, the pensioned impostor, Wellington."

After Belgium, Germany. First Cologne; then, up the Rhine, to Bonn, Coblenz, Mannheim, Karlsruhe. After that, Switzerland. They went to Basel, and then to Sécheron, near Geneva, where, on 27 May 1816, Byron first met the poet Shelley and where, for a time, he settled down.

Byron had strong views about Switzerland. It was, he wrote, "a curst selfish, swinish country of brutes, placed in the most romantic region of the world. I never could bear the inhabitants, and still less their English visitors." In a letter written in Italian in 1821, he remembered Switzerland as "perhaps the most expensive country in Europe for foreigners," a detail he put down to the fact that the Swiss were the "most cunning and rascally [people] on earth—in everything that has to do with money—and deceit—and greed."

In spite of all that, Switzerland was a resting place, and a beautiful one. He rented a villa that had once sheltered the poet Milton, two miles from Geneva. Shelley took a house a few hundred yards away, and they saw much of each other over the next three months. At the time, Shelley was living through his own turmoil. In 1814, he had left his wife and eloped with Mary Godwin. Now he and Mary had come down through France to Switzerland, bringing with them Mary's stepsister, Claire Clairmont.

Claire, a teenage girl, almost exactly the same age as Mary, had met Byron in London during his last few weeks in England, the worst time of all, given Byron's circumstances, for a love affair. But they had, as a result of her insistence and ingenuity, become lovers; she completely involved, he inevitably engaged elsewhere. Now she was pregnant with Byron's child, still in love, and soon to be, once again, Byron's lover.

Byron and Shelley were never close friends. Hobhouse says as much and, though his view may be suspect, since he was always jealous of Byron's friendships, Byron himself confirms it. Even in the aftermath of Shelley's extraordinary death in 1822, Byron could bring himself to say no more than that he had admired and esteemed him, acknowledging that he was "as perfect a Gentleman as ever crossed a drawing room."

Differences in lifestyle and politics separated them; and though they were both poets, Shelley could never think of himself as Byron's equal. When Byron read him one of the unpublished cantos of *Don Juan* in 1821, Shelley wrote to Mary: "I despair of rivalling Lord Byron ... and there is no other with whom it is worth contending." He added, later in the same letter: "The demon of mistrust and of pride lurks between two persons in our situation poisoning the freedom of their intercourse. This is a tax, and a heavy one, which we must pay for being human. I think the fault is not on my side nor is it likely, I being the weaker. I hope that in the next world these things will be better managed."

Quite apart from his personal feelings for Shelley, there is something here that belongs to a pattern in Byron's life. He had come to feel that real friendship was rooted only in the deep past. The capacity for making new friends, he had discovered, drained away rapidly with the passing of youth. After that, a man was left only with what, in a letter to Mary Shelley in November 1822, he calls "men-of-the-world friendships."

In that same letter to Mary, he strikes the note that, at first sight, may seem merely cynical, but which says much about Byron as a social animal: "I have had, and may have still, a thousand friends, as they are called, in *life*, who are like one's partners in the waltz of this world—not much remembered when the ball is over, though very pleasant for the time." Passages like these suggest why it was so hard for Byron to move on from failure, to begin again in new surroundings. For him, the past of childhood and adolescence was the secret spring of nearly everything that mattered.

After the recent months of hell, the summer with Shelley in 1816 was, at least, a release. In June, the two went off together for a sailing tour of Lake Geneva. Then, in late August, Shelley's triple ménage returned to England: Shelley to sort out his finances; Mary to work on the writing of *Frankenstein*; Claire to give birth, some months later, to Byron's daughter Allegra.

By the time they left Switzerland, Hobhouse had arrived. Neither he nor Byron had anything pressing to do. So, once again, they set off on the road together. This time they went into the Alps. On the first night of their travels, at Ouchy, on the northern side of Lake Geneva, Byron wrote to Augusta, showing clearly his continued state of mind: "What a fool I was to marry—and *you* not very wise—my dear—we might have lived so single and so happy. . . . We were just formed to pass our lives together."

Byron kept a journal of his Alpine journey for Augusta. In the gorgeous mountain scenery, there was a momentary promise of a retreat from the pain of exile. "I have lately repeopled my mind with Nature," he wrote. They saw shepherds, true images of the calm and freedom of the pastoral life, and so unlike the Greek shepherds Byron had seen, who never moved without their muskets. "This was pure and unmixed—solitary—savage and patriarchal."

They crossed the snowline, played snowballs. They rode to a glacier, which appeared to Byron like "a *frozen hurricane.*" They passed woods of withered pines, stripped bare by a single winter: "their appearance," he noted gloomily, "reminded me of me & my family."

Looking back on his Alpine journey, at the end of September 1816, Byron felt all his accumulated sadness returning. "Neither the music of the Shepherd—the crashing of the Avalanche—nor the torrent—the mountain—the Glacier—the Forest—nor the Cloud—have for one moment—lightened the weight upon my heart—nor enabled me to lose my own wretched identity in the majesty & the power and the Glory—around—above—& beneath me." The best he could say about the past and the failure of his marriage was that he had now gone beyond the desire for revenge.

In this state of mind, he left with Hobhouse for Italy on 5 October. Northern Europe could never be more for him than a temporary resting place. But in Italy he was back in the Mediterranean culture he loved. Now began the search for a new way of life in exile, as he moved from Venice to Ravenna, then to Pisa and Genoa.

There was action enough over the next seven years, before his return to Greece. Prodigious sexual play, political intrigue, the death of Shelley. But the dominant memory of Byron's Italy is the quiet domesticity of his last years there. Long days devoted to the routines of riding and reading; late nights spent on the composition of *Don Juan*.

To his publisher, John Murray, Byron said that he felt more for the Italians as a nation than for any other people on earth. There was a time when he even foresaw a future for himself as an Italian poet. In a letter of September 1812 to Lady Melbourne, he had called Italian "that dearest of all languages"; and in a letter of April 1819 to Murray, he prophesied that, after a further decade of intensive study, he would go on to write his best work in Italian.

Italy could so easily have been the place to settle down for the rest of a lifetime. From 1819, Byron found, in the young Countess Teresa Guiccioli, a woman who would happily have shared his future and—what was much rarer with Byron—a woman with whom a future seemed possible.

But there were two elements at war in his nature. He understood both, yet could never harmonize them. For if he fell quickly into routines, into the life of the day-to-day, he never abandoned the dream of an active alternative. Riding horses, the love of women, the work of the poet, all filled his days, but not his sense of what the totality of a life might be.

For years, in the absence of other possibilities, Byron's active engagement with the world was primarily physical and sexual.

In Italy, passion gradually failed him, victim of an approaching middle age. In the face of this, he chose the natural defense, a domesticated, faithful love with his Countess Teresa. But he struggled to adapt to the challenges of the quiet life. To abandon the call of action was to acknowledge the final failure of youth; it was to accept the arrival of a serenity he sometimes felt he needed, but which he feared like death.

So, he listened, in the end, to the voice that had been there since adolescence. "I will cut myself a path through the world or perish in the attempt," he had written from Harrow School in 1804. In 1813: "Without occupation of some kind I cannot exist." In the same year, from his journal: "I shall never be any thing, or rather always be nothing. The most I can hope is, that some will say, 'He might, perhaps, if he would.' " And from Ravenna, in January 1821, with the excitement of what he believed was a revolution in the making: "It is now the time to act, and what signifies *self*, if a single spark of that which would be worthy of the past can be bequeathed unquenchedly to the future?"

The pattern can be made to seem inexorable, a relentless working out of a destiny formed by the insecurities of childhood, the need to impose, to matter decisively to oneself. Yet the needs that sent him on, confusedly, toward Mesolongi, are also, perhaps, the same needs that lay behind his love of routine and domesticity. "My taste for revolution is abated—with my other passions," he wrote to Hobhouse in 1819. "I want a country—and a home. . . . I am not yet thirty two years of age—I might still be a decent citizen and found a *house* and a family."

Chance or decision: Byron's return to Greece is difficult to read, the motivation hard to decode, since staying or leaving may not, in the end, be radical alternatives, simply the changing faces of a single dilemma.

Byron and Hobhouse arrived in Milan on 12 October 1816. At the beginning of November, they set off for Venice. On the way, they took in Verona, where, as Byron reported to a friend, they remained a day or two "to gape at the usual marvels,—amphitheatre, paintings," what he called, in a marvelous phrase, "all that time-tax of travel."

The north of Italy, he noted with relief, was "tolerably free from the English; but the south swarms with them, I am told." On 10 November, they reached Venice, and there he was to stay until the end of 1819.

He took an apartment off the Piazza San Marco, over a draper's shop, and, in a few days, was in love with the draper's wife, Marianna. This was a time when love still felt like action, and the action revived him. In his gloom at the end of October, he had written to Augusta with a self-portrait of decay: his hair, he said, was growing gray and thin, his teeth loosening. "Would not one think I was sixty instead of not quite nine & twenty?"

But now, a month later, in love amid the charming decay of Venice, everything was changed. The city, he wrote, a week after his arrival, "has always been (next to the East) the greenest island of my imagination." And a week later: "Venice pleases me as much as I expected—and I expected much—it is one of those places which I know before I see them—and has always haunted me the most—after the East—I like the gloomy gaiety of their gondolas—and the silence of their canals."

He determined to enjoy himself. "I am sick of sorrow," he wrote to Augusta in December, "& must even content myself as well as I can—so here goes—I won't be woeful again if I can help it." The tone of his letters to Augusta changes. From Milan, on 2 November, he had signed himself "ever my dearest thine"; from Verona, on 6 November, "ever my own—thy own"; by February 1817, he ends simply "Yrs. ever."

This ability to refocus his emotional and sexual life always laid him open, as he knew, to charges of volatility, or worse. In some famous lines from Canto XVI of *Don Juan*, he faced the problem head on. There he talks of "that vivacious versatility, / Which many people take for want of heart." People, he suggests, are wrong to condemn those who are emotionally versatile, since versatility is more often a curse than the license for pleasure it may seem to outsiders.

What he calls "mobility," a word he defines in the notes to *Don Juan* as "an excessive susceptibility of immediate impressions," is a painful attribute. Those who are emotionally mobile never move on, never lose touch with the past. On the contrary, they relive it through every shift of sentiment, every new attachment. Versatility, the ability to go on feeling but without the ability to forget, is the Byronic nightmare.

The Venice years were full of promiscuity, but this time, so far as we can tell, Byron was occupied only with women. It was a frenzied, rather gloomy, absorption. Still, there were moments when he could make light of it all. When the eighth earl of Lauderdale returned home after spending some time in his company, he began to spread gossip about Byron's latest affairs. But whom could he mean? Byron asked truculently, in a letter to Hobhouse in January 1819: "Since last year I have run the Gauntlet; — is it the Tarruscelli—the Da Mosti—the Spineda ... the Glettenheimer—& her Sister—the Luigia & her mother ... ? —some of them are Countesses—& some of them Cobblers wives—some noble—some middling—some low—& all whores. . . . I have had them all & thrice as many to boot since 1817." In a postscript to the same letter, he concludes: "I shall not live long—& for that Reason—I must live while I can."

He threw himself into the Carnival festivities at Venice in 1817, 1818, and 1819. He leased a great palazzo on the Grand Canal, into which he introduced his favorite animals: a fox, a couple of monkeys, and some dogs. He continued to love the visual splendor of his surroundings. The views of the Rialto and of the Piazza San Marco "are to me worth all the cities on earth—save Rome & Athens."

He grew obese on his debaucheries. Some visitors, no doubt in malicious exaggeration, reported that he had become "a fat ... middle-aged man, slovenly to the extreme, unkempt, with long,

untied locks that hang down on his shoulders, shabbily dressed."
Another visitor in 1818 thought Byron looked about forty. "His
face had become pale, bloated, and sallow. He had grown very
fat, his shoulders broad and round, and the knuckles of his hands
were lost in fat."

Behind the unremitting indulgence lay a failure of the youthful
sensibility Byron so much enjoyed in himself and in others. His
tone now is different from the comparably promiscuous period in
Athens from 1810 to 1811. By some play of the separation of mind
and body, Byron had kept alive feelings of innocence and boyish
fun. Now he had passed beyond that, and the pageant of promiscuity was colored by a sense of deep personal failure.

In April 1818, he heard of the death of his friend and confidante, Lady Melbourne. In earlier days, she had tried to steer him
around the rocks of incest, marriage, and she alone knew what
else. Now, in response to the news, Byron could only quote from
Macbeth: " 'I have supped full of horrors,' " he wrote, in a letter to
his publisher. "The time is past in which I could feel for the
dead . . . events of this kind leave only a kind of numbness worse
than pain."

The self-destructiveness at work is obvious, as Shelley, wide-
eyed, recorded in a letter. Byron, he said, was sleeping with the
lowest of the low, "people his gondolieri pick up in the streets";
associating with "wretches who . . . do not scruple to avow prac-
tices which are not only not named but I believe seldom even
conceived in England." When Byron looked into his own
thoughts, Shelley went on, "what can he behold but objects of
contempt and despair?"

Byron finally found refuge in commitment. On his thirtieth
birthday, 22 January 1818, he had the briefest of meetings with
the Countess Teresa Guiccioli, by birth Teresa Gamba. She had
only just left school. She came from Ravenna and was in Venice
on her honeymoon, having married three days earlier a man of
fifty-seven. A year later, in April 1819, she and Byron met again,
and, by the twenty-second of that month, Byron was already
writing to her about the finality of their adulterous relationship.

"You sometimes say to me," he wrote in Italian, "that I have been your *first* true Love. . . . I assure you that you will be my last Passion." In a way that must have amazed those who knew Byron, though perhaps not those who knew him really well, his words would turn out to be almost true.

His love for Teresa released him from the self-imposed tyranny of sexual conquest. It reopened the real emotions of the past, allowed them to restate themselves with a force that denied the passing of time. To his sister, Augusta, he wrote in May 1819: "It is heart-breaking to think of our long Separation."

He spoke to Augusta of the lovers Paolo Malatesta and Francesca da Rimini in Dante's *Inferno*, lovers who, though condemned to the second circle of hell for adultery, were at least allowed to suffer together. "They say absence destroys weak passions—& confirms strong ones—Alas! *mine* for you is the union of all passions & of all affections." The renewed emotional outpouring is something that is part of his relationship with Teresa, not a contradiction of it.

Teresa was as close as Byron ever came to the ideal, outside the circle of incest and the altogether impossible case of Augusta. She was beautiful and young, "blonde . . . like a Swede or a Norwegian." Impulsive, though not reckless. A sort of Italian Caroline Lamb, he called her, but "not so savage." She had high social status, through birth as well as marriage. Above all, her commitment to Byron was absolute and passionate. Through her love, some of the humiliation of the past was redeemed, some of the self-disgust transformed. "I have been more ravished," Byron wrote, "than anybody since the Trojan war."

From now on, Byron's future was polarized. It would be a life with Teresa; or else he would have to find some other course that legitimately excluded her. She was not a woman who could be simply abandoned for another, nor a woman who could be left for nothing at all.

The tensions of this polarization emerge in Byron's letters from the earliest moments of his affair with Teresa. On the one hand, there is a true commitment. In July 1819, he writes of having abandoned his old sexual habits: "I have sickened myself of that as was natural in the way I went on—and I have at least derived that advantage from the Vice—to *Love* in the better sense of the word—*this* will be my last adventure." And in October 1821 he wrote to his sister about the relationship with Teresa, saying: "This is 'positively the last time of performance.' "

On the other hand, there is the old nostalgia for a life made meaningful through action, and a feeling that love is no longer a sufficient adventure by itself. "I am a little tired of this effeminate way of life," he wrote in August 1819, only four months after the affair began. In the heart of what, from some angles, looks remarkably like happiness, Byron remained at war.

To Hobhouse he wrote: "I feel & feel it bitterly—that a man should not consume his life at the side and on the bosom—of a woman. . . . But I have neither the strength of mind to break my chain, nor the insensibility which would deaden it's weight. . . . I have luckily or unluckily no ambition left—it would be better if I had—it would at least awake me—whereas at present I merely start in my sleep." This mood, captured in the first months of the affair, was perhaps a luxury, a self-indulgence that Teresa's love for him allowed. But it was never far away.

From the summer of 1819 until his return to Greece in 1823, he thought over and over the possibilities of escape. Greece he never mentions in his correspondence until May 1821, just after the outbreak of the Independence War. Even then, it is without any special enthusiasm. All through this period, it is not Europe but the Americas that most interest him. "There is no freedom in Europe—that's certain," he wrote to Hobhouse in October 1819. "It is besides a worn out portion of the globe."

Of the two Americas, the North appealed to him only in passing. To Hobhouse he wrote: 'The Anglo-Americans are a little too coarse for me—and their climate too cold." The real attraction was the South; and, in the end, his indecisiveness was to deprive the world of a Latin American Byron, leaving the way open for the Greek Byron who now seems so entirely natural.

His idea in 1819 was to go to Venezuela, recently liberated from Spanish control by the glorious exploits of Simón Bolívar. He thought of taking Allegra with him, his daughter by Claire Clairmont. He would learn Spanish and become a settler, perhaps even a citizen, of a free country. "I should go there . . . and pitch my tent for good and all," he wrote. "Better be a[n] unskillful planter—an awkward settler—better be a hunter—or anything than a flatterer of fiddlers—and a fan-carrier of a woman."

At the end of 1819, Byron moved from Venice to Ravenna, where Teresa was living with her husband. He took with him a young and very large gondolier named Giovanni Battista Falcieri. One of Byron's most faithful servants, he would be with him until the end at Mesolongi.

Byron was glad to leave Venice. Much as he loved the city, he had grown to dislike the political climate and its influence on the inhabitants. Venice had long been in luxurious decline when she finally lost her independence in the aftermath of the French Revolution. A plaything between two great powers, she came out of the Napoleonic period under the domination of Austria. The people of Venice, Byron wrote, were "perhaps the most oppressed in Europe." They reminded him of a lesson he had learned in Greece: "Where there is no independence—there can be no real self-respect."

Ravenna was different. There he found, among Teresa's family, a model of aristocratic rebelliousness that he much admired. Not that Ravenna was a free city. It had been part of Napoleon's Kingdom of Italy and, after Napoleon's fall, had been returned to the jurisdiction of the pope in Rome. The administration of the Papal States was renowned for its bigotry and corruption. Nevertheless, the old aristocracy of Ravenna enjoyed freedoms that were unknown in Venice.

Prominent among those who were active in the cause of Italian freedom were Teresa's father, Ruggero, and her brother, Pietro. Father and son were to lead Byron deep into Italian politics and, in August 1820, he was initiated into the secret revolutionary society of the Carbonari. Later, after Byron had gone to Greece, Teresa's father would spend six years in prison for his political activities. Pietro, who had fallen under Byron's spell, accompanied him on the Greek adventure, and died in Greece of fever in 1827.

Ravenna was a romantic place for Byron. Its glory lay even farther in the past than the glory of Venice. It had been the capital of the Western Roman Empire and its decline had already begun eleven centuries before. In the early nineteenth century, it was unvisited. On New Year's Eve, 1819, Byron wrote to his wife, with unusual nostalgia: "I speak to you from another country—and as it were from another world—for this city of Italy is out of the track of armies and travellers and is more of the old time."

In Ravenna he moved into the palazzo that Teresa continued to share with her aging husband. This ménage à trois was less extraordinary than it may now seem. Married women in Teresa's milieu frequently had a lover. By convention he was called her *cavalier servente* or knight-in-waiting, and he was expected to be as permanent as the vagaries of life allowed. He had public recognition, enjoyed almost official status.

So Byron was initiated, not simply into the secrets of Italian poltical life, but into the closed erotic system of aristocratic Ravenna. This system was governed by rules unfathomable to an outsider and Byron's astonishment was understandable: "A man actually becomes a piece of female property," he wrote. "[Ravenna] is a dreadfully moral place—for you must not look at anybody's wife except your Neighbour's, if you [go] to the next door but one—you are scolded—and presumed to be perfidious." In another letter, he reported: "I have been faithful to my honest liaison with Countess Guiccioli. . . . I have not had a whore this half-year—confining myself to the strictest adultery."

For all that he made light of it, the role of gallant, or woman's escort—or whatever name is applied to this strange phenomenon—could hardly have appealed to Byron for long. While it was convenient that he did not have to face the social problems of the immediate breakup of Teresa's marriage, his acceptance of his position as an attendant lord implied that Teresa was still sleeping with her husband. That was humiliating, from more than one point of view.

Finally, in May 1820, Byron and Teresa transgressed one of the key rules of the erotic code and were discovered almost in the act of making love by Count Guiccioli. A crisis followed. In July, Teresa left the marital home and went to live in her father's house. She lost the respectability of life with her *cavalier servente* and embarked on a new and problematic course, as public mistress of one of the most famous men in Europe.

From the summer of 1819, Byron had been writing back to friends in England, asking about the political situation there. It was a last, and rather hopeless, attempt to see whether he might yet play some role in English political life. "Do you think there will be a row? . . . civil war or any thing in that line?" he wrote naively to one correspondent on 19 August 1819.

This was shortly after the massacre at St. Peter's Fields in Manchester, when mounted yeomen were sent into a crowd of sixty thousand people who were demonstrating in favor of parliamentary reform. The event, by ironic allusion to the Battle of Waterloo, became widely known as Peterloo and it soon entered popular mythology as a symbol of everything that was wrong with the Tory government. Peterloo led, among other things, to the vivid denunciation of Shelley's *Masque of Anarchy* (1820) and to the founding of the *Manchester Guardian*.

Byron briefly hoped that civil war or something "in that line" would enable him to return to England and take his part. But it soon became clear that the state would survive by pursuing its repressive course. Byron's last hope of an English solution was gone.

His letters home on English politics at this time show him as the moderate reformer he always was. He had a hatred of radical politicians and could never understand Hobhouse's drift toward them. "*Radical* is a new word since my time," he wrote to him in 1820. "It was not in the political vocabulary in 1816—when I left England—and I don't know what it means—is it uprooting?"

Democracy, universal suffrage: these, he believed, were dangerous illusions to hang before the discontented, uneducated poor. Radicals were all tyrants in the making, using the mob to "throttle their way to power." In his letters, he mentions a range of diverse figures, who had very little in common, except that he thought them all models of political excess: Robespierre, during the French Revolution; Tom Paine; Henry Hunt, the man who had helped organize the meeting that was attacked at Peterloo.

Byron wrote to his publisher in February 1820: "If we must have a tyrant—let him at least be a gentleman who has been bred to the business, and let us fall by the axe and not by the butcher's cleaver." Here he reveals himself as the eighteenth-century nobleman he so desired to be. The only safe way forward, he believed, was enlightened government by reforming elements within the aristocracy, and in that process he had long hoped to be of service. "I am and have been for *reform* always," he wrote to Hobhouse in June 1819. The problem was that, in England, it seemed as if reform was being driven by the wrong class of people entirely.

Byron's position was not unusual at the time. Both Whigs and Tories generally saw the working class as unsuited to the responsibilities of politics. Memories of the Reign of Terror during the French Revolution remained strong. At the heart of Byron's political attitudes is the feeling, always with him a little vulnerable, that he belonged to a class that was born to rule.

Since England offered no release, Byron turned to the politics of Italy. His involvement there was to be brief and disappointing. It did much to prepare the way for a final escape into the politics of Greece. For a time, however, it was fun and, at the very least, it was different. In a poem he sent to a friend in November 1820, he recognized the comic side of it all:

When a man hath no freedom to fight for at home,
Let him combat for that of his neighbours;
Let him think of the glories of Greece and of Rome,
And get knock'd on the head for his labours.

At the time, the hopes of revolutionary Italians in Ravenna had been raised by a rebellion farther south, in Naples. This was initially successful against one of the most blindly reactionary governments in Europe and gave hope to patriots all over the Italian peninsula.

In the autumn of 1820, in a gesture that appears to have ended in farce, Byron prepared an address to the insurgents of Naples. He introduced himself as "Un Inglese—amico della Libertà" (An Englishman—friend to Liberty), and referred to "the glorious determination of the N[eapolitans] to assert their well-won Independence." He offered money, along with his services "as a simple volunteer . . . without any other motive than that of sharing the destiny of a great nation." The fate of this glorious address is uncertain. It was possibly swallowed by the Neapolitan courier charged with its delivery, as he faced arrest on his way south.

In February 1821, however, Byron could still write: "It is probable that Italy will be delivered . . . if the Neapolitans will but stand firm, and are united among themselves." He bought arms and ammunition for an uprising in Ravenna and stored them in his apartments.

In his journal entry for 19 February 1821 he found excitement everywhere, even in the natural world: "Came home solus [alone]," he wrote, "very high wind—lightning—moonshine— solitary stragglers muffled in cloaks—women in mask—white houses—clouds hurrying over the sky, like spilt milk blown out of the pail. . . . The war approaches nearer and nearer." All this— the dream of revolution, the prospect of a liberated Italy—was what he called "the very *poetry* of politics."

A few days later it was all in ruins as the Neapolitan rebellion collapsed. "The Neapolitans have betrayed themselves & all the

World," Byron wrote, "& those who would have given their blood for Italy can now only give her their tears." While in a different mood, he drew his own disabused conclusions from the wreckage: "As a very pretty woman said to me a few nights ago, with the tears in her eyes, as she sat at the harpsichord, 'Alas! the Italians must now return to making operas.' I fear *that* and maccaroni are their forte."

The failure of the Italian uprising had two consequences for Byron. In the first place, he had lost a cause. He tried to tell himself that it was not "the *real* Italians" who had betrayed Italy but only "the Scoundrels" of the south, but his disenchantment was general.

The cause was one that had made his continued domesticity in Ravenna more acceptable in his own eyes. Without the illusion of action, he fell easily into the inactivity of depression. "An Italian winter is a sad thing," he noted in his journal. The approach of winter was something he feared. Sometimes he even suspected the onset of madness. "This season kills me with sadness every year," he wrote to Teresa in late September 1820; and, thanking her for a gift of roses, he ended: "Love me. My soul is like the leaves that fall in autumn."

The other consequence of the political failure of February 1821 was that Teresa's father and brother were exiled from Ravenna. Byron, now tied to the whole family, realized he, too, would have to leave, and he hated leaving places. "There never *was* such oppression, even in Ireland, scarcely!" he wrote from Ravenna in August 1821. Pietro Gamba and his father, now refugees, went to Bologna, then to Florence, and finally to Pisa, where Byron joined them at the beginning of November.

Byron left behind him, in the care of his banker, the debris of his vast menagerie: a badger, a goat with a broken leg, and two aging monkeys.

In Pisa, Byron moved into a Renaissance palazzo, the Casa Lanfranchi, on the banks of the River Arno. Teresa lived in another palazzo nearby; and her brother Pietro acted as Byron's secretary, a role he would continue to fulfill until the end of Byron's life.

The Casa Lanfranchi was "large enough for a garrison," Byron reported to his publisher. It was full of ghosts. Fletcher, he said, "has begged leave to change his room—and then refused to occupy his *new* room—because there were more Ghosts there than in the other."

Byron and Shelley were once again much in each other's company in Pisa. Shelley had been living there since January 1820 and had gathered around him a group of friends who shared his literary interests. Shelley was the only one with any talent, but Byron fell naturally into this society. Life promised to be a pleasant, if undemanding, round of sociability, while he pursued his relationship with Teresa, on the one hand, and the writing of *Don Juan*, on the other.

In January 1822, the circle was enlarged by the arrival of Edward John Trelawny. Trelawny was only a little younger than Byron, though he was to survive him by almost sixty years. Easily the most colorful, and in many ways the most interesting, of Byron's acquaintances, he would be at his side when the Greek adventure began in 1823.

Trelawny was the son of outstandingly disagreeable parents. As a boy he had been sent to a school that was remarkable for its brutality, even by the standards of the day. In protest, he had led a mutiny among his fellow pupils and had publicly flogged the assistant master. After a spell in solitary confinement on bread and water, his school days had ended and he left, still only twelve years old, to join the even more brutalized world of the British Royal Navy.

He had been to India, to South America, and to Java, where he had fallen sick in a cholera epidemic. His experiences, even unvarnished, were extraordinary enough. In Pisa, however, some demon drove him to reinvent his past so that it became, not simply dramatic, but magical, legendary. He turned himself into the perfect romantic man of action, a teller of tales in which he was forever the hero. He became a pirate, a lion hunter, the lover of faraway princesses. In Greece, after 1823, he went even further, pursuing in reality a life that looked remarkably like the fictions of his imagination.

For all that, Trelawny's importance in Byron's Greece is limited. Byron found him an amiable companion, but he was never completely taken in. "Trelawny would be a good fellow if he could spell and speak the truth," is a remark plausibly attributed to Byron by several observers. Moreover, the two were only together in Greece for a short time. Byron committed himself to events in the west and ended his life in Mesolongi, while Trelawny went off to engage his vast fantasies with a guerrilla band on Mount Parnassus.

What is interesting is how reckless Trelawny was in Greece, how cautious Byron seems beside him. A comparison between the two, what they did, who their friends were, will say much about the way the Independence War was fought and the kind of problems it raised for all outsiders.

Before Greece, however, there was the death of Shelley and its unforgettable aftermath. Shelley's death and cremation, one of the great set pieces of romantic drama, found Trelawny at the center of events. While Byron, apparently detached but inevitably moved, stood by and wondered at mortality.

In the spring of 1822, Shelley, with his wife and some friends, moved from Pisa to spend a season by the sea. They took a house on the Gulf of Spezia. It was a wild place, and, according to Mary Shelley, the local inhabitants were even wilder. "Our near neighbours," she wrote, "were more like savages than any people I ever before lived among. Many a night they passed on the beach, singing or rather howling, the women dancing about among the waves that broke at their feet, the men leaning against the rocks and joining in their loud wild chorus."

It was not the best of times. Mary was recovering from a miscarriage and found housekeeping in so remote a place difficult to bear. Shelley, for his part, was writing little. As he explained in a letter: "I have lived too long near Lord Byron and the sun has extinguished the glow-worm." The summer, unusually, was without rain, the heat, as always, oppressive.

In May, they took delivery of a boat they had commissioned in Genoa. They had bought her as a plaything for their months by the sea. Shelley wanted to call her the *Ariel*, but for some reason—apparently at Trelawny's suggestion—she was named the *Don Juan*, after Byron's greatest poem.

At the beginning of July, Shelley took his new boat for a short visit to Livorno. He met friends, saw Byron, went with him to Pisa. Then, in the afternoon of 8 July, he set sail again, with two others, to return home.

Trelawny saw them off and then watched through a telescope as they headed out to sea under a darkening sky. Toward early evening a storm broke. The *Don Juan* went down into the Gulf of Spezia, ten miles west of Viareggio, and stories of the death of Shelley began to multiply.

A week after the storm, two mutilated bodies were washed ashore, followed, a few days later, by a third. Trelawny claimed he had seen this third body, before the local health authorities buried it in quicklime on the beach. He identified it as Shelley's. A month passed and then, in the middle of August, he obtained permission to exhume the deformed corpses and cremate them on the spot.

Through all the period of waiting and uncertainty, Trelawny showed himself a model organizer. He had a portable iron furnace built in Livorno for the burning of the bodies and then he descended on the beach, like a Gothic magus, to conduct the last rites. Byron, too, went down to witness the scene, bringing the coffins in his carriage. Then, according to his own testimony, he went for a swim.

A few soldiers and fishermen watched on the burning sand, and Byron's horses wilted in the heat, as Shelley was cremated. Trelawny threw frankincense, salt, sugar, and wine onto the fire. It "made the yellow flames glisten and quiver," he remembered later. Byron seemed also to have been moved by the theatricality of the scene: "You can have no idea," he wrote, "what an extraordinary effect such a funeral pile has, on a desolate shore, with mountains in the back-ground and the sea before, and the singular appearance the salt and frankincense gave to the flame."

This shoreline is still desolate. Once, on a gray July afternoon, I followed Byron's descent, from the mouth of the River Serchio down toward the Tenuta di San Rossore, now one of the official residences of the president of Italy. The day was full of the damp heat of a north Italian summer. Byron's mountains—the Apuane Hills—were almost lost in the gray haze. Along the beach there were huge dead trees, stripped and bleached. Oil drums, old refrigerators, mountains of plastic and glass. Rubbish in every stage of decomposition. People lay out sunbathing in the sunless air, or sweated the afternoon away in bamboo shelters.

Just before San Rossore is the Fiume Morto, the Dead River that carries Pisa's refuse to the sea. I sat for a long time on the concrete retaining wall, watching a man and his young son as they fished, motionless, where the water turns yellow and green.

Here, between the Arno and the Serchio, on 17 and 18 July 1822, Byron came looking for the body of Shelley. What happened out in the gulf will never be known for certain. But of all the versions of Shelley's death, the most romantic is the one repeated in Richard Holmes's biography, *Shelley: The Pursuit*. According to this account, Shelley went down with his ship under full sail, a grandly suicidal gesture worthy of a poet only weeks away from his thirtieth birthday. Making no attempt to save himself, he surrendered to the waves in the fullness of youth.

What effect this mythic end had on Byron is hard to say. He must have felt the horror of sudden death, but he might have envied it, too, for its suddenness. Perhaps Shelley's death was the one Byron should have had, rather than the slow draining away of his life in Mesolongi. Perhaps the cremation on the beach was the romantic apotheosis he might also have wanted. But Byron gives little away, says little about his feelings, neither then nor later.

From the spring of 1822 onward, Byron's life was a succession of crises. On 20 April his daughter Allegra died, aged five. In July, Teresa's father and brother were banished once again, and were forced to leave Pisa for Genoa. The death of Shelley, with its long-drawn conclusion on the beach, completed the cycle of disasters.

The Pisan group broke up. At the same time, Byron's health began to deteriorate. After a long swim in the sun on the day of Shelley's cremation, his skin blistered and peeled. This was followed by fever and a period of chronic sickness. To combat the effects of his illness, he ate less and less. Shelley's cousin, Thomas Medwin, wrote that he had "starved himself into an unnatural thinness." All that winter he was sick and by the spring of 1823 he had still not recovered. "I have not been so robustious as formerly," he wrote on 2 April, "ever since last summer, when I fell ill after a long swim in the Mediterranean."

In the middle of September 1822, Hobhouse arrived in Pisa for a short visit. It was to be the last time the two of them ever met. Byron was preparing to join Teresa's exiled family in Genoa and the visit passed amid the chaos of removal. Byron finally left Pisa at the end of September, riding in the same Napoleonic carriage that had brought him out of England in 1816.

The winter was cold and damp. Byron continued to diet and often ate alone. He was, in his own words, "as temperate as an Anchorite." His letters give the impression of a life winding down, while another begins to shape itself in confusion. Failure, loss of health, the approach of middle age, had all diminished his energy. His present seemed an aimless state of wandering from town to town, his emotional world one of love for Teresa, marked by ever decreasing passion.

．　　．　　．

There came a point when it seems he would have welcomed almost any offer of escape. When the call to action finally came, however, it was so tentative it might easily have passed unnoticed. It is contained in a letter from Hobhouse, dated 2 March 1823. The letter is an innocent ragbag of gossip, with a few thoughts on the political situation of the day. Hobhouse even talked of the possibility that Byron might come home to England for a month or two. Then, in what looks like an afterthought, he added a final sentence: "Blaquier is going thro' Genoa on a sort of mission to Greece—he will call on you."

Edward Blaquiere, former Royal Navy lieutenant and, like Hobhouse, a member of the recently founded London Greek Committee, was indeed on a mission of sorts. At Hobhouse's suggestion, he called on Byron in Genoa on 5 April 1823. There he handed Byron a lifeline and Byron, very cautiously, took it. From then on, the return to Greece became every day more certain.

Nine

I am ashes where once I was fire,
  And the bard in my bosom is dead,
What I loved I now merely admire—
  And my heart is as grey as my head.

—Byron, "To the Countess of Blessington," 1823

A biographer's dream of a life is one full of action, finally rounded out in tranquillity. The time for loose ends, the luxury of a measured retrospection. As the pace gracefully falters and the hero is conducted toward death, the biographer is left behind with all the satisfaction of a well-filled life. The early years, the years of fame; then, at last, into the twilight or the gathering gloom. A model of completeness that any observer, from either side of the grave, might wish for themselves.

Reality intrudes, of course, insists that death often arrives in the middle of the night, with the project half-finished, the letters unanswered, the lawn uncut. Such sudden endings eliminate the space in which meaning has time to form. For an unfinished story is simply that—unfinished, the sense scattered across the missing pages.

But worse, still, than a life that ends abruptly is the life that drifts into silence, unredeemed even by the illusion that death is its own form of drama. Byron's last surviving letter from Greece, written in Mesolongi on 9 April 1824, lacks even the hint of an ending. He wrote simply to check on his bank balance and to protest that Lord Blessington had bought a boat from him without paying for it. After this last and altogether unmemorable letter, Byron rode out on his horse, got wet in the rain, and died ten days later.

On 4 March 1824 he had written: "It were better to die doing something than nothing." His domestic death, yet so far from home, seems a mockery of the old desire for action. But in a small rainy town in the middle of a long war, there was not a great deal for anyone to do, except wait for the coming of spring. Then, according to the seasonal rhythms of the Independence War, the Turkish navy would sail down leisurely from Constantinople, the paths through the mountains would dry out, and the thoughts of men would once again turn to fighting. On 17 March, Byron wrote to Teresa with news of the first swallow; but by then his death was only a month away.

No heroism, no climax, no meaningful end. Yet it would be perverse to wander through Mesolongi today and pretend that nothing of importance had ever happened there. In the Garden of the Heroes, on the northern edge of town, Byron's statue appears as natural as the palm trees that surround it, more natural certainly than either would be in England. So there is the problem for the biographer of Byron's last days. Two stories, apparently irreconcilable; one of drab decline, the other of unforgettable sacrifice.

There is no shortage of witnesses for the last days of Byron's life. A number of those who knew him in Mesolongi have left records of what he did or said at the time. They were men who came, like Byron himself, because Mesolongi was the center of political power in western Greece; or else, like Teresa's brother Pietro Gamba, they were there because Byron was there.

The testimony of these witnesses is always interesting, but it faces in different directions and gives a range of Byrons to suit all prejudices: self-destructive, despairing, jovial, calculating. Byron lost in drink, Byron on the edge of nervous collapse. Byron as bureaucrat and administrator, Byron as banker to a nation.

It is too easy to say that he was all of these things, went through all of these moods. Yet those who observed Byron most closely were indeed struck by the constant changes in him. Julius Millingen, in his *Memoirs of the Affairs of Greece*, wrote:

> It may literally be said, that at different hours of the day he metamorphosed himself into four or more individuals, each possessed of the most opposite qualities. . . . In the course of the day he might become the most morose, and the most gay; the most melancholy, and the most frolicsome; the most generous, and the most penurious; the most benevolent, and the most misanthropic; the most rational, and the most childish . . . the most gentle being in existence, and the most irascible. . . .

Nothing in Byron's character is more susceptible to misinterpretation than this infinite variety. It seems inevitable that a man possessed by such capacity for change must be merely erratic in all things, and the charge has often been made. Byron the inconstant is a label that has survived down the years. Of all those who observed him in the last months, one of the few to engage with the complexities of his changing nature was George Finlay, participant in the Greek War and subsequently its historian.

Finlay's own copy of *Memoirs of the Affairs of Greece* is now in the library of the British School at Athens. Against Millingen's passage, quoted above, Finlay made a penciled note in the margin: "This very true, and it was strange pliability of character, joined to the deep powers of his mind, that enabled him to receive all these impressions with such force that the past or the future had no influence on the present."

Here Finlay registers what Byron in *Don Juan* called "mobility": the painful receptivity to immediate impressions. Finlay scarcely knew Byron. He met him on the island of Kefallinia in

October 1823, then saw him again in Mesolongi in February 1824. But he was an acute observer, and, in the following passage from his *History of the Greek Revolution*, he showed how far he was able to follow Byron in his understanding of the paradox of change:

> Both [Byron's] character and his conduct presented unceasing contradictions. It seemed as if two different souls occupied his body alternately. One was feminine, and full of sympathy; the other masculine, and characterised by clear judgement. When one arrived the other departed. In company, his sympathetic soul was his tyrant. Alone, or with a single person, his masculine prudence displayed itself as his friend. No man could then arrange facts, investigate their causes, or examine their consequences, with more logical accuracy, or in a more practical spirit. Yet, in his most sagacious moment, the entrance of a third person would derange the order of his ideas,—judgement fled, and sympathy, generally laughing, took its place. Hence he appeared in his conduct extremely capricious, while in his opinions he had really great firmness.

For all its gender bias, this is deeper than the judgments of many of those who knew Byron better, those whom the mobility of his character threatened or repelled, or those who, like Shelley, were simply dazzled by the sun.

The pattern of ever changing moods, set against an underlying constancy, makes the biographer's task a delicate one. Anything said about Byron's state of mind in the final months of his life can be opposed by a dozen examples in contradiction. This quickly gives the impression of a man living in turmoil, the image of Byron that so often survives at the end. The situation is made more complex still by the fact that he was a famous man when he returned to Greece. For fame hardens reactions, and many of the surviving accounts are colored by an anticipation of the man

Byron was supposed to be, rather than by the experience of the man he was.

Over the years, Byron's motives in returning to Greece have been the subject of long and detailed suspicion. There are two main lines of criticism, at first sight mutually contradictory. It has been said that Byron was an impetuous adventurer, a romantic grown old before his time; that he was driven back to Greece in a last attempt to recover a youthful world in which he had once been happy. Or else that Byron was a pathetic, indecisive figure who returned to Greece almost by accident, caught out of his depth in a situation he neither foresaw nor understood.

Byron as futile actor, Byron as helpless spectator. Either way, Greece often seems to be a cause from which he emerges without credit, restored only by the transformations of history in the wake of a pointless death. The criticism is as relentless today as it ever was, not least in England, whereas Greece itself offers an alternative vision, a country where the generosity of Byron's act is still largely uncontested.

In April 1821, Shelley and his wife, Mary, were in Pisa when they heard news of the outbreak of the Greek Revolution. "Greece has declared its freedom!" wrote Mary on 2 April, in a letter to Byron's former lover, Claire Clairmont. As if the end were inevitable and already in sight, she concluded: "What a delight it will be to visit Greece free."

A few weeks later, on 20 May 1821, Byron mentions the Greek War for the first time in his own correspondence. To Hobhouse he says simply: "Our Greek acquaintances are making a fight for it." The governments of Europe, he added, will find themselves in a dilemma, frightened by the example of revolution, but happy at the possibility of the defeat of Turkey. Two weeks later, on 4 June, he wrote to his old friend Thomas Moore: "The Greeks! what think you? They are my old acquaintances—but what to think I know not. Let us hope howsomever."

The contrast says a good deal. There is an unreality about Mary Shelley's enthusiasm, a naiveté about her idea of Greek freedom. Byron, on the other hand, was cautious from the very beginning; conscious of the political context in which the Greek War would be fought, fully aware that, because of the small-scale nature of Greek society, some of the insurgents were bound to be people he had known.

At no point in Byron's surviving correspondence is there a trace of Mary Shelley's uncomplicated rejoicing. Byron inches toward Greece at the speed of the snail and without deep passion. Not because he didn't believe in the value of what he called over and over again the "cause," but because he understood from the start how messy it was all going to be. The best an outsider could do was to wish the cause well and hope for a speedy end.

The first hint that Byron was thinking of going to Greece comes on 14 September 1821, almost two years before he finally left Italy. Strangely perhaps, and no doubt by coincidence, it is in a letter to his wife, Annabella, that the idea first surfaces. He talks to her of his disappointment with contemporary Italian politics; then says: "At present I am going into Tuscany—and if the Greek business is not settled soon—shall perhaps go up that way."

To his friend Thomas Moore, a few days after this, he wrote: "I wanted to go to Greece lately." He blamed his relationship with Teresa for his failure to do so, talking of "the tears of a woman who has left her husband for a man and the weakness of one's own heart." By August 1822, he was still in Italy and still blaming his love affair for his indecisiveness. Had it not been for Teresa, he said in a letter to Moore, he would long ago have gone to South America or to Greece.

When he thought of escape and compared Greece with the Americas, a painful difference always drew him across the Atlantic, rather than back to the East. South America had Bolívar, the North had Washington: two revolutionary heroes Byron could wholeheartedly admire. Greece had no leader of that stature. It was a fragmented country, backward, controlled in practice by dozens of local chieftains whose aim in life was generally the mere accumulation of power.

Since his first visit to Greece, Byron's political views had slowly evolved. He had moved, unwillingly at first, but irreversibly, toward a belief that republican government was the logical choice for the future. He had even come to believe that it would one day be the salvation of England. In his journal in 1821, he wrote: "There is nothing left for Mankind but a Republic—and I think that there are hopes of Such—the two Americas (South and North) have it . . . all thirst for it—Oh Washington!"

In 1800, the French novelist Benjamin Constant, looking back over the early years of the Revolution and Napoleon's rise to power, had written:

> The struggle of which we have been the witnesses and often the victims has always been at heart the struggle of the elective system against the hereditary. This is the main question of the French Revolution and, one might say, the question of the century.

For all his continuing attachment to the virtues of a hereditary nobility, Byron had moved a long way by the 1820s. He had grown to admire republicanism as the only way out of the frozen politics of old Europe. "Whenever an American requests to see me," he wrote in his journal, "I comply . . . because I respect a people who acquired their freedom by firmness without excess." That was Byron's ideal revolution: firmness without excess. It was a model he knew could have no meaning in Greece, and his commitment to republicanism there was to be severely undermined by experience.

It is not strange, then, that Greece continued for many months as a fluctuating, never very positive, image in Byron's mind. Byron wanted to escape. This was partly for the sake of escaping, the hope of a new start—and Greece could hardly be that. At the same time, however, there was something vaguely moral and redemptive about his desires. He needed to escape in order to do something with his life, and it was this, in the end, that would carry the day for Greece.

He never expressed his search for commitment in a complex way. He feared moral posturing, hypocrisy, more than almost anything. Often, indeed, he wrote so simply that he sounds decidedly naive, as in a letter of September 1822, where he talks of a plan "to go amongst the Greeks or Americans—and do some good."

Of course, when Byron talked of doing good, his motives were as complex as anyone's. Few virtues are harder to penetrate than altruism, after all. But there was something else, something particular to his own recent history. When Thomas Moore saw him in Venice in October 1819, he found Byron haunted by the idea that his reputation in England would persecute him beyond the grave. This was the time when Byron wrote Hobhouse one of his bitterest letters of exile: "You must not talk to me of England. . . . I had a house—and lands—and a wife and child—and a name there—once."

Of all these, only his name was conceivably recoverable. The rest was hopeless. His house and lands had been sold and it was as clear as could be that he would never see his wife and child again. As the years passed, however, attitudes toward him in England were hardening. His sexual abandon, his loathing of English society, the writing of *Don Juan*, with its moral and religious provocations—all of this made him more than ever the outcast, his name more than ever reviled.

Doing good, as he liked to call it, was a chance to restore some self-respect. In March 1823 he wrote: "I am at this moment the most unpopular man in England," which, whatever its truth, reveals an anguish undiminished by time or distance. In *Don Juan*, he had claimed to have "shunned the common shore" and skimmed the "Ocean of Eternity." But eternity threatened to be a lonely resting place. A return to Greece might heal present anguish and cure whatever wounds the future held in store after his death.

For all that, his concerns should not be simply misread as a search for glory. As Byron pointed out himself, he had known enough of fame to understand its instability. He did not want more of that, but the cleansing satisfaction of a job well done. Very occasionally, in his correspondence about Greece, more romantic desires come to the surface; but what is generally remarkable about the letters he wrote before leaving Italy is their practical tone. He knew what he wanted out of helping Greece; or, at least, knew what it was sensible to want. In general, that is what he pursued.

From the autumn of 1822, Byron was increasingly anxious to sort out his finances. He made efforts to pay off old debts, to realize his assets, in case of a sudden move. So when Edward Blaquiere, agent of the London Greek Committee, came to call on him in April 1823, he found an easy conquest. But even then, at the moment when escape suddenly looked so close and so easy, Byron never lost sight of his own limitations and the limits of the situation.

To Hobhouse on 7 April 1823 he wrote to report on his meeting with Blaquiere: "[I] have even offered to go up to the Levant in July—if the Greek provisional Government think that I could be of any use.— —It is not that I could pretend to anything in a military capacity . . . nor is it much that an individual foreigner can do in any other way—but perhaps as a reporter of the actual state of things there—or in carrying on any correspondence between them and their western friends—I might be of use—at any rate I would try."

This is the basis on which Byron was willing to go back: on a fact-finding mission, for which his previous experience of Greece and his international fame as a poet suited him well. Yet still, for two months after Blaquiere's visit, he hesitated before making a final decision. There were always obstacles: Teresa, his uncertain health, an unsettled lawsuit in England. On 23 May, however, he was writing: "I am doing all I can to get away"; and, on 15 June: "I am at last determined to go to Greece."

In his anxiety not to appear the adventurer he knew many would think he was, Byron placed himself firmly under the guidance of the London Greek Committee. In a letter to the secretary of the committee, John Bowring, in May 1823, he made it clear that he would obey their instructions to the letter, "whether conformable to my own private opinion or not." This approach was sensible in theory. In practice, it did him no good, since most members of the committee knew much less about Greece than he did himself.

The London Greek Committee was formed at the Crown and Anchor Tavern on 3 March 1823. Its foundation was a symbol of a changing political climate in England. In 1822, the British foreign secretary Castlereagh had committed suicide and he had been succeeded by George Canning. Castlereagh, whom Byron called "the most despotic in intention and the weakest in intellect that ever tyrannised over a country," had been a firm believer in the value of collective security. Europe's only defense against revolution, he had argued, was for the major powers to hold an authoritarian line against all change, whatever its source.

Under Canning, the policy atmosphere was immediately different. He was much less interested in the alliances that had bound Europe together since the fall of Napoleon. "Things are getting back to a wholesome state again," he remarked, "every nation for itself and God for us all." Byron admired Canning, called him a genius, one who was "worth all the rest in point of talent." A small revolution in Greece could be easily accommodated within Canning's worldview. The formation of the London Greek Committee was an early response to this opening space.

Anyone who has ever been involved with solidarity work will recognize the atmosphere of the Greek Committee, its strengths and failings. The late-night meetings, the heady resolutions, the infectious excitement of exotic politics; the sectarianism, which sometimes stems from policy differences, more often from simple clashes of personality; the way work is done by a handful of people, already overstretched by commitments elsewhere. "All the efforts, money, time & talking," Hobhouse wrote of the Greek Committee, "all come from the same set of people . . . about four or five good men & true."

Familiar, too, are the heartbreaking ventures into the outside world, the attempts to raise consciousness among the hostile and indifferent. Blaquiere, an endless campaigner, wrote after visiting a couple of English cities on behalf of the Greek cause: "I could not have thought this country possessed two places so degraded and narrow minded."

The Greek Committee also shared the high seriousness that is characteristic of solidarity movements the world over. Always under siege from charges of irrelevance, of being more concerned with other people's business than their own, solidarity groups find a natural refuge in high-mindedness. So Hobhouse, in a letter to Byron of June 1823, took care to advise him on how to handle his relations with the committee. He knew how much Byron distrusted solemnity: "You must not be waggish," he wrote. "I recommend you only to show the grave side of your face . . . do not be jocose with your admirers of the committee."

Of the many problems facing solidarity groups, the most serious is how to deal with bad news; how to handle the unpalatable truths that are part of every struggle, the devastating revelations that strike at the idealism that sustains solidarity itself.

I remember long discussions within the El Salvador solidarity movement in the late 1970s, as it became clear that Roque Dalton, the nation's finest poet, had been murdered by his own comrades in the Revolutionary Army of the People. Everyone resisted the truth for as long as possible, and even longer—not out of a collective mendacity, but because it was impossible to believe he could have died in such a way. Few understood at the time how brutal were the divisions in the liberation movement. Finally, not knowing what to do with the truth, we chose simply to ignore it.

Byron was a genuine victim of this kind of treachery. Not

knowing what was happening in Greece, he looked to the London Greek Committee for advice, telling Hobhouse what he had told John Bowring: "I shall confine myself to following . . . directions." But the weeks went by and no one gave him any directions. So he kept on waiting in Genoa, thinking of how to leave Teresa, of the sort of welcome he might expect in Greece.

He knew that going into the war zone would not be "a party of pleasure." He had met some of the European officers who had been to Greece in the early years of the war and who were returning in disgust at what they had seen. But with no secure knowledge of recent events, and in the absence of guidance from London, he fell into the simplest of traps. Blaquiere had gone to Greece after meeting Byron in Genoa, and, because of his connections with the London Greek Committee, Byron believed he could rely on the information that he was sending back in his letters.

Hobhouse, in a letter to Byron of July 1823, wrote: "[Blaquiere] is not our agent [that is, not an agent of the committee]. We pay some of his expenses & he writes us letters." Nevertheless, Byron saw no reason to doubt his advice; in any case, he knew of no one who was better placed.

Blaquiere has been universally damned. He understood something of the nature of war, for he had been a naval officer during the days of the struggle against Napoleon. But he was a propagandist by nature, not a witness. From Greece, he wrote Byron the kind of letters he thought would appeal. He wanted Byron to come, fully realizing the propaganda value his presence would have for the Greek cause: "Anxious to see your Lordship in this land of heroes," was the typical conclusion to one of his letters at the end of April 1823.

William St. Clair suggests that Blaquiere was "guilty of every easy trick of suppression, distortion and smear that marks the unscrupulous partisan or the unshakeable fanatic." The judgment is unnecessarily harsh. Yet, without Blaquiere's enthusiasm, it is true that Byron would probably never have returned to

Greece. The irony, often unnoticed, is that in the end Blaquiere had a change of heart. He wrote to Byron in Genoa, advising him not to make the journey while conditions remained as they were. But when the letters arrived, Byron had already set sail. The warnings followed him on, down to the Greek islands. By then, however, he had gone too far in his commitment to the war and there was no turning back.

> My dear T.—You must have heard that I am going to Greece. Why do you not come to me? I want your aid, and am exceedingly anxious to see you. Pray come, for I am at last determined to go to Greece; it is the only place I was ever contented in. . . . They all say I can be of use in Greece. I do not know how, nor do they; but at all events let us go.

Byron's invitation to Trelawny, romantic and a little world-weary, was sent on 15 June 1823. Trelawny immediately responded and arrived in Genoa as Byron was making the final preparations for departure.

As usual, Byron was not traveling empty-handed. He had chartered a boat called the *Hercules* to take him to Greece. He had ordered medical supplies, enough to last a thousand men for two years. He bought arms and ammunition for the cause and some scarlet and gold uniforms for himself and his staff. He had two neo-Homeric helmets made, one for himself, one for Trelawny. His own, now exhibit 3715 in the National Historical Museum in Athens, has the family coat of arms and the motto of the Byrons: "Crede Byron" (Trust Byron).

He engaged a young Italian doctor as his personal physician, a man named Francesco Bruno, fresh from university; and he took Teresa's brother, Pietro Gamba, "a very fine, brave fellow," Byron called him; Pietro, he said, was "wild about liberty," and, ever since the failure of Italian hopes in 1820, he had wanted to go to Spain or Greece to fight for freedom there.

On 13 July, Byron, Trelawny, Gamba, and Bruno went on

board the *Hercules*. They embarked four of Byron's horses and one of Trelawny's, along with a bulldog, and an enormous Newfoundland called Lyon. This Newfoundland appears in a contemporary picture of Byron in Mesolongi, its head rising almost to Byron's elbow. Lyon would survive the Greek experience to accompany his master's body back to England in 1824. There were also half a dozen servants, including the ever devoted Fletcher and the equally devoted Tita Falcieri, the gondolier who had been with Byron since his Venice days.

More important than any of this was the fortune Byron carried in cash and bills of exchange. Byron was, by now, a very wealthy man. In 1819 he had received payment on the sale of his lands at Newstead; and in 1822 he had inherited a share in a large estate on the death of his mother-in-law. Money, not fame, would determine his prestige and status in Greece. "Cash is the Sinew of war as indeed of most other things—love excepted and occasionally of that too," Byron had written to his banker in April 1823.

The *Hercules* was first becalmed, then driven back to Genoa by a storm. It was not until 16 July that they finally got under way. They then took another five days to cover the eighty sea miles to Livorno. There they took on another volunteer in the Greek cause, James Hamilton Browne. From Livorno, Byron sent a few lines to Teresa and a considerably longer letter to the German poet Goethe: "If ever I come back [from Greece]," he wrote, "I will pay a visit to Weimar to offer the sincere homage of one of the many Millions of your admirers."

They finally left for Greece on 24 July. Byron enjoyed the voyage and it passed without incident. Onboard ship, he fenced with Pietro Gamba and boxed with Trelawny to pass the time and to prepare for whatever trials lay ahead. "You never know a man's temper until you have been imprisoned in a ship with him, or a woman's until you have married her," wrote Trelawny. "I never was on shipboard with a better companion than Byron, he was generally cheerful, gave no trouble, assumed no authority, uttered no complaints."

At the beginning of August, the *Hercules* came in toward the Ionian Islands, retracing Byron's first youthful approach to Greece: the same sea, bluer than the Italian, the same bleached mountains of a dry country, a relief after the wet heat of an Italian summer. "My old seas and mountains," as Byron had once called them, in a letter to his mother, "the only acquaintances I ever found improve upon me." Kefallinia lay to the north, Zakinthos to the south, and it was one of those Greek midsummer days that seem beyond mortality.

Blaquiere had suggested in his letters that they make for the island of Zakinthos. On the advice of James Browne, however, they landed at Kefallinia. Browne knew the Ionian Islands and their politics. Since the downfall of Napoleon they had been under British protection; each island had its own British resident or governor. The resident at Kefallinia was Lieutenant-Colonel Charles James Napier and he was a man with unusually strong pro-Greek feelings. In 1821 he had published an anonymous pamphlet called *War in Greece*, which was the first publication on the Greek War by any English writer.

At Kefallinia Byron and his entourage could be certain of a warm welcome, even though the cargo they carried so obviously flouted the neutrality that Britain observed in the face of the Greek War. Napier was to become a good friend and informant, and Byron was deeply grateful for his kindness.

It was on 3 August 1823 that Byron and his party landed at Argostoli, the capital of Kefallinia. Argostoli has one of the finest settings of any Greek port and, in Byron's time, it had style and elegance. Here, as in the other Ionian Islands, the architectural tradition was unmistakably European. Venice had held the territory for four hundred years and it had never been subject to the economic deprivations of Turkish rule. Of this elegant past, however, nothing survives today, for almost every town and village in the island was flattened by a great earthquake in 1953.

In Argostoli Byron was only a few miles from the war on the

Greek mainland, but it was a secure and comfortable place, somewhere to think and decide what to do next. The process was to take him almost five months, and no aspect of Byron's activity in Greece was ever so criticized as this lengthy period during which he apparently did nothing. Even Thomas Moore, one of his oldest friends, wrote to condemn him for enjoying a holiday in the sun, "instead of pursuing heroic and war-like adventures."

Byron, however, had landed to find that the political situation in Greece was confused and discouraging in the extreme. Moreover, he had, in the words of Pietro Gamba, "a great dread of being taken for a searcher after adventures." The futility of adventuring in the chaotic world of contemporary Greek politics would soon be demonstrated by Trelawny, who left for the war zone in early September and went on to become a guerrilla fighter. His action was immensely colorful but of no value to anyone but himself. That kind of headlong dash was never part of Byron's makeup and in Kefallinia he settled for the unheroic option of waiting.

At the same time, Byron knew his own temperament, the old temptation to inertia and the reassurance of habit. He feared the charge of idleness and worked hard to counter it. But once in Argostoli he had simply no idea what to do. To John Bowring, secretary of the London Greek Committee, he had written a few days before leaving Italy: "I await the commands of the Committee. . . . It would have given me pleasure to have had some more defined instructions before I went." Then on 24 July, off Livorno, he had written again to Bowring, in an even more explicit tone of resentment and unease: "As the Committee has not favoured me with any specific instructions as to any line of conduct they might think it well for me to pursue—I of course have to suppose that I am left to my own discretion."

He had arrived without instructions and his discretion was valueless, since, though he knew Greece well, he understood next to nothing about what was happening in Greece at the time. Worst of all, he had counted on finding Blaquiere in the Ionian Islands. But Blaquiere was in Corfu, on his way home to England.

Byron's dismay is clear from a letter he wrote to him immediately on arrival in Argostoli: "Dear Sir,—Here am I—but where are *you*?—at Corfu they say—but *why*? . . . what ought I to do? . . . the Greek news is here anything but Good."

Trelawny recorded Byron's sense of betrayal at finding himself on this mission with no agenda: "Byron was sorely vexed," he wrote. "The truth flashed across his mind, that he had been merely used as a decoy by the committee. 'Now they have got me thus far they think I must go on. . . . They are deceived, I won't budge a foot farther until I see my way.' "

Byron's despondency in the early weeks was something he made no effort to hide in his letters. To Napier, in September 1823, he wrote: "It is lucky for me so far—that fail or not fail I can hardly be disappointed—for I believed myself on a fool's errand from the outset"; and to Teresa, in early October: "I was a fool to come here but being here I must see what is to be done."

To those back in England, the situation must have looked straightforward. Even now, with the passing of years, Hobhouse's naiveté is embarrassing: "If you go to Greece," he had written to Byron in June 1823, "I do not see the necessity of your staying long—Just go to headquarters and look about you and come away again—A few days or weeks . . . would be quite sufficient." While in December 1823, when his attention had long ceased to be focused on Greece, he wrote: "I think you have done a very wise not to say a very spirited and honorable deed by going to Greece . . . you may depend upon it that it is looked upon quite in the proper light here."

This division, between the airy simplicity of words and the inevitable contradictions of reality, is common enough, but no less disheartening for that. The strange thing is not that Byron was slow to act in Greece, but that, having seen the situation close up, he chose to remain at all.

"Just go to headquarters," Hobhouse had written. The problem for Byron was all in that phrase. For it suggests the order and discipline of conventional war, a war of acknowledged leaders, agreed-upon chains of command. The Greek conflict was anything but that.

To call it the Greek War of Independence is already to go a long way. It is true that some of those who fought saw themselves as Greeks—or, rather, as Hellenes—and that some had an idea of what national independence might mean. Many, however, fell into neither category. Most Greeks called themselves Romans, as they had done since the time of the Roman occupation of Greece and as, familiarly, they still do today. And independence for many meant simply freedom from the immediate and local pressures of the Turkish state.

At the heart of the Greek War is a contradiction. The war was planned or dreamed mainly by the Greeks of the Diaspora, by men who were conscious of the position of Greece in the wider European world. These men lived in Constantinople, Odessa, Marseilles, or Amsterdam. The war, when it came, however, was fought mainly by local chieftains, the *kapetanei*, backed by the peasantry, the lower clergy, the shepherds of the mountains, and the sailors of the Greek islands.

Somewhere in between these two main groups were the resident upper-class Greeks, many of whom had achieved power and riches under the Turks. During the war they threw their influence this way and that, consistent only in their struggle for survival and the protection of their interests.

The Greeks of the Diaspora were driven by the ideal of a nation-state, a modern Greece to which they might return in triumph as conquering heroes. The *kapetanei*, on the other hand, were fighting largely for local power. To them the idea of a nation-state, with a strong central government, was not simply alien but deeply threatening. One of the main sources of the discontent that led to the outbreak of the Greek War in 1821 was hostility to authority. Once fighting men had thrown off this authority, they were unlikely to submit to a new one, particularly at the hands of expatriate Greeks who often knew nothing about the daily lives of the people they dreamed of liberating.

In time, some of the *kapetanei* did come to think on more than a local scale: men like Kolokotronis and Makriyannis, who remain popular icons in Greece and live on as street names in almost every quarter of modern Athens. But the gulf that separated them from the educated Greeks of the Diaspora was still vast. William Henry Humphreys, who was in Greece in the early months of the war, recalled that the Greeks who had returned from France to fight "vaunted the sacrifices they had made in quitting the luxuries of Paris to serve their country." They talked of opera around the dinner table, dressed in smart uniforms, and played at war.

Kolokotronis, on the other hand, is described by Humphreys as "a fine-looking savage," one who "exactly answered the description usually given in romance of a bandit chief." He was the classic representative of a premodern age. He was skilled in telling the future from the bones of sheep and he often decided military matters under the influence of dreams. Almost his entire clan had been massacred by the Turks in the early years of the nineteenth century. When, in the 1830s, he dictated his autobiography, he began: "I was born in the year 1770 . . . under a tree on the hill called Ramavouni."

If Byron's sense of romance might have drawn him, like Trelawny, to the *kapetanei*, his common sense, as well as his natural class affinities, made him side with the European Greeks. "I did not come here to join a faction but a nation," he recorded in his journal in September 1823. Byron understood that Greek freedom would be difficult to achieve without European assistance—political, military, and financial—and he knew that such support would be dependent on the existence of a constitutional state with a clear identity.

What Byron needed above all was a Greek nation builder, someone reliable, authoritative, and preferably heroic, through whom he could express his own practical commitment. In the absence of a Greek Washington, or of any Greek figure who combined the skills of the statesman and the military commander, Byron in the end joined forces with an expatriate Greek from Constantinople, Alexandros Mavrokordatos. His decision to do so, which he finally made in December 1823, would determine the course of the remainder of his short life.

Mavrokordatos came from a famous and wealthy Greek family that had been established in Constantinople in the early years of the seventeenth century. He had served the Turkish state as a high administrator before going into exile in 1818. For Byron he was, by reputation, "the only civilized person . . . amongst the liberators," "the only *Washington* . . . kind of man" among the Greeks. At the turn of the year, the war drew Mavrokordatos to Mesolongi and Byron would soon follow on behind.

If, as soon as he reached Kefallinia in the summer of 1823, Byron understood that the situation in Greece was alarming, it took him a while to see that it was potentially disastrous. The War of Independence had broken out in 1821; in the first two years of fighting, the Greeks had met with much success. By seizing control of the Peloponnese, they had taken the first steps toward the creation of a national state. The two years that followed, though, were a time of civil war in which different groups, individuals, or whole regions competed for the spoils of the conflict.

Mavrokordatos had been elected president of Greece in January 1822. By the spring of 1823, however, he had become an internal exile on the island of Hydra, after Kolokotronis had forced him from office. Byron could not have arrived in Greece at a worse moment. As he said to Hobhouse, in a letter of 11 September 1823, "I must not conceal from you and the Committee that the Greeks appear in more danger from their own divisions than from the attacks of the enemy." Even at that stage, however, he did not fully understand the depths of the crisis on the Greek mainland.

Once in Argostoli, Byron sent out messages in all directions, seeking information. He wrote to Blaquiere in Corfu. He wrote to Metaxas, the military governor at Mesolongi. Most important, he wrote to Markos Botsaris, the Suliote chieftain, whom Mavrokordatos had recommended as "one of the bravest and most honest of the Greek captains," and who was fighting in central

Greece. Then, finally, on 6 September, Trelawny and Browne left for the Peloponnese, carrying letters from Byron to Tripolitza (modern Tripoli), nominally the seat of the Greek government.

A week after arriving in Kefallinia, Byron and his companions decided to take a holiday in Ithaca (modern Ithaki). The closest island to Kefallinia, Ithaca was the terminus for the wanderings of Odysseus and a place that Byron, in the days of his youthful enthusiasm for Greece, had once thought of buying. It was an ideal retreat amid the realities and the fantasies of war.

Trelawny went with him, along with Browne, Francesco Bruno, Pietro Gamba, and the servants. They left the port of Argostoli, in the southwest of Kefallinia, and rode for six hours across the island to Ayia Evfimia, in the northeast. The heat was overpowering, the paths through the mountains, Byron wrote, "worse . . . than I ever met in the course of some years of travel in rough places of many countries." From Ayia Evfimia they crossed the Ithaca strait in an open, four-oared boat, landing at sunset about six miles from Ithaca's capital, Vathi.

They saw no houses, no human signs. Byron wanted to spend the night in one of the many caves along the coast, but Gamba was afraid for his companion's health. So while Byron and the others swam in the warmth of early evening, Browne and Gamba went exploring. They walked for an hour and found a house where they were offered shelter. The whole party moved in for the night and, on the next day, they left for Vathi and the hospitality of the British resident on Ithaca, Captain Wright Knox.

In the days to come they roamed the island in the leisurely way of tourists. They visited some ancient stones that were known locally as the School of Homer and where they came across a Greek Orthodox priest whom Byron had last seen at Livadhia in 1809.

They went out to the Arethousa spring, south of Vathi, a legendary place where Odysseus, on his return from Troy, had found his loyal swineherd Eumaios. The sound of falling water is rare in Greece. It is magical in August, and Byron noted in his journal that the Arethousa spring was a sight "which alone would be worth the voyage." It survives today, though it is less fine than it was in Byron's time, for the course has been much damaged by earthquakes. It lies below a limestone cliff two hundred feet high, called, after Homer, the rock of Korax or "Raven's Crag."

On Ithaca, Byron met refugees from the Greek War, families who had fled from the fighting in the Peloponnese. He provided for them financially, in a gesture that set the tone for much of his work in Greece. There was, no doubt, in all his generosity, something of the patrician delight in helping the deserving poor. Yet his behavior was entirely in the spirit of Greek society.

Greece was, as it remains, a country of paternalistic relationships, a place where to be lucky means having a rich uncle or an influential cousin. Byron, whether in Ithaca, Kefallinia, or later in Mesolongi, fell easily into a social role for which his own temperament had long prepared him.

Moreover, giving always has a political value. The fact that Byron had committed his fame to Greece mattered a good deal in the wider world, and would matter enormously after his death. But it counted for almost nothing in Greece itself. There what mattered, as he knew, was money.

Money was prestige; it was influence and power. The scarlet and gold uniforms he had brought from Italy may have pandered to some personal arrogance, but they were also entirely justified by their effect. Byron knew how to impress, knew the importance of creating an appeal that was immediate and material. The Europeans who worked with Mavrokordatos soon noticed how much he was disadvantaged by the plain clothes he wore, in contrast to the dazzling Albanian dress of the *kapetanei*.

Byron was alone in Greece, with no authority except what he could win by his own actions. Once, in Mesolongi, he placed six eggs in a line on the ground and then picked them off, one by one, with his pistols. The gesture, in what was then a frontier town, was doubly impressive. He was a fine shot by any standards. But he was also shooting with English pistols, more beautiful, more expensive, above all more accurate, than anything the Greeks around him possessed. Exhibitionism too was a way to power.

On 17 August the party returned from Ithaca to Kefallinia. On the way back to Argostoli, Byron fell ill. How seriously is unclear. The two most extravagant accounts come from Browne and Trelawny, and they show Byron succumbing to a violent physical and mental attack. Both accounts, however, are unconvincing in the detail.

Byron's temporary illness may have been due to the fatigue of travel in the heat of a Greek summer, or it might have been the forerunner of a serious convulsive attack he suffered in mid-February 1824. That Byron himself was not unduly worried by his health in the summer of 1823 is suggested by his own account of the very different circumstances six months later. In his journal for 17 February 1824, he recorded that he had suffered "a strong shock of a Convulsive description" two days previously, and he commented: "This is the first attack that I have had of this kind to the best of my belief."

Once back in Argostoli, Byron quickly recovered. But he was much disturbed by reports from Greece and soon he began to recognize that the situation on the mainland was deteriorating with every week that passed. The first bad news to reach him— though it turned out to be false—was that Mavrokordatos was dead. Had it been true, it would not have been surprising, since Kolokotronis tried at least twice to have him assassinated. The reality, if less final, was still deeply troubling. For Mavrokordatos was in hiding, in fear of his life.

More bad news followed quickly. Markos Botsaris, one of the most trustworthy of all the military leaders, had fallen in action in the mountains of central Greece. A letter from Botsaris, full of enthusiasm, inviting Byron to join him, reached Kefallinia on 22 August. By then Botsaris was already dead. So, as Pietro Gamba wrote: "Of the two patriots whom Lord Byron and Europe most esteemed, and to whom he was particularly recommended, one was no more, and the other was a refugee."

In November, Byron became aware of Greece's full descent into civil war. His position throughout these months was that he would only move from Kefallinia on the instructions of what he called, in October 1823, "the actual G[ree]k G[overnment]." Increasingly, however, the Greek government had no identity, or rather it was an identity that had fractured along local, regional, and personal lines. Kolokotronis controlled the Peloponnese, while another of the *kapetanei*, Odysseus Androutsos, held central and eastern Greece.

The Executive Council and the Legislative Senate, established under the Constitution of 1822, had become one of the prizes in the conflict. Different factions fought to claim them for their own ends. At times there were rival Executives sitting in different places. Byron's correspondence reveals his frustration in trying to locate the "actual," constitutional government of Greece, as opposed to the simple center of military power. He sought the government at Tripolitza (11 September), at Salamis or Aegina (6 October), and at Nafplio (29 October).

The situation in Greece was one of almost total anarchy. Gamba summarized Byron's position: there "was little good to be reaped from proceeding at present," he wrote. "To learn the real state of affairs, to become acquainted with the men concerned, and to be known to them, was the best method of acquiring an influence which he [Byron] might afterwards employ in settling their internal discords."

This was sensible from most points of view. The only informed criticism comes from Finlay. "Was Cephalonia [Kefallinia] the place to do this?" he wrote, in a penciled note opposite the passage in Gamba's book. Kefallinia was, in Finlay's eyes, too much on the periphery of the conflict. Byron's refusal to leave made him dependent on reports he had no means of verifying and which, in any case, often came so slowly that they were overtaken by events.

It is true that Byron never seems to have fully comprehended what was happening in Greece during the months he spent waiting in Kefallinia. He learned in general that Greece was being pulled apart by factionalism, but the detail apparently escaped him and that inevitably blurred his understanding.

Finlay himself arrived in Kefallinia in October 1823. He created an immediate impression—Byron told him later that he thought he was the ghost of Shelley. He departed the following month for the Peloponnese and the heart of the political and military struggle. It is always interesting to speculate on what might have happened had Byron followed him. But there is no reason to doubt Byron's own instinct that a foreigner in Greece in the autumn of 1823 was unlikely to be able to play the role of mediator, that he had only his reputation, and perhaps his life, to lose.

Until the beginning of September Byron continued to live onboard the ship that had brought him from Italy. This he did partly for privacy and partly to avoid embarrassment to the British resident, Charles Napier. On 4 September, however, he made a move to the village of Metaxata, a few miles inland and to the southeast of Argostoli. There he rented a small villa for himself, Gamba, Dr. Bruno, and the servants, a house that still stood at the time of the great earthquake in 1953. Metaxata, Byron wrote to Teresa, was "a very pretty village—with fine scenery of every description."

Julius Millingen, who was sent out to Greece by the London Greek Committee and who became surgeon to the Byron Brigade in Mesolongi, visited Byron in Metaxata in November 1823: "On my arrival," he wrote, "I found him on the balcony of the house, wrapt in his Stewart tartan cloak ... attentively contemplating the extensive and variegated view before him, terminated by the blue mountains of Aetolia, Acarnania, and Achaia." This became the very image of Byron's inactivity, the romantic contemplation while all Greece suffered before him.

Millingen recorded that Byron was drinking heavily and that he overindulged in pills to keep his weight down. He wrote:

"I frequently heard him say, 'I especially dread, in this world, two things, to which I have reason to believe I am equally predisposed—growing fat and growing mad.' "

All through these months Byron was pursued by the representatives of Greece's warring groups, seeking his approval as a means of gaining his money. Millingen observed that Byron showed great firmness in resisting these political, as opposed to humanitarian, claims on his purse; and, since Millingen was not exactly dazzled by the Byron he found in Metaxata, the observation has credibility.

Mavrokordatos sent a letter, to which Byron replied on 1 October with masterly tact. Writing in Italian, he said how much he regretted that Mavrokordatos was currently "separated from the management of public affairs"; he added that "nothing would be dearer to me than to work with you in this cause," while reaffirming his position that he could only intervene at the request of the Greek government, whatever and wherever that might be.

The master of the Peloponnese, Kolokotronis, sent an envoy, appropriately named Anarghiros (the name means "without money"). He almost succeeded in getting Byron to leave for the Peloponnese and "the residence of the . . . government" in early November. Many other lesser figures, too, made the pilgrimage to Metaxata or sent their agents.

Millingen said that Byron "was deaf to the voice of flattery, and withstood both the allurements of ambition and the powerful enticement, which romantic enterprises could not fail to exert on his warm imagination . . . he calmly sought to discover, amidst so many contradictory and unfavourable statements, the path that would best lead him to the attainment of his wish, which was the welfare of his newly-adopted country."

Byron was assailed in Kefallinia, as he would be again in Mesolongi, by Suliote refugees. The tribes of Suli had been expelled from their home in the western mountains of Greece by

Ali Pasha in 1803. Many had died at the time, in the fighting or under torture. Others had dispersed to the Ionian Islands, where they led the displaced lives of a conquered people.

The Suliotes, even in their homeland, had never been an orga-nized political force. They had worked together only in time of war and for limited aims. After their dispersal in 1803 they were a fractured and embittered group. They had no role in the commu-nities where they settled; they despised agricultural work, having been soldiers, shepherds, and brigands in their former lives. Wherever they went, they antagonized the local population, though the romantic glow of their former resistance to authority touched many outside observers.

The Suliotes were still able to fight and they were willing to offer their services to anyone who might help them recover their homeland. Having been destroyed by Ali Pasha, they came back to help him in the 1820s, when, in his own desperate struggle for survival, he offered to let them return to Suli. They fought against Ali under the Turks; and they fought against the Turks under the Greeks, in the War of Independence, when the small force com-manded by Markos Botsaris became justly famous.

Almost immediately on arriving in Kefallinia, Byron took about forty Suliote warriors into his pay. This was partly out of romance for a people he had celebrated in *Childe Harold*, and partly from the shrewd conviction that a man without a private bodyguard looked naked in a Greece at war.

According to Millingen, the Suliotes were regular visitors to Metaxata. As in Mesolongi later, they proved more trouble than the nostalgia of supporting them was worth. They were, Byron says in his journal, simply bent on "extortion." So in September he obtained arms for them—which was difficult to do in neutral Kefallinia—and sent them into mainland Greece to fight.

Amid all the political confusion and the dark rumors from Greece, life at Metaxata continued in ways that any well-born Englishman would have recognized. The right sort of people visited each other, left their cards, had dinner, talked, went riding. One who called often to see Byron, a Dr. James Kennedy, was perhaps the oddest and least predictable of all his acquaintances in the final months of his life.

James Kennedy was an army officer stationed in Argostoli. He was immensely pious and Millingen says that when Byron arrived "he confidently undertook the task of converting him." Far from discouraging his efforts, Byron gave all the appearance of enjoying them. To his sister, Augusta, on 12 October, he wrote of Kennedy: "I like what I have seen of him"; while Kennedy, for his part, left a record of his *Conversations on Religion with Lord Byron*, before dying of yellow fever in Jamaica in 1827.

Certainly there was some sport in this relationship—Byron suggested in a letter that the beauty of Kennedy's wife was more likely to win converts than the beauty of his theology. Byron was more intelligent, quicker than Kennedy, and ran him in circles. Even so, when he went to Mesolongi, he accepted the curious task of acting as agent for the English Bible Society. "On his arrival there," Millingen recalled, "he piled up at the entrance of his receiving-room the numerous Bibles and religious tracts, that had been intrusted to his care, and seldom neglected to offer copies to his visitors."

Toward the middle of December 1823, Byron's mood, as reflected in his letters, began to sound unambiguously cheerful, for the first time since his arrival in Greece; and, for the first time, he began to speak positively about the prospect of action. Behind this renewed optimism lay a series of developments that Byron seems to have half grasped and half misread.

All through the autumn of 1823 the Greek fleet had remained in port on the island of Hydra. This was a waste of one of the Greeks' best assets, since their armed merchant ships had proved highly effective against the Turks. The reason for the inactivity says much about the state of the country at the time: the ships remained in port because no one could or would pay the sailors to take them out to sea. In November, Byron, with an expansive gesture, put up £4,000, and this finally enabled the fleet to set sail.

Coincidentally, at this time, Mesolongi had come under Turkish siege and was blockaded by sea. It was not the first time, nor would it be the last. In a previous siege in October 1822, Mavrokordatos had distinguished himself through his talents as an organizer and administrator. Now, late in 1823, when Mesolongi was again under siege, the inhabitants of the town asked for his recall.

All the pieces fell together. Mavrokordatos came out of hiding to sail with the Greek fleet for Mesolongi, supported by Byron's vast resources. The fleet arrived off Mesolongi on 11 December. With all the care that Byron had taken to avoid siding with one faction or another, circumstances now brought him inescapably into the camp of Mavrokordatos.

Mavrokordatos, for his part, played the Byron card with great skill. It was greatly in his favor that Byron was known to support him. In December, the Legislative Senate wrote to Byron asking him to join Mavrokordatos in Mesolongi. While from Mesolongi itself, Mavrokordatos wrote the letter that pierced all Byron's caution: "You will be received here as a saviour. Be assured, My Lord, that it depends only on yourself to secure the destiny of Greece."

Ten

for we are young no longer. . . .

—Byron to Lady Byron, 28 December 1820

In a street that leads off the main square in modern Mesolongi, someone has written on a wall the English words: "Fuck Agrinio. . . ." The unexpected, casual scrawl is years old. Whenever I go back to Mesolongi, I walk down the street to look and it's always there, scarcely fading.

Agrinio is a small and harmless town about twenty miles to the north. The writing on the wall, hardly original, it is true, still reminds us of two things. Of the dull hatreds we often reserve for those closest to us; and of the fact that there are worse places in the world than Mesolongi. Those writers who have, for so long, given Mesolongi a bad name, as the ultimate outpost at the end of the world, should spend a weekend in Agrinio and meditate on an eternity there.

For such a famous place, Mesolongi has remained extraordinarily intimate. This, no doubt, is because its fame, outside Greece, is almost all literary. Foreigners don't come here much. It is a long drive from Athens and it isn't near any of the places where

tourists usually go. You couldn't visit Mesolongi as an afterthought, on the way to the beach or an ancient monument.

Greeks come in large numbers, especially schoolchildren, for
whom the pilgrimage is part of an education in citizenship. It's a
town of small squares and palm trees; and, though reinforced
concrete came to Mesolongi in the 1960s, as everywhere in
Greece, there are still some stout old houses, with iron balconies
and peeling facades, pink and orange.

These old houses are an obvious invitation to the past. Famous
people have lived in Mesolongi. Byron's Maid of Athens, Theresa
Makri, was one of them. Though she never married Byron, she
did marry an Englishman. He was a teacher of English who was
appointed British vice-consul in Mesolongi in 1862. On her marriage, she became Mrs. Black. Respectable, certainly, though not
obscure, since the shadow of Byron never left her.

Kostis Palamas, another of Mesolongi's famous residents and
one of the outstanding poets of modern Greece, remembered
going as a young boy to Mrs. Black's afternoon receptions.

Palamas is a bridge between the old Greece of Byron's Theresa
Makri and the modern world. He lived on until 1943, when
Greece was once again under occupation, this time by the
Germans. In death he became, like Byron, an icon of rebellion and
resistance. For at his funeral, while German officers looked on, a
vast crowd sang the Greek national anthem and returned to the
old cry of "Long live Freedom!" Today, the house where he lived
in Mesolongi has been turned into a museum of his long life.

Close by is the house that once belonged to the Trikoupis
family. The clan, already distinguished in the eighteenth century,
dominated the politics of Greece in the nineteenth. Spiridon
Trikoupis, born the same year as Byron, delivered the funeral oration over Byron's body. He wrote a famous history of the Greek
Revolution, was brother-in-law to Mavrokordatos, and was Prime
Minister of Greece in the post-Independence period. His son
maintained the family tradition. A European Greek par excel-
lence, he died in Cannes on the eve of the twentieth century.

·   ·   ·

I returned to Mesolongi one December, after years away. As you come south toward the town, following the route of Byron's first visit in 1809, you pass a sign by a pile of builders' rubble. It says, in English and Greek: "Welcome to Mesolongi, the Town of Liberty." Farther down the road there is a stone marker, with the words: "Every free man is a citizen of Mesolongi."

I arrived in the early evening. Two old women were shaking olives from a tree by the roadside. In the growing darkness a red neon sign suddenly lit up, high on the roof of a building. It flashed the word "Liberty," in English. This might make you fear the worst, and, as you come closer, your fears might seem confirmed, for the sign turns out to be an advertisement for a furniture store.

There is a Restaurant Liberty, a Liberty Super Market, a Hotel Liberty, all within a few yards. Even a shop selling sinks and odd collections of metal piping sells them in the name of Liberty. But it's all right. That is the extent of the exploitation of Mesolongi's past, and it's harmless enough.

This is the only town in Greece that you can enter in the old way, through a gateway in the defensive walls; and it is an approach that has enormous symbolic value. For it was here, on a night in April 1826, that the population of Mesolongi tried to make their escape through Turkish lines, after suffering a year under siege.

The plan was born of complete desperation. Many were too weak to leave, suffering from sickness and starvation. So they remained behind to blow the town to pieces as the Turkish forces entered. The rest planned to march to safety across the mountains to the east and might have made it, if they had not been betrayed by an informer and ambushed. As it was, only a fraction of those who passed through the gate of Mesolongi survived to reach exile in the town of Amfissa.

It is these events that have given Mesolongi a heroic reputation. It is the Byron connection that has made that reputation international. The impact of the massacre was immediate and immense throughout Europe. One of the most famous responses was Delacroix's painting *La Grèce sur les ruines de Missolonghi*, the *Guernica* of the Greek War.

"The conduct of the defenders of Mesolonghi," says Finlay, "will awaken the sympathies of freemen in every country as long as Grecian history endures." The town had shown, he wrote, a heroism "rare in the Greek Revolution—rare even in the history of mankind." The attempted escape is still known simply as the *Exodos*, and is remembered every year in a procession.

More than two hundred years before the Greek War, an English traveler, Sir Anthony Sherley, had already foreseen the role Byron would be called on to play. In the early seventeenth century, he had written: "If the little remnant of people, which is left there [in Greece] had courage; or if they have courage, had also armes; or if the Princes Christian had but a compassionate eye turned upon the miserable calamity of a place so near them . . . I do not see . . . but the redemption of that place and people were most facile . . . and the glory would be immortal to the Actor."

Once the way was open to Mesolongi, Byron responded with helpless enthusiasm. He and Mavrokordatos would work together; they would operate beyond the clash of factions and the messy relativism of the Greek civil war. Mavrokordatos would be the national figure Greece needed, Byron the fellow traveler, with an open purse and an irreproachable dedication to a glorious cause.

To a correspondent on 23 December 1823, Byron wrote: "Till now—I could have been of little or no use—but the coming up of Mavrocordato—who has not only talents but integrity, makes a difference." And to his old friend Thomas Moore, on 27 December: "The state of parties . . . has kept me here till *now*; but now that Mavrocordato (their Washington . . .) is employed again, I can act with a *safe conscience*."

The degree to which the call to action altered Byron's judgment is easy to see from his letters. Until that point, his entirely sensible view had been that, whatever role he might play in Greece, he had no future as a military leader. The Greeks, he had written, "won't obey a stranger—unless he has a force of his own sufficient to make himself respected." Over and over, he had said that what was needed was an experienced military man with a regular force under him; and as late as 10 December 1823, he was writing to the London Greek Committee recommending Napier as "*our* Man to lead a regular force, or organize a national one for the Greeks."

But now he began to talk wildly of military action of his own. He and Mavrokordatos would attack the Turks in Prevesa or Patras. He would march into battle at the head of a company of Suliotes. Or, most unrealistic of all, he would take his Suliotes over to the Peloponnese and sort out the warring factions there: "We must go over . . . and try the effect of a little *physical* advice— should they persist in rejecting *moral* persuasion," he wrote on 23 December. This was pure madness, fortunately never pursued.

From the time when Byron was still in Italy, he had wanted Mavrokordatos to be the man for Greece; or, at least, was at a loss to know who might be better. His willingness to see him as far more than he could ever be was understandable. Wrong-headed, perhaps, but not foolish. For Mavrokordatos had many talents. Above all, he was a survivor. In the post-Independence period, his political career went on and on, finally coming to an end only in 1855. He saw off many of the leading figures of the war, into death or retirement.

After he had exiled himself from Constantinople in 1818, Mavrokordatos had settled in Pisa. The Shelleys knew him there and it was Mavrokordatos who, on 1 April 1821, brought them the first news of the Greek uprising. Mary was enthusiastic about the man her husband called "our turbaned friend." She exchanged lessons with him, English for classical Greek.

Percy Shelley, for his part, was more ambiguous. He dedicated his drama *Hellas* to Mavrokordatos, but when he mentions him in his letters, the tone is lukewarm. "I reproach my own savage disposition that so agreeable, accomplished and amiable a person is not more agreeable to me," he wrote to Claire Clairmont. In another letter to Claire he reported that a ship had arrived to take Mavrokordatos off to the war in Greece: "He is a great loss to Mary and *therefore* to me . . . but not otherwise."

Most of the foreigners who knew Mavrokordatos had deep reservations about him. Partly this was a kind of almost racial antipathy. Foreign observers often had little idea of the background from which he came and of the inevitable compromises forced on a Greek who had been the high servant of Turkish masters.

Leicester Stanhope, who was sent out by the London Greek Committee in November 1823, wrote: "Mavrocordato is a clever, shrewd, insinuating, and amiable man . . . but he pursues a temporizing policy, and there is nothing great or profound in his mind. He has the ambition, but not the daring or the self-confidence required to play a first part in the state. . . . What, after all, can you expect from a Turk or Greek of Constantinople?"

Julius Millingen commented: "Happy would it have been, had Mavrocordato known the extent of his qualifications. . . . The greatest fault in his character . . . was a total want of firmness. He was incapable of pronouncing '*no*.' " Many, like Millingen, noted his complete lack of physical presence: "His stature was much below the usual size; and his carriage altogether too unmartial to impart much confidence to a half-civilized people, who prize external appearance so much."

At the same time, Millingen was alive to the qualities in Mavrokordatos that drew Byron and others to him. "He was, perhaps, the only man in Greece," Millingen wrote, "who united . . . unadulterated patriotism, and the talents which form a statesman. He alone was capable of organizing and giving a proper direction to civil administration."

If Mavrokordatos was a famous temporizer, this was partly a matter of character, partly the result of his long service in Constantinople, and partly due to the fact that he lacked a significant power base in Greece. He had no personal followers under arms, as did the *kapetanei*, and so he was forced to seek influence by other means, through diplomacy or shadowy compromise.

That he should have been associated with Mesolongi from the earliest days of the Revolution is in itself an indication of the weakness of his situation. It is true that Mesolongi was strategically important, since it commanded one of the two approaches to the Peloponnese. It was the key to control of western Greece. Nevertheless, it was never central to the struggle on the mainland. It was simply one of the few towns that was not dominated by the *kapetanei* and this gave Mavrokordatos room for maneuver.

On the outbreak of the Greek War, Mavrokordatos chose to go to the Peloponnese. When he reached it, in August 1821, however, he saw very quickly that he had no role to play there. In September he went on to Mesolongi instead and began the process of political organization. He convened an assembly of representatives from the liberated areas of western Greece and persuaded them to adopt a constitution.

It was from Mesolongi in 1822 that Mavrokordatos, by then president of Greece, launched a disastrous military expedition that forever colored his reputation. His campaign was designed to enhance his prestige as a national leader and to relieve his Suliote allies who were fighting the Turks in the northwest. It ended in the Battle of Peta, which saw the destruction of the Philhellene Battalion, along with the idealism of the international volunteers in Greece. "Of all the blunders committed by Mavrocordatos in his long political career," wrote Finlay, "this was the greatest and the most reprehensible."

After Peta, all of western Greece was back in Turkish hands, except for Mesolongi, which remained, from that time on, a vulnerable outpost of Greek power. So it was to a Mesolongi under siege that Byron prepared to sail at the end of 1823, a return to the small town on the edge of a lagoon where in his youth he had once spent a few unmemorable days.

Byron hired two boats to take his party across the sea from Kefallinia. He refused the offer of a Greek ship, so as to avoid compromising British neutrality. They embarked on 29 December and arrived at the island of Zakinthos on the morning of the thirtieth. There Byron took on yet more cash to add to his vast reserves. They left for Mesolongi at 6:00 P.M. the same day.

Byron approached the war zone in an apparently equable frame of mind. In his Italian days he had been fond of quoting the eighteenth-century French writer Marmontel, to the effect that "Revolutions are not to be made with rose-water." Even so, he was going into a situation that might have made anyone pause. The Greek War so far had been fought with few rules and much horror. Indiscriminate massacre was common from the outset and neither side normally took prisoners, except for the purpose of torturing them to death.

The dominant image that survives from the early months of the War of Independence was the sack of Tripolitza in October 1821. Tripolitza, the largest town in the south of Greece, was besieged for several months by Kolokotronis and others. Finally, on a day of stifling heat in early October, the town fell. Thousands of Turks were slaughtered and the town's Jewish population put to torture; a single massacre in a ravine outside Tripolitza carried off two thousand Turks, mainly women and children. Finlay remembered seeing the heaps of unburied bones, bleached by winter rain and summer sun, when he passed by two years later.

Insofar as this kind of savagery was politically directed, it had the same aims as the ethnic cleansing of the former Yugoslavia in the 1990s: to forge unity among those who participated in the slaughter and to prevent any subsequent return to the status quo.

Insofar as it was spontaneous, it was the release of the accumulated hatreds and day-to-day frustrations of hundreds of years of foreign occupation.

Tripolitza was a disaster for the reputation of the Greeks in Europe. It made it all too easy to argue that the Greeks were barbarians who deserved no help in their freedom struggle. Within Greece it was equally a disaster, since the spoils of war at Tripolitza, as elsewhere, fell to the *kapetanei* like Kolokotronis. This strengthened their hand and weakened an already impoverished national government.

Byron had given long thought to these problems. He knew the temper of the Greek War and how it was being fought, how it looked to outsiders. To Hobhouse in April 1823 he had written: "If I go there [to Greece]—I shall do my best to civilize their mode of treating their prisoners." In the short time that he was in Mesolongi he did what he could. He saved lives, relieved suffering, set out the lines of an alternative to traditional butchery. In February 1824, for example, he rescued thirty Turkish prisoners from the Greeks—men, women, and children. He sent them out of the war zone, to Patras and Prevesa, at his own expense.

Money, too, had long preoccupied him and very early on he had identified it as the key to the Greek crisis. He recognized that even his own private fortune could make little difference to the long-term course of the war. Before he left Italy, he had already backed the idea that Greece should finance its struggle through a loan on the international market. Whoever controlled the proceeds of such a loan would have a crucial role in the internal politics of the war. His experience in Greece itself further convinced him that there was no other way to redress the balance of power in favor of the European Greeks he instinctively favored.

The story of the eventual Greek loan is murky and tangled and Byron did not live to see its end. Two Greek deputies arrived in London to negotiate the deal in January 1824. The impression they created even on those disposed to be sympathetic was wholly negative. "They carried on their discussions . . . as if they were trading for old clothes," wrote Bowring to Byron in February 1824. The philosopher Jeremy Bentham wrote to Simón Bolívar in August 1825: "Such a compound of ignorance, groundless suspicion, insincerity, faithlessness, incivility, negligence, quarrelsomeness, weakness of judgment, pride, vaingloriousness, frivolity, and in the whole together incapacity for political business, I could not have conceived unless I had witnessed it.... I have but too much reason for the apprehension that they are but a fair specimen of their Countrymen at home. A guerrilla warfare seems to be all they are fit for."

From the Greek point of view, the negotiations were equally unsatisfactory. The terms, when finally agreed, were usurious. Greece was to borrow £800,000, which, after all deductions, resulted in a genuine loan of only about £300,000. Moreover, the money was secured on "the whole of the national property of Greece." This meant the very land of Greece itself.

It was no wonder that the loan was a bitterly divisive issue. An agreement, however, was signed in London on 19 February 1824, and the first installment arrived at Zakinthos at the end of April. By that time Byron was already dead. Nevertheless, the expectation of the loan and the knowledge that Byron had been named as one of the commissioners in charge of its distribution gave him great influence during the months he spent in Mesolongi.

Byron and his party had to run a Turkish blockade off the western coast, in order to reach their destination, and their journey from Zakinthos to Mesolongi was more of a storybook adventure than anything that happened to them subsequently.

Byron made the crossing onboard a swift sailing ship, Gamba on another, slower vessel that carried the horses and baggage. In the early hours of 31 December, Byron's ship was intercepted by a Turkish patrol. That could have led to the sudden end of his Greek experience, if not of his life, had not chance and the confusion of the moment enabled the ship to escape. Even so, it was to be several days yet before Byron reached Mesolongi.

Gamba's ship was also intercepted by the Turks on the way

across. She was taken into custody with all onboard, and her captain was on the point of being beheaded. Then, by one of those coincidences that are plausible only in life, the Turkish commander suddenly recognized the captain as the man who had once saved his life in the Black Sea. Gamba and his party were briefly detained in Patras by the Turkish authorities, then released. They reached Mesolongi on 3 January 1824, by which time Byron had still not arrived.

After their escape from the Turks, Byron's party had found the direct entrance to Mesolongi blockaded. They sailed north of the town instead and, since their ship drew little water, the captain was able to bring her in among the shallows. Byron set ashore a young Greek boy, Loukas Chalandritsanos, and sent him on to Mesolongi, with a letter requesting a military escort.

They had no time, however, to wait for a response. Threatened by the presence of a Turkish vessel, they slipped away up the coast, looking for safe harbor. They went as far as Dragomestre, the modern Astakos, where they remained, held up by wintry weather, until 3 January.

On their way back south toward Mesolongi, they ran into storms and they struggled to make the entrance to the lagoon. Once inside, they dropped anchor just offshore and rested for the night. Byron went swimming, to kill the fleas, so he said, from five days of unwashed traveling. Fletcher was certain that the cold sea and night air caused lasting damage to his master's health, though this may be a natural case of wisdom after the event.

On the following day, 4 January 1824, Byron descended on Mesolongi. Nothing suggests the event was anything but the extraordinary climax he must have desired. An idealized painting of the scene, done forty years later by the Greek artist Vryzakis, hangs in the National Gallery in Athens. It shows Byron surrounded by priests, warriors, and women in fine clothes. In the background, the ordinary people of the town raise their arms in greeting. A man holds on to his baby daughter as she reaches out to embrace the arriving hero. The historical value of the picture is not great, but it confirms that, even in the 1860s, the excitement of this strange event was still alive in the Greek imagination.

Mavrokordatos had told Byron that his presence in Mesolongi would "*electrify* the troops." Partly this was because he could pay their wages, which were long in arrears. But his presence, like his wealth, was also symbolic. By his commitment, he connected Mesolongi to a world outside, gave back to people an image of their own importance, a renewed sense of the purpose of their deprivations. The people cheered, the guns saluted. "It must," says William St. Clair, "have been one of the best moments of his life."

He came ashore in his scarlet uniform. Gamba was there to meet him, his eyes full of tears. The crowd cheered on, Byron waved, then moved off toward the apartment that had been reserved for him. There he met Mavrokordatos, Greek and foreign military officers, and representatives of the civil administration. It was a ritual for which Byron was elegantly suited. Through its glimpse of competing positions, however, it already began to darken the theatrical simplicity of his reception by the water's edge.

Byron took up residence in the same house as Leicester Stanhope, agent of the London Greek Committee. It was on the western edge of town. Mavrokordatos had a house just a few yards away. In those days the area bordered the sea and could be approached by small boats; indeed, in times of bad weather, it was often hard to approach it in any other way. Now, since a reclamation project has opened up a new quarter on the west side, the site lies inland, in a quiet area of solid houses and orange trees.

The house itself looks very large in surviving pictures. Such pictures are, perhaps, an exaggeration. One eyewitness reported that Byron's house "was small and incommodious, though one of the best in town." It was blown up on the night of the *Exodos* in April 1826. Only a few stones survived, out of which a commemorative monument was raised in 1924, on the hundredth anniversary of Byron's death. Now there's only a simple plaque in Greek to mark the site. It says: "Here was the house where Lord Byron lived from 5 January and [where] he died on 19 April, 1824."

Byron and Stanhope and their entourage lived upstairs, Stanhope on the second floor, Byron on the third. A bodyguard of Suliotes camped out below them. Byron's drawing room, Millingen recalled, looked more like an armory than the residence of a poet: "Its walls were decorated with swords, pistols, Turkish sabres, dirks, rifles, guns, blunderbusses, bayonets, helmets, and trumpets, fantastically suspended." Here, at last, was the very image of war.

Mesolongi was much changed from the place Byron and Hobhouse had seen in 1809. Millingen wrote: "[The town], at the time I landed [December 1823], was enjoying its halcyon days. An immense concourse of strangers filled its bazaars and streets; scenes of merriment were day and night repeated in its numerous cafés; and in every direction marriages and feasts were celebrated." Millingen's Mesolongi was an almost medieval vision, a romance of mandolins and timbrels.

The French officer Maxime Raybaud, who is one of the most reliable of the foreign witnesses in Greece, came to Mesolongi in August 1821, when he found the town poor and filthy. A year later he was back and found it much improved. It had been tidied up, cleared of "the disgusting refuse [that] normally litters all the towns of the East."

At the same time, the population had doubled, with an influx of refugees and fighting men. When Byron was there, all the chiefs of western Greece, from the plains of Arta to the mountains of Parnassus, had gathered for a General Assembly. Four thousand soldiers had followed their commanders to Mesolongi and Millingen observed "with much displeasure, the haughtiness and harshness with which these men treated the unarmed inhabitants."

Byron was a strange hero in this warlike, but fundamentally inactive, town. He soon recognized the limitations that the season placed on dreams of movement and conquest. All those who were eyewitnesses, as well as a few who were not, have written memorably about the winter in Mesolongi. The torrential rains, the streets deep in mud; the struggle to walk, the frequent impossibility of riding. The season does not last long, by the standards of northern Europe, but it coincided exactly with Byron's stay. This was not a time for doing anything. Instead, and inevitably, Byron found an atmosphere of restlessness, petty intrigue, and insubordination.

He seems to have accepted the position easily enough. Poised, as so often in his life, between the hope of change and the comfort of routine, he settled down; and while he waited for larger possibilities, such as an attack on the Turks or the arrival of the Greek loan, he turned to the day-to-day problems of life in a besieged town.

One of Byron's first initiatives in Mesolongi was to have an inventory drawn up of the remaining stocks of ammunition. He found that if the town came under sustained attack, there were supplies for only ten days of fighting. Of the few available cannons, more than half, having no platforms, were buried up to their axles in mud. The defensive walls of the town were only four feet thick and rested on poor foundations in marshy ground.

It is often said that Byron was an unstable actor in Mesolongi. William Parry, who arrived in the town at the beginning of February, is one of the main propagators of this line of thought. He was sent out from England by the London Greek Committee to organize a brigade of artillery and, for a few weeks, worked closely with Byron. He believed the poet's death was due more to psychological than physical causes; that his heart was broken by his disappointments in Greece, his inability to reconcile the warring parties, "to direct all hearts and minds, as his own heart and mind were directed, to the single object of liberating Greece."

This romantic view is not easily reconciled with the tone of Byron's surviving correspondence; and if there was an unstable actor in Mesolongi, it was clearly Parry himself. Parry's book, *The Last Days of Lord Byron*, is a work of committed, almost passionate, sympathy, but biographers who are drawn to its vision of Byron have to struggle with the all too obvious defects of Parry's character. There is much evidence that the book was not his own unaided work; that he was a drunk, a bully, and a coward. Most important of all, he was mentally unstable to the point of insanity.

That Byron should have felt frustration, even despair, in Mesolongi is only natural. But there is nothing to suggest that he felt these and nothing else, that they alone drove him on from day to day. Many of his letters from Mesolongi give the impression of a man sensibly preoccupied with remaining busy. He engaged in endless administrative tasks, organizing, talking, persuading. Some of his letters from this time come as close to being dull as any he ever wrote and scarcely suggest a mind overthrown by disappointment.

It is often claimed that Byron was ideologically adrift in this sea of organizational problems, that he labored in Mesolongi with no sense of direction. A recent book says simply: "He lacked ideological commitment in a setting that required it, if any progress . . . was to be made." This remark goes to the heart of Byron's last days in Greece. For, if its truth is accepted, all further questions are closed. All that is left is a picture of Byron floundering toward death, in the face of circumstances too vast for his comprehension.

In fact, Byron was attempting to work with men who were highly driven ideologically, and the comparison between them is entirely in his favor. It is hard to read Stanhope's letters, for example, without feeling sympathy for Byron's infinitely more flexible attitudes. Stanhope wrote to Bowring on 18 December 1823: "It is my practice, when the natives visit me, to draw their attention to those points which are most essential to their welfare." Or, to the same correspondent, in February 1824: "You must never forget that you are not administering to men [in Greece] but to children."

Or, in a similar vein, the Swiss journalist Johann Meyer, who died at the fall of Mesolongi in April 1826: "We felt here, more perhaps than in any other part of Greece," he wrote in March 1824, "the necessity of instructing people, of teaching them religion and morality, as the only basis on which to found true liberty." Meyer is remembered by a street name in modern Mesolongi. But Byron wrote of him: "Of all petty tyrants he is one of the pettiest."

Men like Stanhope and Meyer knew only too well what they wanted to do in Greece. Stanhope was motivated by ideals of a secular republican state, with liberty of the press and universal education. His models for Greece were Switzerland and the United States. These visions were not absurd in themselves, but they came close to being so in the Greek context.

Stanhope founded a Greek newspaper, the *Hellenica Chronica*. It ran from January 1824 to February 1826, financed by the London Greek Committee, with Meyer as editor. It attracted considerable interest in the Ionian Islands and in London, but it was virtually unread in Greece itself. Many Greeks could not read at all and, moreover, the *Hellenica Chronica* was written in a formal language (the *katharévusa*) that was largely unintelligible even when read aloud. A further venture into journalism by Stanhope was the Italian-language *Telegrafo Greco*, which was launched in March 1824. Stanhope recommended for its motto: "The world our country, and doing good our religion."

After all this, it is a relief to turn to Byron and a wonder that he managed to work with Stanhope at all. Byron had long accepted that certainty was one of the great enemies of truth. To his publisher, John Murray, he wrote in May 1817: "Opinions are made to be changed—or how is truth to be got at? we don't arrive at it by standing on one leg? or on the first day of our setting out." Or, as he put it in *Don Juan*:

> *But if a writer should be quite consistent,*
> *How could he possibly show things existent?*

This is the Byron who, in 1821, argued for the superiority of poetry over prose, on the grounds that poetry "does not systematize—It assails—but does not argue."

Yet Byron had also written, as early as 1813: "I never was consistent in anything but my politics ... my redemption depends on that solitary virtue." He had no time for ideological precision, but, as George Finlay recognized, this did not mean that his opinions rested simply on air. "I have never been a Christian," said the French writer André Gide, "but I have always been a believer"; and there is something of the same quality in Byron's politics.

Stanhope was able to recognize Byron's sense of purpose in Mesolongi. A letter from James Hamilton Browne appears in Stanhope's book *Greece in 1823 and 1824,* in which Browne wrote: "Lord Byron was a man who, from the ardent nature of his disposition ... would, most probably, have tired of the Greek cause, where so many jealousies and dissensions exist." To which Stanhope added a note: "Yes, he would have tired, but never have abandoned the cause. Lord Byron's was a versatile and still a stubborn mind; it wavered, but always returned to certain fixed principles." While Finlay wrote: "No stranger estimated the character of the Greeks more correctly than Lord Byron ... to nobody did the Greeks ever unmask their selfishness and self-deceit so candidly."

If the foreigners with whom Byron had to work were often uncongenial, the Greeks were no easier. Byron's relationship with Mavrokordatos, in particular, was bound to be difficult, since the glorious rhetoric that had brought Byron to Mesolongi soon faded before reality. At the same time, Byron was a sophisticated enough observer to understand that Mavrokordatos, like all the other major figures in the war, had an agenda to pursue. The ultimate purpose of that agenda was something Byron could still support.

All Byron's biographers retell a story from Millingen that suggests a complete breakdown soon occurred in relations with Mavrokordatos. Millingen says that Mavrokordatos was jealous of Byron's popularity; that Byron gradually lost respect for him, and that in the course of an evening's conversation he insulted him in English (their normal language of communication was Italian), in front of several witnesses.

The account is plausible. Millingen claims to convey Byron's own words, and it is one of a series of stories that apparently show Byron losing his self-control under the provocations of life in Mesolongi. In fact, the story is almost entirely a fabrication.

This is clear from a penciled note made by Finlay in his own copy of Millingen's book. An incident of some sort took place on the evening in question, but Finlay notes expressly that Millingen wasn't there to witness it. Finlay himself was there and later told Millingen what had happened, but the story, he says, was not the one Millingen reported in his book. This leaves simply a mystery, one less peg on which to hang the popular conception of Byron "living constantly at the edge of his physical and mental strength," as his great biographer, Leslie Marchand, puts it.

It is highly likely that relations with Mavrokordatos were strained. Byron and Mavrokordatos "felt no mutual esteem," as Finlay recognized. But there is no surviving account from a reliable witness, least of all from Byron himself, that enables an accurate assessment to be made. To John Murray, Byron wrote on 25 February 1824: "[Mavrokordatos] is an excellent person and does all in his power—but his situation is perplexing in the extreme." This studied discretion is also part of Byron's politics. He knew how much was at stake.

At the other end of the spectrum of Greek life were the Suliotes. In Kefallinia Byron had engaged about forty of them, out of nostalgia and a misguided sense of their usefulness. Now in Mesolongi he took five hundred into his pay, agreeing to maintain them for a year.

It was obviously a dubious decision. But Byron was still, even at the end of January, talking of an attack on the Turks in which he would march with his own band of men. Gamba confirms that he showed at times a reckless desire for military engagement, while in a document of 17 February, Byron signed himself "General Noel Byron, Col. of the 1st Regt. of Suliotes & Com[mand]er in Chief of Western Greece." This, of course, was all fantasy, but it is clear that Mavrokordatos encouraged it and did what he could to legitimize it, as a means of keeping Byron by his side.

The best that can be said for Byron's renewed association with the Suliotes is that it brought him influence with a potentially explosive section of Mesolongi's population. The Suliotes had no desire for military action. For most of them the idea of Greek liberty was meaningless. "They owned that they did not like to fight against stone walls," as Gamba reported. They hadn't been paid, and they had no means of subsistence. At the same time, they were bored; they did not belong in Mesolongi, and they were distrusted, despised, or feared by the Greeks around them.

On 19 February, an incident occurred that showed how dangerous the Suliotes were. One of the bravest of them was involved in a brawl with Lieutenant Sass, a Scandinavian volunteer in Greece. Sass was shot in the head and cut with a dagger, so that his arm was almost severed from his body. "He remained alive, but senseless and speechless, about an hour," Parry recalled, "and then the existence of the adventurous but unfortunate Sass terminated for ever."

In the aftermath of the death of Sass, Mesolongi was filled with rumors. People feared the Suliotes would sack the town. Byron's house was surrounded, with the Suliotes threatening to murder every foreigner they could find.

Byron intervened, sent for the Suliote commanders, restored calm. But he knew he could deal with the Suliotes no longer. "Nothing, during [Byron's] residence at Mesolonghi, distressed him more than the conduct of the Suliots [*sic*] whom he had taken into his pay," wrote Finlay. "He saw that he had degraded himself into the chief of a band of personal followers, who thought of nothing but extorting money from their foreign leader." Byron offered them a month's pay to leave Mesolongi in peace and go elsewhere. In March, Mavrokordatos reported that, "après mille et mille difficultés," they had finally gone.

Even so, it is possible to overplay the psychological damage of the Suliotes in Byron's last days. It is only too easy to see them as the symbol of a Greece Byron had carried with him since his youth, a Greece now revealed to be the illusion it had always been. A Greece of mighty warriors, guardians of an age-old liberty.

But nothing in Byron's own words or conduct suggests that he felt this way. In a note written a few days before the death of Lieutenant Sass, when he was already at his wit's end over the behavior of the Suliotes, he shows all that one might expect: anger, disappointment, a desire for an end, but nothing more. "Having tried in vain at every expence—considerable trouble—and some danger to unite the Suliotes for the good of Greece—and their own—I have come to the following resolution.—I will have nothing more to do with the Suliotes—they may go to the Turks or—the devil,—they may cut me into more pieces than they have dissensions among them, sooner than change my resolution. . . ."

The finality of death weaves irresistible patterns for the biographer, at once assembling and dissembling. It is true that, given the early deaths of both his parents, Byron was probably destined to die young. But there was nothing inevitable about his death in Mesolongi. That, in the end, was simply bad luck, perhaps simply the chance of the weather. Once he was dead, however, everything begins to look fated. The failure of ideals, the disappointments, betrayals, all the threads of a life inexorably unwinding.

From another perspective, the story of Mesolongi is simply the story of life in most besieged towns. As in Homer's Troy, the reality is that things go on and on; what is most characteristic is not what happens, but the apparently endless tale of what does not.

Much of Byron's time seems to have been spent unmemorably and not unhappily. Many people came and went. There were always things to do, few of them critical. There was a small earthquake toward the end of February and a false rumor of plague on 12 March. On 30 March, Byron was made a citizen of Mesolongi. From time to time, there were mutinies among the soldiers, owing to the quality of the bread, which, said Byron, "neither native nor stranger could masticate (nor dogs either)."

In the evenings there was always conversation, the kind of unrestricted conversation among men that Byron loved. There was riding, when the weather improved, and the pleasures of his huge dog, Lyon. "In conversation and in company he was animated and brilliant," said Parry; "but with Lyon and in stillness he was pleased and perfectly happy."

Finlay remembered that Byron often spoke of his childhood in Aberdeen. Of his youth, the England of Cambridge and London, of his friends, like Hobhouse. Finlay talked to him of Newstead Abbey, Byron's old country house, which had been sold in 1817 and which Finlay had visited in 1821. It is almost impossible not to see a picture of Byron lost in nostalgia, rather than a Byron who was simply and naturally nostalgic in the company of Englishmen.

For most of his life Byron resisted nostalgia better than most. One of his last letters from Mesolongi was to the earl of Clare: "I hope that you do not forget that I always regard you as my dearest friend," he wrote, "and love you as when we were Harrow boys together." The words invite a sense of pathos, of a life that has taken all the wrong turnings, to end so far from home. But, again, Byron is resistant. His letter to Clare reveals, not the pain of distance or decline, but something of the old Byronic insouciance. Here is the familiar sexual wit, now directed at the misfortunes of Clare's younger brother, who has gone off with someone else's wife; here is all the happy intimacy of the vast gentleman's club that is the British aristocracy.

If there is a real point of tragedy in Byron's last days, it is beyond what happened in Mesolongi. It lies, rather, in his reiteration of an old dilemma. The unresolved conflict that he saw, rightly or wrongly, as having shaped his life: Marathon or Sounion, public or private, self-sacrifice or self-indulgence.

One thing that the return to Greece had seemed to promise was resolution. In Kefallinia, however, he had chosen to remain the observer, while others acted out the obscure, savage pageant of the Greek War. Now, though he was in Mesolongi, the situation was somehow no different. He could hardly come closer to the war than to commit himself to a town under siege; that surely was what it meant to join a cause. But though the effects of war were everywhere, the war itself was elusive, and life continued to be a matter of waiting and watching.

Byron knew, of course, that a life of action, like a life of passion, was a kind of literary illusion, in some ways no more than a figure of speech. To Thomas Moore, in July 1821, he wrote: "There is no such thing as a life of passion any more than a continuous earthquake, or an eternal fever. Besides, who would ever *shave* themselves in such a state?" The search for a life fulfilled in action was inevitably futile, for even in the heart of war he discovered merely an accumulation of old habits.

Nevertheless, the fantasy never left him, and it was all the more painful now because, at the very moment that he sought the apotheosis of life-as-action, he found that he was irredeemably in love with a young and beautiful Greek boy, Loukas Chalandritsanos.

When Byron had visited the island of Ithaca in August 1823, he had met the Chalandritsanos family. They had taken refuge there from the fighting on the mainland. Byron gave the family financial support, as he supported other refugee families in

Ithaca. During the summer Loukas was away, fighting under Kolokotronis in the Peloponnese. But he later rejoined his family and came into Byron's service, first on Kefallinia, then later in Mesolongi. Byron was deeply involved with him. This last love of his life, however, like the first, for his cousin Mary Chaworth, was hopelessly unrequited.

In Mesolongi Byron wrote a poem full of the pain of it all. It is headed simply "January 22nd 1824. Messalonghi," to which Byron added a note to explain the occasion: "On this day I complete my thirty sixth year." Byron had written almost no poetry since leaving Italy. Now, as he turned thirty-six, he came out of retirement, the aging boxer before a doubting audience, but with all his faculties still intact.

Gamba recalled the circumstances: "January 22.—This morning Lord Byron came from his bedroom into the apartment where Colonel Stanhope and some friends were assembled, and said, with a smile, 'You were complaining, the other day, that I never write any poetry now:—this is my birthday, and I have just finished something, which, I think, is better than what I usually write.' "

It is a moving poem and shows how little the experiences of a lifetime had changed his sense of life's irreconcilable polarities. It begins with a plea for the validity of the personal, the right to go on loving even in a hopeless cause:

> *'T is time this heart should be unmoved*
> *Since others it hath ceased to move,*
> *Yet though I cannot be beloved*
> *Still let me love.*

It goes on to speak of the guilt and the loneliness of love; and then, as if driven by a logic of despair, it opens out into the wide world of politics and war. Here, in Mesolongi, is not the place to talk of love, since here, above all, is the possibility of an escape into heroic and meaningful death:

> *But 't is not* **thus**—*and 't is not* here
> *Such thoughts should shake my soul, nor* now
> *Where glory decks the hero's bier*
> *Or binds his brow.*

> *The Sword—the Banner—and the Field*
> *Glory and Greece around us see!*
> *The Spartan borne upon his shield*
> *Was not more free!*

The Spartan image of the warrior returning dead upon his shield is the ultimate denial of the personal, the supreme affirmation of the value of public service. Byron turns to Greece as the alternative to the guilty pain of love, the promise of deliverance into the peace of a valued sacrifice:

> *If thou regret'st thy youth, why* live?
> *The Land of honourable Death*
> *Is here—up to the Field! and give*
> *Away thy Breath.*

> *Seek out—less often sought than found,*
> *A Soldier's Grave—for thee the best,*
> *Then look around and choose thy ground*
> *And take thy Rest.*

The tragedy is not so much that circumstances refused Byron a meaningful death—after all, posterity would soon create myths enough to redeem him. The tragedy is that in the very act of embracing a public role he reveals his enormous regret for the inner life—for love, however tortured, for youth, the memory of being twenty-one, the Greece of sunshine and sea, before the war.

"There I was always in action or at least in motion," Byron wrote to Lady Melbourne of his first visit to Greece. This memory is of a time when action was its own pleasure, motiveless and happy. Greece began as a celebration of the physicality of life itself. It ends as a fantasy of stillness and death.

•   •   •

> *When I am dead, and doctors know not why,*
> *And my friends' curiosity*
> *Will have me cut up to survey each part . . .*

—John Donne, "The Damp"

On 15 February, Byron fell seriously ill from some kind of convulsive attack. "It was very painful," he noted in his journal, "and had it lasted a moment longer must have extinguished my mortality—if I can judge by sensations.—I was speechless with the features much distorted—but *not* foaming at the mouth—they say—and my struggles so violent that several persons . . . could not hold me—it lasted about ten minutes—and came on immediately after drinking a tumbler of Cider mixed with cold water in Col. Stanhope's apartments."

On 16 February, leeches were applied to his temples, with the aim of bringing down a high fever. He bled profusely and continued to do so for a long time after the leeches were removed. Millingen says that Byron's Italian doctor, Bruno, was alarmed at his failure to stanch the blood and that he called him in to help. This may be only a partial truth, however, since Millingen and Bruno were in competition after Byron's death to avoid responsibility for their failure to save him.

From now on Byron lived in the shadow of mortality. He was troubled and perplexed by the attack. He believed it might have been due to the conditions in Mesolongi, or perhaps to the lack of exercise brought on by bad weather. Perhaps, he wondered in his journal, it was the result of excessive drinking, or any combination of the public and private tensions to which he was exposed.

A letter to his sister, Augusta, on 23 February, told her that he was by then feeling much better. But he said he suspected the attack was epileptic in character. He asked Augusta to warn his wife, so that she might "take some precautions" over his daughter Ada. His doctors disagreed about the nature of the attack, Millingen apparently ruling out the possibility of epilepsy, Bruno inclined, at least for a time, to believe in it.

The threat to his reason predictably troubled Byron more than any threat to his life, and he became deeply gloomy. Millingen writes:

> From this moment a change took place in his mental and bodily functions. That wonderful elasticity of disposition, that continued flow of wit ... by which his conversation had been so highly distinguished, returned only at distant intervals; for he fell into a state of melancholy. . . . He felt assured that his constitution had been irretrievably ruined by intemperance; that he was a worn-out man. . . . Flashes before the eyes, palpitations and anxieties, hourly afflicted him.

Millingen's view, once again, may not be the whole truth. Only a few days after the convulsive attack, when the Suliotes threatened the peace of Mesolongi in the wake of the death of Lieutenant Sass, Byron was fully able to take charge; and, weak though he was, Stanhope noted, "the more the Suliots raged, the more his calm courage triumphed."

What remains curious is the fact that Byron chose to stay on in Mesolongi. He could so easily have left. His banker, Samuel Barff, offered his country house in Zakinthos, where he could have recovered his health without loss of face. It is often said that his pride kept him where he was, but that is an explanation that only conceals, for plenty of proud men came to Greece and left in disgust.

It is remarkable how little Byron changed under the stresses of Mesolongi. To Samuel Barff, on 10 March, he wrote: "I cannot quit Greece while there is a Chance of my being of any (even *supposed*) utility—there is a Stake worth millions such as I am— —and while I can stand at all—I must stand by the Cause,— —When I say this—I am at the same time aware of the difficulties—and dissensions—and defects of the Greeks themselves—but allowances must be made for them by all reasonable people."

How different is the language from Stanhope's authoritarian condescension. Disgust with the situation is something Byron almost never shows; which is interesting, since, of all the alibis that pride gives itself when times are hard, disgust is one of the easiest and most natural. His decision to stay on in Mesolongi is even more striking in the light of Finlay's shrewd observation that "whatever abstract enthusiasm he [Byron] might feel for military glory was joined to an innate detestation of the trade of war."

All through Byron's stay in Mesolongi, the political situation in Greece remained precarious. There were persistent rumors about the extent of the civil war on the mainland and it seems as if Byron, like most others, continued to be uncertain about where the balance of power lay. In late February, Byron reported to John Murray news that a Turkish army of a hundred thousand men was advancing in eastern Greece. In the face of this threat, unity among the Greeks remained the unrealizable aim of any disinterested participant in the war.

Byron continued to hope that the opening of the campaigning season would concentrate the minds of the war leaders; but, more than anything, he counted on the arrival of the first installment of the Greek loan. On 7 April, he wrote: "Almost every thing depends upon the arrival—and the speedy arrival of a portion of the loan— —to keep peace amongst themselves—if they can but have sense to do this—I think that they will be a match and better for any force that can be brought against them for the present."

On the local level, Byron continued to maintain the corps of artillery—commonly known as the Byron Brigade—that he had formed soon after his arrival in Mesolongi. It was, he wrote proudly, "the only *regularly paid* corps in Greece." At the beginning of February, William Parry came from London to take up a commission as major to the brigade. He arrived on a ship chartered by the London Greek Committee, and he brought military and medical supplies.

Parry's appointment led to the resignation from the brigade of some of its best officers. Finlay, too, refused to serve under him, noting privately that "a drunken mountebank was not the person to do anything for the good of Greece." As for the supplies that had been sent from London, the Greeks declined to move them, saying it was beneath their dignity. Much of the valuable equipment lay still unused at the fall of Mesolongi two years later.

Undeterred, Byron continued to contribute money in all directions. He funded a hospital for the poor, which was a useful service in a town as dislocated as Mesolongi; and he worked to humanize relations between Greeks and Turks, as unpromising a task as can be imagined.

Several Turkish women who had escaped slaughter in the early days of the Revolution came to him for protection and he helped them all. One Turkish survivor, a girl aged nine, he even thought of adopting. He fantasized about sending her to England, as a companion for his daughter Ada. "She is very lively and quick," he wrote, "and with great black Oriental eyes." Millingen reported that she had been found naked and shivering. Her younger brother had had his brains dashed out against a wall by the Greeks, a detail that gives some idea of the world in which Byron had to work.

On the diplomatic front, the main interest during the final weeks of Byron's life centered on the war leader Odysseus Androutsos. Odysseus, whom many of the Europeans called Ulysses, controlled much of eastern Greece, including Athens. From the time Byron arrived in Mesolongi, Odysseus had been promoting the idea of a congress in the town of Salona (modern Amfissa), near Delphi. His aim, allegedly, was to explore the possibility of unifying the forces of western and eastern Greece. Assisted by a number of foreigners, including Finlay, he worked hard to persuade Byron and Mavrokordatos to join him in the common cause.

Odysseus, like Kolokotronis, was the complete bandit chief. Beside him, Mavrokordatos looks no more than one of the minor bureaucrats of the Revolution. Edward Trelawny met Odysseus in the Peloponnese after he left Byron on Kefallinia in September 1823. While Mavrokordatos struck him as "a poor, weak, shuffling, intriguing, cowardly fellow," Odysseus was the very soul of his imagined Greece.

Odysseus had served as a page in Ali Pasha's court when he was young, and a much disabused Finlay later wrote of him: "His character was a compound of the worst vices of the Greeks and Albanians." By which Finlay meant that he was deceitful, vindictive, avaricious, and ferociously cruel.

Trelawny's life was, for a time, bound in fascination to Odysseus. They fought together as guerrillas. They went on raiding parties and besieged towns. They lived in a fortified cave on Mount Parnassus, where Trelawny married Odysseus's thirteen-year-old half-sister and narrowly escaped assassination at the hands of two agents in the pay of Mavrokordatos.

Odysseus was as colorful a figure as any in the war and as duplicitous. He later came to terms with the Turks, in what Finlay called "the most celebrated instance of treachery among the Greeks during their Revolution." He was murdered on the Acropolis during the night of 16 July 1825. He died, wrote Finlay, "like his patron and model, Ali of Joannina, a sacrifice to his own selfishness; and he will be execrated as long as the memory of the Greek revolution shall endure."

Odysseus had enormous charm. He won over not only Trelawny, which was easy, but Stanhope, too. Stanhope left Mesolongi on 21 February to go to Athens to work with Odysseus on the Salona project. From Athens, on 6 March, he wrote to Byron: "I have been constantly with Odysseus. He has a very strong mind, a good heart, and is brave as his word; he is a doing man; he governs with a strong arm, and is the only man in Greece that can preserve order."

Stanhope apparently believed that Odysseus shared his own interest in bringing about a unified government in Greece. Whereas Odysseus wanted Stanhope primarily in order to get his hands on the Greek loan, and he wanted Byron for the same reason. Both Mavrokordatos and Byron had good reason to be suspicious of the invitation to Salona. Mavrokordatos feared for his life, while Byron, too, had much to lose, not least as a hostage against the arrival of the Greek loan.

Nevertheless, on 19 March Byron wrote to Stanhope to say that he and Mavrokordatos would "go to Salona to meet Ulysses." He confirmed his intention in a letter written the same day to the secretary of the London Greek Committee. To his banker, Samuel Barff, on 22 March, he summed it up: "In a few days—P[rince] Mavrocordato and myself—with a considerable escort intend to proceed to Salona at the request of Ulysses and the Chiefs of Eastern Greece—to concert if possible a plan of Union between Western and Eastern Greece—and to take measures offensive and defensive for the ensuing Campaign."

It is possible that Salona would have seen the ruin of Byron's reputation in Greece. The situation, however, is too complex for meaningful speculation. It is also possible that some good might have come of it all, though that seems unlikely with hindsight. Most probably, Byron and Mavrokordatos would have been skilled enough to defend their corners and the results of Salona would have been of passing interest. In the end, the weather made all the decisions. Travel from Mesolongi was impossible during March and early April, and soon after that, Byron was dead.

"My dearest T.—The Spring is come—I have seen a Swallow today—and it was time—for we have had but a wet winter hitherto—even in Greece." Byron's letter to Teresa Gamba is dated 17 March 1824. The relief at the promise of spring is palpable. Byron had been deeply frustrated by the winter weather in Mesolongi, as everyone in his circle was aware. He had felt shut in, unable to take exercise; above all, unable to go riding.

Millingen wrote: "The rain falls in torrents almost every day; and in the intervals of sunshine, the streets and roads are so covered with water and mud, that it is equally impossible to ride as to walk. Lord Byron suffered greatly from the confinement."

On 4 April, Byron and Pietro Gamba rode out together. "There was less appearance of rain," Gamba noted, "than there had been for almost three months." For a few days afterward Byron seemed unwell, but on 9 April, even though the weather was threatening, they rode out again. They were overtaken by heavy rain and returned to town soaked through. Two hours later Byron was shivering violently and complaining of fever and rheumatic pains.

On the next day the shivering would not leave him. But he took his horse out into the olive woods around Mesolongi and appeared in good spirits. It was the last time he was able to ride. That evening Finlay and Millingen came to see him and found him lying, feverish, on a sofa. He had spent much of the day, Millingen reported, reflecting on a prediction made, when he was a boy, by a famous fortune-teller in Scotland: "Beware of your thirty-seventh year."

On the night of 10 April, Byron slept little. On the morning of the eleventh he was so unwell that, according to the frequently unreliable Parry, he agreed to leave Mesolongi for Zakinthos. Unlikely as this was, it is clear that his health was deteriorating quickly.

Since his convulsive attack on 15 February, he had eaten little. Millingen says that this was on the orders of Dr. Bruno. Fletcher told Augusta that Byron "would not even take a Dish of fish which his [*sic*] the only Good thing we have here." By now he must have been weak, though his diet of bread, olives, and oil was not unhealthy and many have survived on it for far longer than Byron spent in Mesolongi.

All day on the twelfth he kept to his bed, complaining that he could not sleep. On the thirteenth the fever had subsided, but the pain in his bones and head still troubled him. He was melancholy and irritable, Gamba remembered, and though he rose from his bed he no longer had the strength to leave the house. Outside, a sirocco was blowing, the warm winter wind bringing ever heavier rains. Parry says it rained so much that "the country around was flooded, and Missolonghi for the time became a complete prison."

From 14 April Byron was confined to his bedroom. Only Gamba and Parry, the doctors, and his two servants, Fletcher and Tita Falcieri, were allowed to see him. Even so, it seems that no one yet recognized that his condition might be mortal. Then, on the fifteenth, toward noon, Fletcher called on Millingen. He said that Byron wanted him to consult with Bruno about the best way forward. Millingen agreed.

Bruno told Millingen that Byron "laboured under a rheumatic fever"; that during the last two days the fever had much increased; and that he had repeatedly proposed bleeding, but that Byron had consistently refused.

Byron seems indeed to have shown many of the symptoms of rheumatic fever, one of the classic diseases of poor countries and poor conditions. It is an illness that begins with attacks of shivering, along with severe pain and swelling in the joints. The patient feels restless and very thirsty and there can be neurological complications, producing the sudden, twitching movements known as Saint Vitus's dance.

The precise cause and course of Byron's illness will never be known for certain, however, for the medical record is too fragmentary. It is also, at times, contradictory.

Millingen examined Byron. He, too, was convinced that bleeding was absolutely necessary. Byron again refused. At length, however, he promised that if the fever increased during the night he would allow Bruno to bleed him.

In the meantime, Millingen recommended a solution of

tartarized antimony and potassium nitrate (saltpeter) in twelve ounces of water. This was a concoction commonly used as an emetic. It is highly toxic and can provoke sudden death from circulatory collapse; it was certainly the last thing Byron needed. Millingen's thinking, however, illustrates the disastrous philosophy behind the whole process of treatment that Byron was to suffer: he prescribed the medicine, he wrote, "with a view of lowering the impetus of the circulating system."

It is possible, perhaps even quite likely, that Byron would have died whatever had been done. That was certainly Millingen's view when it was all over. It is clear, however, that the doctors, by their intervention, greatly assisted the natural course of events.

Had Byron survived to witness his own ending, he would hardly have been surprised. When he suffered a severe attack of fever in the Peloponnese in 1810, he was attended by two Albanian servants who, he said, "saved my life by frightening away my Physician." To Lady Blessington he once remarked: "Medical men do not sufficiently attend to idiosyncrasy, on which so much depends, and often hurry to the grave one patient by a treatment that has succeeded with another. . . . All that I have seen of physicians has given me a dread of them."

Byron's doctors proceeded, inevitably, by the methods they had been taught in medical school. The principle behind their treatment of fever was to reduce the strain on the heart. They had to work with little understanding of what fever was; they had no insights into the bacterial origins of infection; above all, they did not recognize how serious it was to weaken their patients by the forms of treatment they prescribed.

Millingen believed that Byron's nervous system had for some time been in "a continued state of erethism [abnormal excitement]." His aim, therefore, was consistent, attempting to relieve both the mind and body of his patient by lowering the "impetus" of the circulatory system. This, according to the medical fashion of the age, pointed to bloodletting on a grand scale;

and this, in turn, would lead to the further, fatal weakening of his patient.

The holistic approach represented by Millingen inevitably had its effect on Byron's reputation after his death. For if Byron's whole being had simply collapsed under the stresses of life in Mesolongi, then the line taken by Parry and others seems only natural as a consequence: "That the disappointment of his ardent hopes was the primary cause of his illness and death, cannot, I think, be doubted," was how Parry expressed it. While Millingen comes close to saying that Byron had lost the will to live.

Finlay, too, added his influence to the romantic, terminal view of Byron's illness. In June 1824 he wrote: "Such hearts as Lord B.'s must become old at an early age, from the continual excitement to which they are exposed." There is, however, nothing in the correspondence of Byron's last weeks and days to support this attitude. There is no sense in the letters of continual excitement or the edge of the precipice. On the contrary, the impression they give is of a mind resolutely set for the long haul; and if Byron was tempted to despair, he was able to hold this permanently in check, for the voice never once intrudes.

A commitment to therapeutic bleeding lay at the heart of the training Byron's doctors had received. In this, Byron was exceedingly unlucky. Bloodletting had been valued since classical times, but as a therapy for a limited number of conditions. It was a practice that had always had its detractors. During the period of the Napoleonic Wars, however, military doctors turned to bleeding as the universal solution to everything, and the effects had passed down into the medical schools.

Bleeding was still a panacea in Byron's time, the first and often the only line of defense against almost every disease or problematic condition. It was commonly used, for example, to counteract the effects of excessive eating or drinking. The principle was that, by lessening the total volume of blood in the system, the heart's work would be lightened. In the eleventh edition of the *Britannica*, which appeared shortly before the First World War, bloodletting was still recommended for treating the early stages of acute pneumonia, for pleurisy, bronchitis, and convulsive attacks.

The real craze for bloodletting corresponded approximately with Byron's lifetime. It continued until the 1830s, after which there was a gradual moderation. The same edition of the *Britannica* registered the shift in attitudes that had taken place by the early years of the twentieth century. It noted: "Unfortunately, in years gone by, blood-letting was used to such excess . . . that public opinion is now extremely opposed to it."

Ironically, one of the main nineteenth-century opponents of bleeding was the English physiologist Marshall Hall, who was almost exactly Byron's contemporary. His *Observations on Blood-Letting* of 1830 coincided with the height of the fashion and signaled the start of its decline. In the mid-1820s, however, there was never much chance that Byron would escape radical bloodletting at the hands of his young doctors. After he was dead, Bruno and Millingen would argue, not over whether the treatment was the right one, but over who had been responsible for delaying its application.

"I never was bled in my life—but by leeches—," Byron had written to Hobhouse in March 1823. "Perhaps the tape and lancet may be better," he added. "I shall try on some great emergency." Patients and their families almost always preferred local blood-letting by leeches to general bloodletting by "tape and lancet." In the latter process, a bandage was tied around the arm, so that the veins of the forearm would swell, and then an exposed vein was opened with a knife.

When Millingen returned to see Byron on the morning of 16 April, he tried to persuade him that the moment had come for the "great emergency." Byron tried to hold him off, saying he had spent a better night than he had expected. As a result, he had not asked Bruno to bleed him. Millingen replied that unless he agreed to be bled, "neither Dr. Bruno nor myself could answer for the consequences." Then, knowing Byron's fear of madness, he threatened that the disease might make him lose his reason if it remained untreated.

Byron finally surrendered, in a gesture that made his death inevitable. They took about twenty ounces of blood, which was toward the upper limit prescribed by medical training. During the night the fever became stronger than ever and Byron lapsed into incoherence. On the next morning, the seventeenth, it was clear that the doctors had lost control. For the first time, said Gamba, "the medical men seemed to entertain serious apprehensions." There was further bloodletting, and then again, in the afternoon, for a third time.

Byron was terribly distressed from lack of sleep. On 18 April, he got out of bed at 3:00 P.M. and walked to the next room, leaning on Tita Falcieri. Then at 3:30 P.M., two further doctors were called in for consultation: Dr. Treiber, Millingen's assistant, and Dr. Loukas Vaya, who had been physician to Ali Pasha.

According to Millingen, all four doctors agreed that Byron's condition was the result of "rheumatic inflammation." During the night Byron had begun to suffer from involuntary movements in his limbs. Bruno and Vaya proposed the use of antispasmodics, as in the treatment of the final stages of typhus. Treiber and Millingen, however, believed that such a remedy "could only hasten the fatal termination." Instead they recommended the application of leeches to the temples, behind the ears, and along the course of the jugular vein.

Bruno's account of the final days is very different from Millingen's and the two versions are impossible to reconcile. Both men were agitated, out of their depth, increasingly desperate at the thought of the responsibility that fell upon them for the death of one of Europe's most famous men.

Gamba says that toward 4:00 P.M. on the afternoon of the eighteenth, Byron seemed aware of approaching death. Millingen,

Fletcher, and Falcieri gathered around his bed in tears. Byron held on to Falcieri's hand and the other two, overcome, left the room.

Bruno, as Byron's personal physician, had the casting vote in the disagreement over how to proceed. Accordingly, Millingen says, he chose to administer an antispasmodic potion, a strong infusion of valerian with ether. The convulsions and delirium increased. Byron spoke to Fletcher for the last time, "recommending him to call on his sister, on Lady Byron and his daughter, and deliver to each the messages, which he had repeated to him before." A second dose of medicine was administered half an hour later. Byron uttered a few broken phrases and sank into sleep.

What Byron thought or said as his life drew to an end escapes us. There is testimony enough, but much of it sounds unconvincing. Millingen's celebrated version certainly does not read like Byron, and, in any case, Millingen was always happy to invent dialogue to suit the moment. Even so, his words have long been accepted into tradition: "To terminate my wearisome existence I came to Greece.—My wealth, my abilities, I devoted to her cause.—Well: there is my life to her. . . . Let not my body be hacked, or be sent to England. Here let my bones moulder.—Lay me in the first corner without pomp or nonsense."

More convincing, because less rhetorical, are Pietro Gamba's recollections. Byron, he says, talked confusedly in those final hours of his sister, Augusta, and his daughter Ada. At some point he spoke in Italian, perhaps still thinking of them, of everything that was far from Mesolongi: "Io lascio qualche cosa di caro nel mondo" (I leave behind me something precious in the world). After which he added in English: "For the rest, I am content to die."

At about 6:00 P.M. on the eighteenth came the bleak ordinariness of the last words: "I want to sleep now"; an ordinariness made memorable only by the coincidence of finality. Attempts were made to rouse him, but in vain. Bruno reported that "in that state of most profound sleep he continued the whole night." Many leeches were applied to his forehead and Byron quietly bled his way toward death.

Once only, at around 6:15 P.M. on 19 April, he opened his eyes, to close them almost immediately and forever. A few years before, in Ravenna, he had written: "A deathbed is a matter of nerves & constitution—& not of religion;—Voltaire was frightened—Frederick of Prussia not." Millingen, writing from Mesolongi three months after his death, confirmed that Byron had died, "to say the melancholy truth, like a man without religion."

At the point of death, Byron's old ally, Nature herself, intervened and the transformation into myth of these miserable last hours began. "At the very time Lord Byron died," wrote Parry, "there was one of the most awful thunder storms I ever witnessed." The lightning played over the mountains, the fishing boats in the lagoon, the countryside in flood; and the Greeks, in their superstition, says Parry, took it as a sign and exclaimed among themselves: "The great man is gone!"

Epilogue

Yet once more let us look upon the sea. . . .

—*Childe Harold's Pilgrimage*

There is a frontier in Europe, marked on few maps, but no less important for all that. It runs eastward from Galicia in northwestern Spain, turns south to pass between Valladolid and Madrid, takes in a fringe of coastal France, descends on Rome, then runs down the coast of old Yugoslavia into Albania and Greece. This is the line that marks the northern limit of the olive tree. Below it is what the scholar Fernand Braudel calls the "true" Mediterranean.

Byron's story lies, polarized, on either side of this line. In his youth the oppositions are still simple: it is the cold of England against the warmth of Greece, clouds against sun, beer against wine. Gradually the complexities deepen: Greece is clarity against England's confusions, space against confinement. Always, of course, freedom against tyranny. In the beginning, the freedom of the body, bronzed and promiscuously indulged; later, that strange, obscure pursuit of freedom through others.

After Byron's death, there were good reasons for leaving his body in Greece. In June 1819, in the bitterest moments of exile, he had written to his publisher, John Murray: "I am sure my Bones would not rest in an English grave—or my Clay mix with the earth of that Country:—I believe the thought would drive me mad on my death-bed could I suppose that any of my friends would be base enough to convey my carcase back to your soil—I would not even feed your worms—if I could help it."

Millingen believed that, in this, Byron had been consistent to the end—"Let not my body be hacked, or be sent to England"—and he told Pietro Gamba so. But Gamba apparently replied "that a great man belonged to his country; and that it would be a sacrilege to leave his remains in a place, where they might, one day, become the sport of insulting barbarians." It is possible, too, that Byron changed his mind or wavered on the approach of death, as Fletcher, Parry, and others claimed. At all events, the decision was taken to return him to England.

The Greeks first took their leave. All shops, except those selling food and medicines, closed for three days. The Easter festivities were suspended and there were three weeks of general mourning. On 21 April, Byron was carried to the Church of Ayios Nikolaos in Mesolongi for a funeral service. A black mantle covered the rough coffin, and upon it were placed a helmet and sword and a crown of laurel.

The following day, Spiridon Trikoupis delivered the funeral oration. Among the senior Greek political figures there was no doubting the enormity of the loss. "All Greece is his sepulchre," said Trikoupis, recalling the famous words of the Athenian statesman Pericles in 430 B.C.: "The whole earth is the sepulchre of famous men."

Gamba wrote of the funeral service: "The wretchedness and desolation of the place ... the wild and half civilised warriors around us; their deep-felt, unaffected grief; the fond recollections; the disappointed hopes ... all contributed to form a scene more moving, more truly affecting, than perhaps was ever before witnessed around the grave of a great man."

The citizens of Mesolongi appealed for some material share in the departing Lord Byron. As a result, his lungs were deposited in an urn and left behind. Trikoupis declared that the town would "ever watch over" the relic, symbol of Byron's love for Greece. It disappeared when Mesolongi fell, two years later.

In the English text of the funeral speech by Trikoupis, the Greek word for "lung," *pnevmonas*, was translated, by error or elaboration, as "heart." And to this day, even in the best of guide-books, the story is told that Byron left his heart in Mesolongi.

· · ·

> *And I have loved thee, Ocean! and my joy*
> *Of youthful sports was on thy breast to be*
> *Borne, like thy bubbles, onward . . .*
>
> · · · · · · · · · · · ·
> *For I was as it were a child of thee,*
> *And trusted to thy billows far and near. . . .*
>
> —*Childe Harold's Pilgrimage*

The love affair with the Mediterranean goes on and on and few are completely immune. Byron, it is true, would have hated the crowds, but the tourists who arrive each day by thousands all through the long Greek summer are the natural heirs of his own youthful Greece. The nude beaches and smoke-filled tavernas would now be his hunting grounds, and the bars where Greek army conscripts gather, lonely and far from home. As the *Greek Gay Guide* says: "It is easy to approach a boy; the people here are friendly and communicate easily."

This is the Greece of sun, sea, and the body, a world Byron discovered, made his own. Curiously, despite all the invasions, it is a Greece that still invites a fantasy of intimacy and belonging:

> *Place me on Sunium's marbled steep,*
> *Where nothing, save the waves and I,*
> *May hear our mutual murmurs sweep. . . .*

It is the country of eternal youth, framed by the eternally old. The holiday brochures are filled with ancient columns, plodding donkeys, and old women in black. These images live on, side by side with the glittering sea and the ripening flesh, proof that the serenity of age follows naturally on the frenzy of youth.

I was spending the summer in France, in an old house deep within a valley. One side of the valley was thick with trees; the other, looking toward the southern sun, was arid and sandy, with low shrubs and struggling pines. It was an isolated place and for days no one came by.

In the early morning I used to watch dragonflies cruising the stream and buzzards in the dead apple trees below the house. Outside, in the barn, old farming implements rusted quietly away in the dusty sunshine. At night, I read by a huge window that opened onto the darkness of the valley; and moths, drawn to the only light for miles around, fell like snow against the glass.

Before the end of August it was already autumn. It rained for a week without ceasing and the wind blew so hard I kept the shutters drawn against the gray sky. Sometimes, far away, a car passed by on the wet road, with the sound the sea makes on still nights. Listening to the wind, I thought sometimes of summer storms in the Aegean, when the wind howls out of a clear blue sky; or of the warm winds in autumn, which blow up, sand-laden, from Africa. And so, driven by the most commonplace of nostalgias, I went back to Greece.

I left on a day when clouds swirled about the roof of the car and the sky was the color of the road ahead. But as I drove south through Italy, the year turned back on itself and it was summer again. I didn't think of Byron then, or for a long time afterward, though it was Byron's Greece that I wanted to see and feel.

For a while, after I returned, things seemed no different from the way I had remembered. Of course, Greece was noisier than before, faster, richer, and with more crowds. But the sea still looked the same, the countryside smelled the same. The same stunningly incomplete landscape of bare mountains, with half-built, half-ruined houses.

As time passed, however, I began to wonder what to do and where to go. This came as a shock, since Greece was a country where once I could happily do nothing for days on end. I thought of the changes, asked myself if they were in Greece or in me. I had seen higher mountains and wilder since I was last here, but there was more to it than that.

Increasingly, I wanted a reason for being where I was. Not when things went well, of course. But at the moments of all those minor disasters that travel brings—missed boats, sickness in cheap hotels, the loneliness of eating in strange places. Increasingly, I wanted to know why I was putting up with it all, when in the past putting up with it was what made travel so marvelously different from the comfort of everyday life.

I have never wanted to travel in anyone's footsteps. I once followed a sixteenth-century madman called Lope de Aguirre on a journey through Peru and Brazil. But that was different. For, as I read the chronicles of those who were with Aguirre on his great journey, it was clear that for most of the time no one had any idea where he was going. That made it an easy path to follow, free and unconstrained. And then, much of the traveling was down the waters of the Amazon, where all idea of footsteps vanishes into absurdity.

Now, however, I began to understand that dull page boy who followed Wenceslas—the delights and rewards that come with limitation. And, ceasing to wander on my own, I began the search for company.

I had long been interested in Byron. He had first come to Greece pursuing no cause but his own self-satisfaction. Then, years later, he had returned, and with a purpose. So I followed him, through northern Greece and Albania, Akarnania and the Peloponnese. I went back to many places I had known, but each time now I tried to imagine him there. And eventually I went back to Mesolongi.

•   •   •

Not far from the place where Byron died in Mesolongi, on a large tract of wasteland lined with orange trees, a new Byron Museum is being built. From here, on the west side of town, the road runs straight down to the sea, past some old military aircraft and a couple of disused tanks. Beyond is a causeway that leads out to open water and the tiny village of Tourlida.

It's a long walk down the causeway. Tourlida's brightly painted bungalows rise out of the sea on stilts before you; and, looking back, you see one of the best views of Mesolongi, lying low in the water, a skyline with nothing higher than its churches.

Perhaps there's no better fate for a town than to be quietly famous. This is a place grown used to self-respect, satisfied with the road that has been traveled. Like one of those nineteenth-century women *d'un certain âge*.

In the main streets, sides of beef and enormous fish hang in shop doorways. Baskets of eels, boxes of fruit. At night, nothing moves through Mesolongi, for it is bypassed by the main road that runs from Nafpaktos to Agrinio. Before dawn, the church bells ring, the dogs and roosters reply, then peace descends once more.

A waiter passes by, riding a bicycle down the main street. He carries a circular tray suspended from a chain, with a cup of black coffee and a glass of water on it, unself-consciously balanced. A fantasy of the intimate.

Mesolongi's Town Hall is on the main square. Inside is a small museum. In the entrance, there is a map showing the progress of the final siege of the town, from April 1825 to April 1826. A succession of black lines marks the advance of the Turkish forces, month by month, as the defenders were forced back. Like a hammer driving a wedge ever deeper into the base of the peninsula on which the town is built.

To the left are the rooms of "Lord Byron's Memorial." Here are pictures of Ioannina, Arta, Delphi. The wide emptiness of the Attic plain. The remoteness of Sounion. There is a Suliote in his "shaggy capote"; a glass case with a miniature cricket bat; and a copy of Byron's commission as a colonel of artillery in the Greek army.

The ground floor is all Byron's. The floor above is dedicated to the Greeks. It is full of paintings of stern warriors with pistols in their belts and fine mustaches. Odysseus Androutsos, Markos Botsaris. Battle scenes with terrified horses, smoke, and fearsome explosions.

How different the warrior faces in these pictures are from those of the European Greeks, who look as if they would have been at home in any salon of the nineteenth century. And no less different from the shaggy, hangdog features of Mavrokordatos, whose portrait is also here. As you move from one floor of the museum to the other, the size of the problem that confronted Byron becomes ever clearer. This is a portrait of Greece divided, by class and time and expectation.

For a different view, the place to go is the Garden of the Heroes. In English the very name is almost an embarrassment, inviting suspicion or ridicule. But the idea of the hero is still secure in Greek. The *Kipos ton Heroon* backs onto the fortification wall of Mesolongi and is one of the loveliest of gardens, full of flowers, palm trees, and firs, and the songs of birds. It was planned as a memorial to the revolutionary past, from the moment Mesolongi returned to Greek hands in 1829.

From the entrance, a paved pathway leads straight ahead toward the retaining wall on the far side. Toward the end of the path is a statue of Byron. It is a monument he might have liked, though in general he distrusted such things. For as he once wrote: "A bust looks like putting up pretensions to permanency—and smacks something of a hankering for *public* fame rather than private remembrance."

Here he is young and slim and handsome. His head is turned to his right, as if refusing to acknowledge the place of honor. At the base of the statue is a small garden and when I was last there, in early December, there were still some fading yellow roses blooming in the sun. There is an inscription in a Greek so formal, so archaic, that the official guidebook provides a translation for Greek visitors.

What is most moving in the garden is the sense of shared space. Byron has his place of honor, undenied. But all around are memorials to the other foreigners who gave their lives for Greece. To the Germans, Americans, Swedes, Poles, French, Swiss, and the rest. Then there are the memorials to the Greeks, to the Suliote commander Botsaris, to those who fell in the first siege of Mesolongi in 1822, and to all those who fell, anonymously, in the great *Exodos* of 1826.

It is here that Byron's sacrifice is most revealing, the Greek cause most compelling. In England the old, parochial controversies still ramble on, about Byron's character, behavior, or sexuality. Here all details fade, leaving only the nostalgia of an extraordinary internationalism.

Byron's politics have much to say to the late twentieth century. At first sight this may seem strange. His motives for returning to Greece were obscure, after all, and he never gave anything but the simplest account of his aims. His commitment looks, from some angles, almost casual. Today, however, with the collapse of old habits, old ideals, it is easier to see the strength in this, where only a few years ago the limitations appeared overwhelming.

The ability to think systematically once seemed the best guide to the authentic in politics, the only defense against losing one's way. There was a time when nothing was thought worth attempting that did not have its place in the great scheme of the world. Today, such inclusiveness seems an ever more archaic virtue, ever more vulnerable to the realities of change. Byron always saw the potential tyranny in the systematic, and his hostility to it has stood the test of the modern world.

There is another way, too, in which Byron's approach speaks to our time. Traditional revolutionary politics always demanded an abnegation of the self, an almost religious denial of the value of the personal. This, too, once seemed a reliable claim on authenticity. Byron's commitment, on the other hand, begins with the self and, no doubt, ends there, too. He sets no model, refuses to generalize.

By all the old rules he should have abandoned the Greek cause, for want of political ballast. But he did not; and there is no reason to think Stanhope was wrong when he said he would never have given up, even had he lived. Byron's approach, so often derided, resists abstraction. It is a commitment to the here and now of the world, problematic and elusive.

In the Monastery of Pendeli, where Byron began his sexual tour of old Athens, there is a flag in a glass case, with the slogan of the 1821 revolution: *Freedom or Death.* The words have had a long life. The slogan returned during the Spanish Civil War in the 1930s, and in 1979, through the wet heat of a Nicaraguan winter, I heard the same cry of *Patria libre o morir.* Now, it may be, the words have finally lost their power to inspire, with the collapse of the ideas that once underpinned them. In a way, it's hard to think of them as real now, as having any meaning outside the past.

A few months ago, on an October afternoon, I left the Albanian port of Saranda for Greece. I traveled in a ship crowded with Albanian refugees. Some of them spoke Greek and we talked on the way across, about the poverty they were leaving, the better life they hoped to find. At Corfu the handful of foreigners and Greeks got off. The Albanians were roped into a corner of the deck and I stood and watched from the shore as they began to face all the humiliations of the unwanted.

A Free Country or Death . . . The old politics, the old enthusiasms seemed far away, in the face of this most routine of situations. I thought of Byron then. Of that easy pragmatism that never excludes the possibility of indignation. The language of the last letters from Mesolongi, so unheroic, so purged of illusion, is what in the end confirms Byron's authenticity as a political animal.

The paradox, however, remains. This minor adventure in Mesolongi has spread its influence promiscuously in time and space, beyond those who knew Byron, beyond Greece, beyond Europe.

Those who did know him felt a personal loss at his death, as was only natural. In 1825, Pietro Gamba met Dimitrios Zograffo, once Byron's servant, now a combatant in the war. Zograffo told him that when Byron died "we felt like men suddenly struck with blindness, when the only thing that could equal our sorrow for his loss, was our perplexity for the future."

That is understandable. But what of the Italian Mazzini, who wrote: "The day will come when Democracy will remember all that it owes to Byron"? Or the literary critic from China's May Fourth Movement of 1919, who wrote as if Byron had died only a few weeks before: "He stands on the crest of the waves, showing . . . his pride, his strength, his grandeur, and his sorrow . . ."? Or the demonstrators in Tiananmen Square in June 1989, for whom it appears Byron had never died?

Byron, the heavily laden traveler who came to Greece in search of pleasure, the man who could scarcely move without his teams of horses and servants, his bedsteads and fine linen . . . Byron, the eighteenth-century English gentleman, the temporary resident of Mesolongi in a dull season. It is a long way from this to the figure Shelley called the Pilgrim of Eternity.

André Gide once wrote that happiness is to be found, not in freedom, but in the acceptance of a duty. Happiness was a rare thing in Byron's life, the idea of duty a little serious, perhaps, for a gentleman. But Greece played a vital part in what happiness there was, just as it provided the motivation for that strange, inexplicable commitment at the end. A commitment that gives a shape to Byron's vast dissatisfactions and has enabled him to float free in the eye of posterity. The project completed, not in life certainly, nor even in death, but in that supreme lightness of baggage that we still, sometimes, call immortality.

Bibliographical Note

Oscar José Santucho's bibliography, *George Gordon, Lord Byron*, covers the years 1807 to 1974. It refers only to material in English and is over six hundred pages long. In the writing of the present book, I have profited greatly from Santucho's labors. In addition, I have tried to take account of the most interesting material published since 1974, and of work in French, Italian, Spanish, and modern Greek. It is clear that much remains to be disinterred from Greek archives, and that Greek sources in general have a great deal to say to those interested in Byron. Many questions, concerning the kind of society Byron found in Greece and the political developments with which he had to contend, will only be answered after further work in this area.

Given the volume of material and the inaccessibility of some of it, there seemed no purpose in adding a bibliography here. It would be wrong, however, not to cite the three contemporary peaks of Byron scholarship: Leslie A. Marchand's edition of *Byron's Letters and Journals*, 13 volumes (1973–1994); the same author's *Byron: A Biography*, 3 volumes (1957); and Jerome J.

McGann's edition of *The Complete Poetical Works*, 7 volumes (1980–1993), magnificently indexed by Carol Pearson. No writer on Byron could do without these and it is a pleasure to record the debt. Finally, I would like to acknowledge all I have learned from G. I. Kokosoulas, *Mesolongi, 1830–1990*, a work on that most underrated of Greek towns, written *con amore*, by a native son.

Index